ISL∕

OF THE SOUTH AND SOUTHEASTERN UNITED STATES

Also by Sarah Bird Wright

FERRIES OF AMERICA
A Guide to Adventurous Travel

ISLANDS

OF THE SOUTH AND SOUTHEASTERN UNITED STATES

Sarah Bird Wright

Peachtree Publishers, Ltd.
Atlanta · Memphis

*In memory of my parents,
Elise and R. Oscar ("Rock") Grant,
Who raised their children on the best island they knew.*

Published by
PEACHTREE PUBLISHERS, LTD.
494 Armour Circle, NE
Atlanta, Georgia 30324

Design by Patricia Joe
Maps by Tom Roberts

Manufactured in the United States of America

10 9 8 7 6 5 4 3 2 1

Library of Congress Cataloging in Publication Data

Wright, Sarah Bird.
    Islands of the south and southeastern United States / Sarah Bird
  Wright.
       p.   cm.
     Bibliography: p.
     ISBN 0-934601-69-0
     1. Southern States—Description and travel—1981—Guide-books.
     2. Islands—Southern States—Guide-books. I. Title.
   F207.3.W75   1989
   917.5′0443—dc19   89-30326
                                                          CIP

CONTENTS

PRICE CATEGORIES

RESTAURANTS:

Average cost of a meal for one (excluding beverages, tips, and taxes)

$ Under $12   **$$** $12–$20   **$$$** Over $20

LODGINGS

Accommodations:

Price for a standard double, high season, exclusive of taxes: $ Under $60   **$$** $60–$90   **$$$** Over $90

Note that many establishments have a wide range of prices, according to location and season.

Villas:

Daily price, high season, for a standard one-bedroom villa with kitchen, which is offered in many of the newer developments (to be designated as Villa in the text):

$ Under $75   **$$** $75–$100   **$$$** Over $100

Condominiums:

One or more bedrooms, rented weekly, high season:

$ Under $400   **$$** $400–$500   **$$$** Over $500

While every care has been taken to assure the accuracy of the information in this guide, the passage of time will always bring change, and consequently the publisher cannot accept responsibility for errors that may occur. All information is based on that available at press time; the prudent traveler will avoid inconvenience by calling ahead.

INTRODUCTION

> *Away with a corrupt world! Let us breathe the air of enchanted islands.*
> —George Meredith

Islands really need no introduction. Who has not longed to escape, like Paul Gauguin, to a tropical island, shedding cares and transmuting life into an idyllic existence? Lawrence Durrell once wrote of the universal yearning people have toward islands: "The mere knowledge they are on an island, a little world surrounded by the sea, fills them with indescribable intoxication."

Fictional and fabled islands have long engaged the imagination and embodied the romantic conception of escape, and perhaps the transformation of mundane lives, from the island on which the magician Prospero and his daughter Miranda were shipwrecked in *The Tempest* to the one sought by Jim Hawkins in Robert Louis Stevenson's *Treasure Island.* On a mythical island in the western sea, the Hesperides, daughters of Atlas, guarded the tree bearing golden apples. The Isles of the Blest, or the Fortunate Islands, were placed in the Western Ocean in Greek mythology, and peopled by immortals; there perpetual summer and abundance reigned. The greek sorceress Circe reigned over the island of Aeaea, turning the companions of Ulysses into swine. Jonathan Swift's Gulliver visited the flying island of Laputa, inhabited by abstract philosophers. Tennyson's dreamy Lady of Shalott inhabited an island near Camelot, preoccupied with her weaving and detached from reality. These Lilliputian domains were of manageable proportions, as were the series of islands in D. H. Lawrence's story "The Man Who Loved Islands."

Writers have always, it seems, had an affinity for islands. Victor Hugo lived on Guernsey, Lawrence Durrell and his brother Gerald on Corfu, and George Orwell on Jura. The islands of the Southeastern part of the United States have attracted many writers; Hemingway wrote of Key West and Anne Morrow Lindbergh of Captiva; John D. MacDonald set many of his Travis McGee mysteries on Gulf islands. Pat Conroy has celebrated life on the South Carolina Lowcountry islands, writing of Daufuskie in *Prince of Tides,* and Eugenia Price, Phyllis Whitney, and Sidney Lanier wrote of the Georgia coastal islands. James Michener and John Barth have both recorded the flavor of the Chesapeake Bay, and Marguerite Henry immortalized the ponies of Assateague Island in *Misty of Chincoteague.* Shirley Ann Grau wrote of Cajun life on Grand Isle, Louisiana (disguised as the Isle aux Chiens), which she knew from childhood summers there, in *The Hard Blue Sky.*

Islands have been a particularly congenial subject to artists also, for they inhabit virtually every developed island, displaying their work in local galleries as well as in more distant ones and in museums. Among the American artists who have depicted islands are Andrew and James Wyeth, who have portrayed Monhegan in Maine (James Wyeth now lives there in the former home of Norman Rockwell), James Audubon, who did some of his bird studies on Key West, Ernest Lawson, a landscape painter who depicted Key West, Winslow Homer, known for a famous series of watercolors showing sailboats in the Key West Harbor, and Frederick Remington, who spent three years painting on Key West. It was at Key West that Dwight Eisenhower began painting. The northern coastlines attracted John Martin, and James Addison Palmer, Jr., has captured the unique spirit of Hilton Head and the Lowcountry islands nearby. Thomas Cole and the Hudson River School of artists painted scenes on Mount Desert Island, Maine, and Bob Timberlake has portrayed Bald Head Island, North Carolina.

The present volume aims to give a portrait of islands in 12 southern states, beginning in Maryland and going as far south as Louisiana. It is the first in a series about United States islands, which began as an outgrowth of a previous book, on ferry boats (*Ferries of America: A Guide to Adventurous Travel*). Both the ferry book and the present one really had their genesis in my childhood on a North Carolina island, Wrightsville Beach. My research about ferry boats had taken me to many islands, large and small, and it seemed that a practical guide to them would be useful to prospective visitors and boating people, as well as to current island residents and armchair travelers.

The series is intended to be an anthology of islands rather than an encyclopedia. Some have been omitted because they were too urban and others because they were privately owned, or, though publicly owned, not accessible for ecological or other reasons. Some of those included are admittedly well-settled tourist enclaves, yet they are still attractive to visitors, especially off-season. Others are sparsely settled, with a small year-round population and a large seasonal influx of visitors. One island, Portsmouth, in North Carolina, even has a ghost town; erosion and shifting sands caused an alteration in shipping channels and brought about its decline. A good many, fortunately, are now protected as state or national parks.

Life proceeds at an adagio pace on some islands; on others there is a thriving cultural climate, with museums, theaters, concerts, dinner cruises, and party boat rental. It is almost a given on popular islands from Ocracoke to Sanibel that residents are mounting a frenetic effort to fend off commercial development, or at least ensure that it is tasteful and not inimical to the environment. Even tiny Smith Island, Maryland, in the Chesapeake Bay, faces threats by developers. Often, however, high-rise condominiums seem only a remote concern; the boating life is paramount, with spacious marinas and a welcoming attitude toward transient yachtsmen. Still others are known for their excellent golf courses and for abundant fishing.

The topography of the islands chosen varies almost as much as their ambiance. Some have been largely stable, geologically, for centuries; others have only recently been wrestled into being by tangling mangrove swamps, or mounded by torrential currents. The southeastern islands include sandbars and coral reefs, manmade river islands and hurricane-severed slivers. Some beaches have been eroded, nourished, and renourished. Certain islands are rich in legend, have coves where buccaneers once took refuge; others have a Gothic flavor, with moss-hung live oaks shading oyster-shell paths. The very approach to an island, even if by car, has a never-failing allure. The trees thin and part, and the bold bridge or causeway spans the spiky marshes. A prescient glimpse of foamy blue/green water, perhaps graced by sails, hints at the island to come. If the island is beyond the Intracoastal Waterway, there may well be a drawbridge, probably raised and towering over the throbbing cars, adding a last moment of mainland tension before the island, in Prospero's words, "'twixt the green sea and the azur'd vault," begins to settle the spirits and work its calming magic. The ideal arrival, of course, is by boat, when the prospective island begins as a tiny speck, perhaps signalled by a lighthouse, and gradually attains mass and shape, as do one's expectations.

The better to formulate these expectations, the book has sections on location, size, access, history and description, points of interest, sightseeing, parks, beaches, camping, marinas, restaurants, lodging, and seasonal rentals; for each entry there is a contact address and telephone number for further information.

In 1783, James Boswell and Samuel Johnson made a celebrated tour of Scotland, sailing through the Hebrides. Boswell expressed a desire to buy the island of Inchkenneth, and said his brother had always talked of acquiring an island. "Sir," said Dr. Johnson, "so does almost every man, till he knows what it is." Even Dr. Johnson, however, might approve of these islands of the Southeast, at least for a pilgrimage, for, in varied ways, each has its own individuality and special appeal.

ALABAMA

The early settlement of Alabama by diverse European nations has resulted in a broad spectrum of influences and cultures. In 1507, a map of the world by Martin Waldseemuller, a young German geographer/cartographer, was published; it showed the outline of Mobile Bay. Alonso Pineda, a Spanish explorer, was the first white man to enter Mobile Bay, in 1519. In 1540, Hernando de Soto crossed the upper central part of the state and planted a Spanish flag. The French established a colony on Dauphin Island (then called Massacre) in 1699, and began a settlement at Mobile in 1711, trading trinkets to the Indians for furs. The English gained possession of Mobile in 1762, and continued trading cloth and firearms with the Indians for furs. Dauphin Island was ceded to Spain in 1762, to England in 1763, and back to Spain in 1783. In 1798, the state was part of the U. S. Territory of Mississippi, but it became the Alabama Territory in 1817 and entered the Union in 1819. By the middle of the 19th century, Alabama was the leading cotton producing state in America.

The name "Alabama" comes from a Choctaw word for "thicket clearers." The state has a variety of landscapes, ranging from the forested and craggy northern Highlands to the ancient swamps, cypress forests, tropical gardens, and fine beaches of the Gulf Coast Delta. Dauphin Island is marked by woodlands, live oaks, sea oats, and sandy beach, and is the site of historic Fort Gaines. There are a number of permanent homes and it is much visited by tourists in summer.

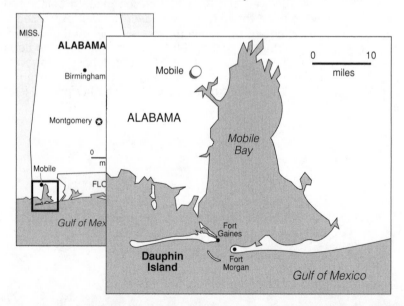

ALABAMA

DAUPHIN ISLAND

Area Code 205

LOCATION   30 miles south of Mobile.

SIZE   17 miles by approx. 1 mile.

ACCESS   ***Car:*** By toll-free 4-mile bridge and causeway from mainland Mobile County (Rt.
163). ***Ferry:*** From Fort Morgan (Von Bergen
Ltd., 2901 Byrnewood Dr., Theodore, AL 36582; 205/973–2251). ***Air:***
The island has a 3,000-foot paved airstrip. There is commercial air
service to Mobile. ***Private boat.***

HISTORY AND   Dauphin Island is Alabama's only barrier is-
DESCRIPTION   land. It was known to early explorers; the
Spaniards surveyed it in the 16th century.
In 1699, Pierre Le Moyne, Sieur d'Iberville, was sent by Louis XIV to
establish a colony on the Gulf. He discovered Massacre, now Dauphin
Island, and a colony was established there. The island was named
"Dauphin" to honor the king's son. In the 18th century, French and
British adventurers on Dauphin Island traded gaudy trinkets to the In-
dians for fur. The island was once the capital of all French Louisiana.

A few years ago, Hurricane Frederick ravaged the island, destroying
the bridge to the mainland and damaging many facilities on the island. A new bridge has now been finished, and the rebuilding of the
island has been largely accomplished. Today Dauphin Island is a popular vacation retreat. Frances Kennedy, who is compiling a history of
the island, calls it "very quiet, very mild, a special place." There are
about 1,000 year-round residents. The Dauphin Island Fishing Pier is
popular with anglers; in July the island is host to the Alabama Deep
Sea Fishing Rodeo.

POINTS OF INTEREST   Fort Gaines, a five-sided brick fortress
commanding the entrance to Mobile Bay,
was built in the 1860s and was active in
the 1864 Battle of Mobile Bay. Forces here withstood a 3-day siege.
The site includes the Fort, museums, and a gift shop. Additional buildings were added to Fort Gaines following the Spanish-American War.
Each March, a re-enactment of the Federal rendezvous on the island
to attack the city of Mobile is held at the Fort. In September a Civil

Fort Gaines

War re-enactment is held, and in Christmas Civil War re-enactors portray an 1863 Christmas at the Fort.

Also of interest is the Indian Shell Mound, a prehistoric monument built by early Indians and representative of the Indian culture which flourished around Mobile Bay thousands of years ago. There is also a 60-acre Audubon Society Sanctuary which features natural barrier island forest with walking trails.

Fort Morgan, reached by ferry from Dauphin Island, is a National Historic Landmark. It consists of a group of weathered frame buildings, relics of the War of 1812 when it was named Fort Bowyer. It was renamed Fort Morgan in honor the Mexican War hero General John H. Morgan. Among the buildings are a museum, powder magazine, and an old engineer's wharf. A buoy marks the resting place of the *Tecumseh*, 200 yards offshore. (In August 1864, Admiral Farragut shouted his famous command of "Damn the torpedoes! Full speed ahead!" when the Union ironclad sank at the beginning of the Battle of Mobile Bay. She hit a Confederate torpedo and went down with her captain and 93 crew members.)

SIGHTSEEING TOURS   There are no sightseeing tours on the island, but Gray Line has bus tours in Mobile (Box 1711, Mobile 36663; 432–2229).

PARKS, BEACHES AND   **Parks:** Cadillac Square has restrooms and
CAMPING   picnic facilities, and the Audubon Sanctuary has nature trails. **Beaches:** There is an excellent swimming beach. **Camping:** The Fort Gaines Campground (861–3607) has 150 sites, washer/dryers, and a children's play area. It is bordered by the Audubon Bird Sanctuary and is across the street from free boat launching ramps.

MARINAS   Dauphin Isle Marina (861–2201); 5 transient slips; maximum length 75 feet; approach depth 6 feet; dockside depth 5 feet; electric power—yes; restaurant within walking distance—yes.

RESTAURANTS   The Seafood Galley, 1510 Bienville Blvd. (861-8000), across from the public pier, has excellent seafood.**$**

LODGING   The Gulf Breeze Motel, Box 107, Dauphin Island, AL 36528 (861–7344) is on Cadillac Ave. 1 mile west of the water tower; it has 2-bedroom efficiencies with kitchens.**$**

RENTALS   Dauphin Island Real Estate, LeMoyne Dr. (861–8042) and Curtis Gordon Realty, corner of LeMoyne Dr. and Bienville Blvd. (861–3612) are 2 companies handling rentals.

CONTACT   For information on activities at Fort Gaines, contact Fort Gaines, Box 97, Dauphin Island, AL 36528 (861–6992). For general information, contact the Mobile Convention and Visitor Service, 451 Government St., Box 2187, Mobile, AL 36652 (433–6951).

ARKANSAS

Hernando de Soto's expedition is thought to have passed through the region which is now Arkansas in 1541, possibly halting at Hot Springs. There they found the "Valley of the Vapors," where 47 thermal springs gushed from the earth, pure and clear. South of Hot Springs is DeGray Lake, one of the state's newer impoundments. DeGray State Park is on its shores, and DeGray Lodge is situated on its own island in the lake.

The 2 lakes, scenically situated, offer a variety of recreational pursuits; they are also centrally placed for exploring Hot Springs National Park and the Ozarks as well as the remainder of Arkansas, which has been called a "bountiful, individualistic vacation land."

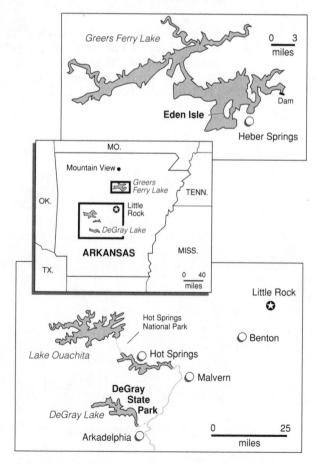

ARKANSAS

DEGRAY STATE PARK

Area Code 501

LOCATION

In DeGray Lake, 11 miles north of Arkadelphia and 21 miles south of Hot Springs.

SIZE

DeGray State Park has 938 acres; DeGray Lodge is on a small adjacent island, reached by causeway.

ACCESS

Car: Via Hwy. 7 from Arkadelphia or Hot Springs. *Air:* There is commercial air service to Little Rock or Hot Springs; Arkadelphia has a private airport 12 miles south of DeGray with a 4,000-foot runway. *Private boat.*

HISTORY AND DESCRIPTION

DeGray State Park lies on the north shore of DeGray Lake. The DeGray Dam, completed in 1972, impounds the waters of the Caddo River to form the lake, which has 13,800 acres. It is known for its fishing (the lake has several species of bass) and recreational opportunities. The Lodge, situated among tall pines and hardwoods, is open year-round and overlooks the lake; there is a lobby with a fire-

DeGray State Lodge and Convention Center

place as well as a spacious restaurant; the building has a contemporary design, with large windows and glass doors. Amenities include an 18-hole golf course, lighted tennis courts, a children's playground, and a courtesy dock for private or rental boats. DeGray Lodge was named one of the 10 best vacation bargains in America by *Better Homes and Gardens* magazine.

POINTS OF INTEREST   The Island Trail (1 mile), on the island, follows the western shoreline of the Lodge property. In the mainland section of the park, the Towering Pines Trail (1/2 mile) is located near the amphitheater. The Green Heron Trail offers guests access to several natural habitat zones.

The DeGray Dam Visitors Center, near the park entrance, has 2- and 3-dimensional displays which illustrate the dam's construction and operational features; Caddo Indian artifacts and a wildlife exhibit are also here, along with a slide exhibit.

Hot Springs National Park is just 21 miles away.

SIGHTSEEING TOURS   At the Lodge, party barge tours, guided walks, and special evening programs are offered.

PARKS, BEACHES AND   **Parks:** The island is part of DeGray State
CAMPING   Park. **Beaches:** There are no recreational beaches on the island, but the lake itself has several swimming beaches. **Camping:** The island itself does not have camping, but the park has 3 camping areas with 113 campsites open year-round. Reservations must be made in advance.

MARINAS   There is a full-service marina with 132 slips on the mainland side of the park, offering rental fishing boats, party barges, canoes, and a houseboat.

RESTAURANTS   The full-service Lodge restaurant also offers children's selections. Among the specialties are catfish, shrimp, and seafood supreme.$

LODGING   The Lodge has 96 rooms and extensive convention facilities; price varies according to location.$$

RENTALS   There are no cottage rentals on the island.

CONTACT   For Lodge reservations, contact Manager, DeGray State Park Lodge, Rt. 3, Box 490, Bismarck, AR 71929–8194 (865–4591);

for general information on the park, contact DeGray State Park, Rt. 3.
Box 490, Bismarck, AR 71929–8194 (865–4501).

EDEN ISLE

Area Code 501
LOCATION   In Greers Ferry Lake, in the eastern foot-
                                hills of the Arkansas Ozarks; the island is
                                5 miles west of Heber Springs.

SIZE   600 acres.

ACCESS   *Car:* Via Hwy. 110 from Heber Springs. *Air:*
                                There is commercial service to Little Rock;
                                Heber Springs has a private airport. *Private
                                boat.*

HISTORY AND   Greers Ferry lake, 50 miles long, is im-
DESCRIPTION   pounded behind a dam that was dedicated
                                in 1963 by President John F. Kennedy. In
the last quarter-century the lake has developed rapidly; there are now
15 public recreation areas on 31,500 acres. Eden Isle, at the eastern
end of the lake, has over 350 exclusive homes. It also has the Red
Apple Inn, a luxurious resort, opened in 1965, which has an 18-hole
golf course, two landscaped swimming pools, excellent tennis facilities, and many other amenities (see Lodging).

POINTS OF INTEREST   The Greers Ferry Lake and Little Red River
                                Visitor's Center is located on the west side
                                of the dam; it has a museum and an audio-
                                visual show.
     Sugar Loaf Mountain Island is 22.5 miles west of Eden Isle; it is
accessible by boat and has a foot trail to the 1,001-foot summit.

SIGHTSEEING TOURS   There are no sightseeing tours on the is-
                                land.

PARKS, BEACHES AND   Parks: There are no parks on the island.
CAMPING   *Beaches:* There are no recreational
                                beaches on the island. *Camping:* Camping
is not allowed on the island, but the lake itself has a number of parks
which allow tent and trailer camping.

MARINAS   The Red Apple Inn has a full-service marina
                                with slips for transient boats. Available for
                                rental are a party barge, ski boats, sail-
boats, lake cruisers, and fishing boats.

RESTAURANTS   The resort dining room has a Mediterranean decor, with outdoor dining and a menu "somewhere between caviar and spoon bread" (they have both). There are soufflés, homemade rolls, and excellent desserts.**$$**

LODGING   The Red Apple Inn is a luxurious resort nestled in the rolling hills of Arkansas and surrounded by Greers Ferry Lake. It was designed by David George of Dallas, a student of Frank Lloyd Wright. The structure, which has handsome timbers and natural moss rock, blends beautifully into the site. It has many fireplaces, works of art, hand-carved furniture from Italy and Spain, tapestries, and individually decorated rooms. The gate to the "After Five Room," retrieved from a Spanish castle, dates from the 16th century. There are 58 rooms, along with kitchen apartments, suites, and condominium units. The Red Apple Inn was selected by the Mobil Travel Guide as one of 16 outstanding inns in the nation.**$$**

RENTALS   There are no rentals on the island.

CONTACT   Red Apple Inn, Box 8900, Eden Isle, Heber Springs, AR 72543 (US except AR 800/255–8900; AR 800/482–8900).

FLORIDA

"Eternal summer gilds them yet," wrote Byron of the isles of Greece, but he might have said the same of Florida's sun-drenched islands. No state has been more identified with tropical pleasures than Florida, with its palm trees, coral reefs, abundant fish, and polychromatic waters. Florida has a rich array of islands, which have escaped the urban ills afflicting the state's mainland.

The state has over 8,000 miles of coastline, counting the land around the bays, and has more beaches than any other state. The eastern and Gulf Coast islands, as well as the Keys, are far more accessible now than when Henry Flagler made the state fashionable and began building his railway in 1883. There is a large population of retirees, mixed with lively young professionals. The busiest season is January through March. If, late on a cold and bleak December afternoon, you decide to satisfy your craving for sunshine by calling a small condominium complex about a winter apartment, don't be surprised if the voice of the owner sounds dim and remote—he may well be speaking from a portable telephone out on a boat, enjoying drinks. Floridians excel at achieving an ideal balance between industry and relaxation.

Florida's islands are remarkably varied; the faint aura of wreckers, pirates, and smugglers lingers in the Keys, where visitors' conceptions have also been imprinted with Humphrey Bogart's films and Ernest Hemingway's novels. Palatial resort hotels, now historic landmarks, may still be found on islands along the Gulf Coast, which have, as well, more modest inns evocative of Florida as it was before 1900. On the east coast, there are also diverse islands, such as Merritt, home of the Kennedy Space Center, and Amelia, rich in Victorian homes and the starting point of Florida's first cross-state railway. Those seeking elaborate resorts or seasonal condominiums have a wide choice throughout the state, and travelers on modest budgets can easily find moderate accommodations. Several islands are state or national parks, inviting day visitors, fishermen, divers, and campers. The Scottish naturalist John Muir, who walked across the state from Amelia Island to the Cedar Keys in 1867, wrote of the Cedar Keys, "the climate of these precious islets is simply warm summer and warmer summer, corresponding in time with winter and summer in the North. The weather goes smoothly over the points of union betwixt the twin summers." This is still true of Florida today, whose islands offer sufficient sand, turquoise water, light, and shells to satisfy the most deprived northern refugee.

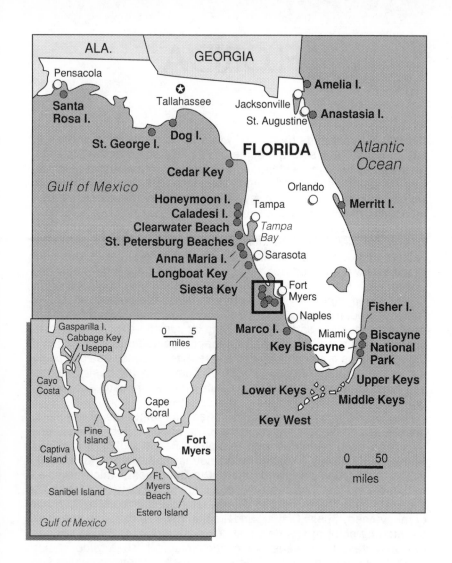

FLORIDA

AMELIA ISLAND

Area Code 904

LOCATION   At the northernmost tip of Florida, across the St. Marys River from Georgia, 32 miles northeast of Jacksonville.

SIZE   13.5 miles long; width varies from ¼ mile to 2 miles.

ACCESS   *Car:* Rt. A1A from Talbot Island. *Air:* To Jacksonville International Airport or Fernandina Municipal Airport (private aircraft only, 5,200-foot paved/lighted runway). *Private boat.*

HISTORY AND DESCRIPTION   Amelia Island, the location of Florida's northernmost city, Fernandina Beach, was named by General James Oglethorpe in honor of Princess Amelia, third child of King George II, born June 10, 110. Fernandina Beach is an appealing seaside port with narrow historic streets. It is the only place in the U.S. to have existed under 8 different flags: French, Spanish, British, Patriots, Green Cross of Florida, Mexican, Confederate, and United States. The island was first claimed for France in 1562; then it was captured for Spain, which ruled it from 1565–1763. The English controlled it between 1763 and 1783 and the Spanish from 1783–1821 (interrupted by the flags hoisted by the Patriots of Amelia Island in 1812, the Green Cross of Florida in 1817, and Mexican rebels in 1817). Spain ceded Florida to the United States in 1821, but the Confederate flag flew over the island from April 1861 to March 1862.

Amelia Island became prosperous soon after the Civil War, when Northern tourists began coming down on the Mallory Steamship Line. The island has had a colorful history; President James Monroe once called Fernandina Beach a "festering fleshpot" because of the pirates and smugglers who anchored there. During Prohibition, the port was a stronghold of rumrunners.

In the late 19th century, great 4- and 5-masted schooners crowded the harbor, and many ornate buildings were constructed. Tourism waned in the early part of the century, but the late Victorian buildings still stood and today the island's 49-block downtown area is listed in the National Register of Historic Places. The modern shrimping industry was founded here early this century; each year, the first weekend in May is celebrated with the Isle of Eight Flags Annual Shrimp Festival of arts, crafts, and entertainments. Fernandina Beach, which once had an erosion problem, has been renourished. It was called "one of the 10 most beautiful beaches in the world" by the host of the television program "Lifestyles of the Rich and Famous," and several movies have been filmed here, including "Naked Under the Sun" and "The New Adventures of Pippi Longstocking."

POINTS OF INTEREST Fernandina Beach has fine old Victorian houses; the 1878 Palace Saloon is the second oldest in the state of Florida and advertises "refreshing libations" in a Victorian atmosphere; it has hand-carved bar murals and antiques. In 1973, 30 blocks were designated an Historic District, and in 1986 additional blocks were nominated to extend its boundaries.

Centre Street, S. 7th, and N. 6th Streets are especially charming, with such buildings as the Lesesne House (1860), the Tabby House (1885), and the Bailey House (1895; see Lodging). Centre Street offers an enjoyable place to stroll, as utility lines were placed underground in the late 1970s; today it is a mini-plaza with benches in each block and landscaping. The old railroad depot houses the Chamber of Commerce; the building is a survival of the days when Florida's first cross-state railroad ran between Fernandina Beach and Cedar Key.

The Florida Museum of Transportation and History, 233 S. Cedar St. (261–7378), has displays on the history of trolleys and electric railroads in Florida during the 19th century.

Amelia Island Museum of History, 233 S. 3rd St. (261–7378), offers two walk-in tours a day, Monday-Saturday, at 11:00 A.M. and 2:00 P.M.

The Mediterranean-style post office building, completed in 1912, has sculptured garlands over the doorways; there are marble stairways inside and a spectacular 2-story Federal Courtroom on the second floor.

The San Carlos Winery, 112 South 3rd St. (277–3236), invites visitors for tours.

The Amelia Lighthouse marks the Amelia Island-St. Marys entrance from the ocean. Believed to be the oldest structure remaining intact on the island, it was completed and lighted in 1839, replacing an earlier lighthouse at the southern tip of Cumberland Island. It was fully automated in 1956.

North of Amelia Island is Georgia's Cumberland Island National Seashore, reached by ferry from St. Marys, GA. South of Amelia is Fort George Island, site of Fort George and the Zephaniah Kingsley Plantation State Historic Site. It is one of the few remaining examples of the plantation system of territorial Florida, and has slave quarters, a carriage house, and a guided tour. The Kingsley (1817) and Don Juan McQueen (1792) houses are among the oldest in the state. The

Mayport-Fort George ferry provides a charming bit of nostalgia, cherished by Floridians and tourists alike.

Between Amelia Island and Jacksonville, a 16-mile scenic toll road, the Buccaneer Trail, leads through undeveloped beach land and over causeways connecting several islands.

SIGHTSEEING TOURS There are walking tours of the Historic District organized by the Amelia Island Museum of History (see Points of Interest).

PARKS, BEACHES, AND CAMPING **Parks:** Fort Clinch State Park covers over a thousand acres at the north end of Amelia Island. It was named for General Duncan Lamont Clinch, an important figure in Florida's Seminole War of the 1830s. Fort construction began in 1847; during the Civil War, it was first occupied by Confederate troops and later by Federal forces. The fort is in an excellent state of preservation. There is a nature trail, and there are living history interpretations by rangers dressed in Union uniforms, who demonstrate the daily chores of the garrison soldier in 1864. You may observe them maintaining the fort, cooking meals, and keeping sentry duty. A 1,500-foot ocean fishing pier, the Amelia Island Park, and several city parks provide additional recreational opportunities. At the southern end of the island, horses can be rented from Sea Horse Stables for trail rides along the beach; reservations are required. **Beaches:** The sand of the Amelia Island beach is fine white quartz; the strand is extremely popular, and wide enough for vehicles to drive along (permits required). **Camping:** There is camping at Fort Clinch State Park, as well as fishing, swimming, and boating; a boat ramp on the Amelia River is available for launching.

MARINAS Fernandina Harbour Marina (261–0355) is the first Florida stop on the Intracoastal Waterway, and for many years was the site of the only Florida marine welcome station. The station was closed in 1985, and the marina completely renovated and expanded. There are 36 transient slips; maximum length 200 feet; approach depth 28 feet; dockside depth 18 feet; electric power—yes; restaurant within walking distance—yes. The waterfront adjacent to the marina also marks the beginning of the historic district with its shops and Victorian architecture.

Amelia Island Yacht Basin (277–4615); 10 transient slips; maximum length 80 feet; approach depth 6 feet; dockside depth 6 feet; electric power—yes; restaurant within walking distance—no.

RESTAURANTS The Crab Trap, 31 N. 2nd St. (261–4749), located in an old warehouse, has a quaint nautical atmosphere. It offers fried and broiled seafood; the Crabbers' Delight, with fish, shrimp, and oysters, is a local favorite.**$$**

The 1878 Steak House and Seafood Restaurant, 12 N. 2nd St., in the Historic District, just off Centre (261–4049), has fresh seafood and a Louisiana Raw Bar. They specialize in steak cooked at the table, as well as seafood. The restaurant has become quite popular with patrons of the new marina.**$$**

Jad's, 4802 Palmetto Walk (277–2350), on A1A, is in a 2-story Charleston-type country home with many-paned windows. They specialize in Lowcountry cuisine, serving she-crab soup, fresh fish en-croute, and interesting shrimp, veal, and chicken dishes.**$$**

The Marina Seafood Restaurant, 101 Centre St., (261-5310), is open for breakfast, lunch and dinner and serves seafood straight from the docks.**$$**

The Sandbar, 3 miles north of the Amelia Island Plantation, on the Intracoastal Waterway (261–4185), is the oldest family-owned restaurant in North Florida. Specializing in seafood since 1932, it has long been a favorite with boaters (no docking, but so good they often take taxis from Fernandina Beach). Patty McNeil is the chief cook; her mother was with the restaurant 17 years. The seafood platters are local favorites.**$$**

The five Amelia Island Plantation restaurants are not open to the public except for Sunday brunch (no reservations required; see Lodging). They range from **$** to **$$$**.

LODGING

Amelia Island Plantation (US except FL 800/874–6878; FL 800/342–6841) is a family-oriented luxury resort community fronting a broad 4 mile beach protected by massive dunes; it has a 2-story inn as well as a number of villas. There is a 27-hole Pete Dye golf course and an 18-hole Tom Fazio masterpiece, along with a tennis park placed amid live oaks dripping with moss, and large magnolia trees. Other amenities include a health/fitness center, paddleboats, canoes, horses for beach riding, supervised children's programs, electric cars, and boardwalks through lighted sunken forest marshland. Chris Evert Lloyd maintains a condominium here.**$$$**

The Amelia Surf and Racket Club, 800 Amelia Parkway S. (261-0511), has kitchen villas, and balconies with ocean views.**$$$**

The Bailey House, Fernandina Beach (261–5390), built in 1895, is a Victorian bed-and-breakfast inn with turrets, gables, fish-scale decoration, and many windows. Effingham Bailey, for whom the house was built, was an agent for a steamship company and it is thought that the outstanding craftsmanship displayed in the home was done by boat-builder carpenters. It is now owned by Tom and Diane Hay; Ken Nolan is the innkeeper. Rates include an expanded continental breakfast (muffins, fresh fruit, beverages, juices).**$$**

Another bed-and-breakfast inn is the 1735 House, 584 S. Fletcher, Amelia Island, FL (261–5878), owned by Gary and Emily Grable. The inn is about 100 years old. The rooms have a suite format, accommodating up to four people, and private baths; rates include a continental breakfast.**$$**

RENTALS   Professional Property Management, Box
                                1022, Fernandina Beach, FL (261–7716),
                                handles vacation accommodations in private cottages, houses, and condos.

Amelia Rental and Management Services, 5225 First Coast Highway S., Fernandina Beach (US except FL 800/874–8679; FL 261–9129), handles vacation accommodations at a number of places.

Amelia Island Lodging Systems, 584 S. Fletcher, Amelia Island, FL (261–4148).

Further listings available from the Chamber of Commerce.

CONTACT   Amelia Island/Fernandina Beach Chamber
                                of Commerce, 102 Centre St., Box 472,
                                Fernandina Beach, FL 32034 (261–3248).

ANASTASIA ISLAND

Area Code 904
LOCATION   East of St. Augustine.

SIZE   18 miles by about ½ mile.

ACCESS   *Car:* Via the Bridge of Lions from downtown
                                St. Augustine. *Air:* There is commercial
                                service to Jacksonville; St. Augustine has a
small airport for private aircraft. *Private boat.*

HISTORY AND   Anastasia Island is a barrier island extend-
DESCRIPTION   ing south from the St. Augustine Inlet to
                                the Matanzas Inlet. Attention is often fo-
cused on St. Augustine, the oldest city in the country, but the staff of the Historic St. Augustine Preservation Board recently reconstructed the history of Anastasia Island itself. There were Colonial settlements on the island; one was located midway on the island. The Spanish regarded the island as useful and had watchtowers on the northern tip; sentries assisted ships through the inlet and warned of approaching enemy vessels. They began constructing a stone fort in 1672. One early landowner was Jesse Fish, who had a 40-acre orange orchard on the island in the 1700s. In 1793, another settler, Lorenzo Rodriguez, obtained a land grant for a parcel of 124 acres; it passed through many hands, but was intact as late as the 1870s. In 1871, the U.S.

Government purchased a 5-acre parcel and erected a lighthouse in 1874, along with keeper's quarters in 1876. The lighthouse is still in use and the keeper's house is operated as a museum. Soon after the turn of the century, H. J. Ritchie and M. R. Bean established a trolley to the island. In 1923, D. P. Davis began developing the island. In 1926 the Mediterranean Revival drawbridge, graced with lordly Carrara marble lions sculpted by F. Romanelli of Florence, Italy, replaced the trolley.

The town of St. Augustine Beach is at the northern end of the island; Crescent Beach is in the middle, and Fort Matanzas is at the lower end. Marineland is just south of Matanzas Inlet. Between the state park and Marineland is a stretch of beach with spacious single and multi-family accommodations, camping resorts, restaurants and recreational offerings.

Nearby St. Augustine is the oldest city in the United States; it was here that Ponce de Leon, in search of the legendary Fountain of Youth, landed in 1513; the first permanent European settlement was established here in 1565 by Pedro Menendez de Aviles.

POINTS OF INTEREST   The St. Augustine Alligator Farm, 2 miles south of the Bridge of Lions (824–3337), was established in 1893; it offers a view of huge alligators and crocodiles, and an alligator wrestling show is a featured event.

The 1874 Lighthouse and 1876 Keeper's House, which is a museum, are at the northern end of the island (see History and Description).

Fort Matanzas National Monument, at the southern tip of the island, extends over an area of 298 acres. It includes the southern tip of Anastasia Island (site of the visitor center). The actual fort, visible from the visitor center, is on Rattlesnake Island. Access is by free ferry. (For information, call 471–0116 or 829–6506). In 1565, Don Pedro Menendez de Aviles, founder of St. Augustine, captured and killed more than 200 French Huguenots who had settled here in an attempt to claim the land for France.

The Cross and Sword, the official state play, is an outdoor drama by Paul Green depicting the story of the founding of St. Augustine; it is held on the northern end of Anastasia Island from mid-June through mid-August.

Marineland of Florida (471–1111), though not actually on the island, is 18 miles south of St. Augustine. It is a township (population 8) which is home to one of the world's most popular marine-oriented tourist attractions. There are dolphin shows, oceanariums, and other aquatic displays.

There are many attractions in St. Augustine, including the Castillo de San Marco National Monument (1672–95) and many historic structures; some are operated as essentially commercial enterprises, but others are administered by the St. Augustine Historical Society. St.

George St., the heart of the historic district, is a delightful narrow pedestrian street, European in flavor and well worth a stroll. There are old tabby, coquina, and wooden houses with balconies, along with restaurants and interesting shops.

The Lightner Museum, in the former Alcazar Hotel, has a large collection of Tiffany glass, a Victorian Village, and other exhibits.

SIGHTSEEING TOURS The *Matanzas Queen*, at the Fort Matanzas National Monument, provides free shuttle service to Fort Matanzas.

In St. Augustine, 2 scenic cruises leave from the Municipal Yacht Pier, the *Victory II* (824–1806) and the *Spirit of St. Augustine* (824–3090), a sternwheeler able to carry 150 passengers.

Also in St. Augustine there are sightseeing trains, 170 San Marco Ave. (829–6545), with guides giving narrated tours of the historic part of the city.

Colee's Sightseeing Carriage Tours, on the St. Augustine Bay Front near the Fort Castillo de San Marco (829–2818), offer narrated tours of the historic area.

PARKS, BEACHES AND **Parks:** The Anastasia State Recreation
CAMPING Area has over 1,000 acres and is the site of the coquina quarries from which the building material for the Castillo de San Marcos was dug. Here there are nature trails, picnic tables, and a bath house. Favor-Dykes State Park is near Marineland; this is a wilderness of piny woods with facilities for camping and recreation. **Beaches:** There are many miles of ocean beach; the stretch within the state park is carefully maintained. **Camping:** There are 139 sites in the State Recreation Area as well as a number of campgrounds on St. Augustine Beach.

MARINAS St. Augustine is a popular stop for mariners, and the sightseeing train has a courtesy van pick-up service at some marinas.

In the vicinity of Anastasia Island, there are several marinas. One of the best-known is Marineland (471–0087); 20 transient slips; maximum length 100 feet; approach depth 6 feet; dockside depth 6 feet; electric power—yes; restaurant within walking distance—yes.

RESTAURANTS Cowboy's, Dondanville Rd. (471–2332), serves seafood, has a casual nautical atmosphere, and overlooks the Intracoastal Waterway; their grilled fish is always popular.**$**

The Dolphin, at the Quality Inn Marineland (*see* Lodging) specializes in seafood and offers oceanfront dining.**$$**

Palermo's Fisherman, 4 Fl. A1A (471–2811), serves Italian and French food, as well as seafood. Breads, pasta, and desserts are made on the premises. Mr. Palermo is a watercolorist and exhibits and sells his beach scenes and historical buildings in the restaurant; his son Paul, who is the chef, has won awards for his culinary creations.**$**

There are many other restaurants; the Chamber of Commerce will send a list.

LODGING   The Conch House Marina Resort, 57 Com-
                               ares Ave., St. Augustine Beach 32084
                               (829–8646), has a marina/dock, and a
pier; it is on the Salt Run Inlet at the northern end of the island.**$$**

Quality Inn Marineland, Hwy. A1A, Box 122, St. Augustine Beach, 32086 (471–1222), has balconies, tennis, golf privileges; it is on the oceanfront and has a marina.**$$**

Sheraton Anastasia Inn, 2050 FL A1A S. at Pope Rd., St. Augustine Beach 32084 (471–2575); this is on the ocean and has a pool.**$$**

There are many other motels on the island; the Chamber of Commerce will send a list.

RENTALS   There are many rentals, both condos and
                               cottages; the Chamber of Commerce has a
                               large folder with the names of some of the
beach house owners. One realtor handling rentals is St. Augustine Shores Realty, 49 Shore Blvd., St. Augustine, 32086 (797–4050).

CONTACT   St. Augustine & St. Johns County Chamber
                               of Commerce, Drawer O, St. Augustine, FL
                               32085 (829–5681).

ANNA MARIA ISLAND

Area Code 813
LOCATION   7 miles west of Bradenton.

SIZE   7½ miles long; a few blocks wide.

ACCESS   **Car:** Highways 64 and 684 from Bradenton.
                               Air: Bradenton-Sarasota Airport has com-
                               mercial flights. **Private boat.**

HISTORY AND   On old Spanish maps, the island was
DESCRIPTION   marked as "Ana-Maria-Cay," named in
                               honor of Mary, the mother of Christ, and
her mother, Ann. About 1840 the first American settlers arrived, and found Cuban fishing camps on the island. Rurick Cobb, the island's second settler, built the first resort, the Oar House, about the turn of the century; it burned in 1980. The island has 3 cities: Anna Maria City, at the northern end, which is largely residential; Holmes Beach,

Anna Maria Island

in the center, the largest city and the hub of commercial activity; and, on the southern end, Bradenton Beach, gateway to Coquina Beach and Cortez Beach.

Anna Maria Island offers more public access to its beaches than Longboat Key, to the south, where parking is severely limited (though there are access points). Tarpon fishing is quite popular from May-July.

POINTS OF INTEREST   In Bradenton, Manatee Village Historical Park (794–1800) has renovated historic buildings. The South Florida Museum and Bishop Planetarium (746–4132) are also in Bradenton; the former is the home of Snooty the Manatee, the oldest living manatee born in captivity; the museum also houses natural history exhibits and historical dioramas. The Gamble Plantation (1845–50) in Bradenton, on U.S. 301, is the only Confederate museum in Florida and the oldest building on Florida's West Coast. De Soto National Memorial Park, 5 miles west of Bradenton, has living history demonstrations related to de Soto's journey from December–April. In April, the de Soto Celebration has a re-enactment of his landing.

Egmont Key, in Tampa Bay, is 3 miles northwest of Anna Maria. Although it is accessible only by boat, this historic, 2-mile-long island deserves a visit. It has beautiful beaches with sea oats, and offers excellent shelling. The 1847 Egmont Key lighthouse and Fort Dade (1900), now crumbling, built during the Spanish American War, are here as well. It is also home to the threatened gopher tortoise. An excursion boat, the *Miss Cortez*, makes twice weekly trips (see Sightseeing Tours). Many people who are staying on Anna Maria Island rent a boat to explore Egmont Key, and there are tours from Cortez (*see* Sightseeing Tours).

SIGHTSEEING TOURS   None on the island, but there are cruises from Cortez on a Mississippi-style stern-wheeler (Seafood Shack Showboat, 794–1236).

The *Miss Cortez* (794–1223) makes excursions to Egmont Key on Tuesdays and Thursdays from Cortez, a fishing village just west of Bradenton on Cortez Road and the Intracoastal Waterway.

In downtown Sarasota, the cruise ship *Le Barge* is docked at Marina Jack (366–6116). Narrated cruises of Sarasota Bay are given, along with special cruises featuring live entertainment and meals.

PARKS, BEACHES AND   **Parks and Beaches:** Anna Maria's four
CAMPING   parks have beautiful beaches. Bayfront Park, on the north end of the island, offers swimming, surfing, shelling, fishing, picnicking, and boating. Coquina Beach, on the Gulf of Mexico, has 96 acres, much of it lined with Australian pines, and provides opportunities for swimming, surfing, and fishing. Cortez Beach adjoins Coquina Beach at Cortez Road. Manatee Beach, on the Gulf of Mexico at State Road 64 West, has swimming, showers, restrooms, a playground, and other amenities. **Camping:** None on the island, but there are campgrounds in Bradenton, Palmetto, and Cortez.

MARINAS   Bradenton Beach Marina (778–2288); 28 transient slips; maximum length 50 feet; approach depth 9 feet; dockside depth 6 feet; electric power—yes; restaurant within walking distance—no.

Island Marina, Holmes Beach (778–6602); 3 transient slips; maximum length 35 feet; approach depth 4 feet; dockside depth 4 feet; electric power—yes; restaurant within walking distance—yes.

Pete Reynard's (*see* Restaurants) has daily slip rentals, if available; maximum length 50 feet; approach depth 4 feet; dockside depth 4 feet; electric power—yes; restaurant within walking distance—yes.

Galati's Boats and Motors, Holmes Beach (778–0755), close to the Anna Maria Yacht Basin; 10 transient slips; maximum length 50 feet; approach depth 9 feet; dockside depth 7 feet; electric power—yes; restaurant within walking distance—yes.

Across the Intracoastal Waterway at Cortez is the Seafood Shack, which has 10 transient slips and sternwheeler cruises.

There are also the Coquina Beach boat ramp, Sarasota Bay and State Road 789, and the Kingfish boat ramp, north side of Manatee Ave. on Palma Sola Causeway.

RESTAURANTS   "Fast Eddie's Place," 101 Bay Blvd., Anna
                              Maria 33501 (778–2251), advertises
                              "warm beer, lousy food," and offers a fam-
ily atmosphere with all-you-can-eat portions.**$**

Harbor House, 200 N. Gulf Dr., Bradenton Beach 33510 (778–
2320), has a gulf view, serves seafood, oysters, clams, and has a
patio bar with live entertainment nightly.**$**

Pete Reynard's Restaurant, 5325 Marina Dr., Holmes Beach 33510
(778–2233) has a revolving Compass Room, and serves a Sunday
brunch with complimentary champagne. They are situated on the bay,
with glass windows and a pleasant night view.**$$**

The Sandbar, 100 Spring Ave., Anna Maria 33501 (778-0444), in
elegant Gulfside surroundings, has a patio popular for watching the
sunset and listening to live music; specialty is the fresh catch of the
day.**$$**

LODGING   Bali Hai Resort, 6900 Gulf Dr., Holmes
                              Beach 33510 (778–6604) is a gulf-front
                              resort with a private beach.**$$**

Blue Water Beach Club, 6306 Gulf Dr., Holmes Beach 33510 (778–
6688) has 129 rooms, all with a view of the Gulf; there are motel
rooms as well as efficiencies and villas.**$$**

Catalina Beach Resort, 1325 Gulf Dr. N., Bradenton Beach 33510
(778–6611); has a private beach and sailboat rentals; there are units
with kitchens and villas.**$$**

Silver Surf, 1301 Gulf Dr., Bradenton Beach, FL 34217 (US except
FL 800/654–4337; FL 800/872–3317) has motel rooms, efficiencies,
and villas; remodeled and expanded in 1987.**$$**

The island has many motels, condominiums, and inns; a full listing
is available from the Chamber of Commerce.

RENTALS   Coconuts Apartments, 100 73rd St.,
                              Holmes Beach, FL 34217 (778–2277) has
                              gulf-front apartments.

Many realtors also handle rentals, including Doug Dowling Realty,
Box 1667, Anna Maria 33501 (778–1222); Dick Wagner, Box L, Bra-
denton Beach 33510 (778–2246) and Helen A. White, Neal & Neal
Realtors, 501 Manatee Ave., Holmes Beach 33510 (778–2261). For
a full list, contact the Chamber of Commerce.

CONTACT   Anna Maria Island Chamber of Commerce,
                              Box 1892, Holmes Beach, FL 33509 (778-
                              1541).

BISCAYNE NATIONAL PARK
Elliott Key, Adams Key, Boca Chita Key,
Sands Key

Area Code 305

LOCATION

21 miles east of Everglades National Park, on Florida's east coast.

SIZE

The area of the islands within the park is 175,000 acres.

ACCESS

Boat only. See Sightseeing Tours for information about tours to these islands. **Air:** There is commercial service to Miami. **Private boat.** Convoy Point, where the Biscayne Park headquarters is located, is reached by taking North Canal Drive east from Homestead. From the Florida Turnpike, take Tallahassee Road (SW 137 Ave.) south to North Canal and then go east.

HISTORY AND DESCRIPTION

The park is a wildlife and historical preserve. Portions of it are on the mainland, where the mangrove shoreline has been carefully maintained. Convoy Point (*see* Access) is headquarters for the park; an information center and visitor services are located here. The remainder of the park consists of small keys set amid magnificent coral reefs, reached by boat travel across over a warm shallow bay.

Biscayne Park was established in 1968, after much controversy. The Upper Keys had been slated for commercial development, but local residents grew alarmed as they realized the natural beauty of the keys and surrounding marine environment might be lost forever. Fortunately, local concern expanded to a national level and the bay and reef tract were preserved. The boundary was adjusted in 1974, and in 1980 Congress designated that Biscayne Monument become Biscayne National Park. Unlike most national parks, its principal beauty comes from its maritime surroundings; here water is emphasized rather than land. It is a paradise for marine life, water birds, boaters, fishermen, snorkelers, and divers, with clear, clean water. The coral reefs are suffused with light and life, and are populated with exotic undersea creatures.

POINTS OF INTEREST

Elliott Key: This is a long narrow key with two docks and a Visitor Center. *Adams Key* is south of it; here there is an information station and a nature trail. *Boca Chita Key* has an ornamental lighthouse, open intermittently. *Sands Key* has popular overnight anchorage sites.

SIGHTSEEING TOURS   Biscayne Aqua Center, Box 1270, Homestead, FL 33030 (247–2400), offers
glass-bottom boat tours and snorkeling
trips to the islands and reefs.

PARKS, BEACHES AND   **Parks:** The mainland park Headquarters is
CAMPING   located at Convoy Point, along with the visitor services. The information station has
exhibits and schedules of park activities. **Beaches:** The islands are
fossilized coral; there are a few very small sandy beaches, but the
coral is not conducive to sand formation. **Camping:** Backcountry
camping is allowed on Elliott Key and Sands Key; you need to get a
free permit at the park headquarters or Elliott Key Visitor Center. There
is a primitive campground also on Boca Chita Key. All trash must be
packed out. Fires are only allowed in camp stoves or designated grills.
There are many mosquitoes; carry bugproof netting and insect repellent.

MARINAS   Elliott Key, Adams Key, and Boca Chita Key
have free boat docks. Elliott Key Harbor
has wet slips for 64 boats ranging in width
from 12 to 18 feet (first come, first served). University Dock, 2 miles
north of Elliott Key Harbor, has a dock and sandy beach.

RESTAURANTS   None.

LODGING   None.

RENTALS   None.

CONTACT   Superintendent, Biscayne National Park,
Box 1369, Homestead, FL 33090–1369
(247-PARK).

CABBAGE KEY

Area Code 813
LOCATION   In Pine Island Sound, east of Cayo Costa
Nature Preserve; Mile Marker 60 on the In-
tracoastal Waterway.

SIZE   100 acres.

ACCESS   **Ferry:** Cruise boat *Tropic Star* from Pineland Marina, Pine Island (283–0015),
every morning at 9:45; there are also tour

boats from Captiva and Fort Myers which stop here (see Pine Island, Captiva, and Fort Myers entries) and the Bocilla Island Club on Pine Island will arrange trips for guests. *Air:* There is commercial service to Fort Myers. *Private boat.*

HISTORY AND
DESCRIPTION
Cabbage Key, which has been called the "living history of Florida islands," was built on top of an ancient Calusa shell mound; it is remarkably unspoiled, despite the numbers of people who come to the inn for lunch and dinner each day. The cozy inn was constructed in 1938 by the son of playwright and novelist Mary Roberts Rinehart. Alan Rinehart and Grace Houghton Rinehart purchased Cabbage Key for $2,500 in 1929, and then spent over $125,000 for the amenities which exist today. Mrs. Rinehart's appreciation for natural beauty was apparent in the planning of the resort; the main building is high on the shell mound, which, at 38 feet above sea level, makes Cabbage Key one of the highest points in this area of Florida. Larry Stultz began running the "Old House" as a restaurant and inn about 40 years ago; it is now owned by Robert Wells, Jr. and managed by Dale Curtis. It has a solar energy system, 5 porches, and 6 working fireplaces. The building tops a sloping lawn, overlooking the marina and a small gift shop. It is not difficult to imagine Hemingway making his home here, sport fishing for tarpon and writing amid the tropical foliage.

POINTS OF INTEREST
The inn is the most memorable feature of the island.

SIGHTSEEING TOURS
None, except that the cruise boats visiting Cabbage Key usually go by other isolated islands in the vicinity of Cabbage Key.

The Inn at Cabbage Key

PARKS, BEACHES AND   **Parks:** None, but there are nature trails.
CAMPING   **Beaches:** There are no recreational
                         beaches; guests are usually taken over to
the Cayo Costa State Park. **Camping:** None.

MARINAS   Cabbage Key Marina (283–2278); 30–40
                         transient slips (according to size boats
                         docked); maximum length 90 feet; ap-
proach depth 7 feet; dockside depth 7 feet; electric power—yes; restaurant within walking distance—yes.

RESTAURANTS   The Inn at Cabbage Key (283–2278) has a
                         pleasant rustic bar and delightful dining
                         room, papered with about 20,000 auto-
graphed dollar bills; in the course of a year, many bills come floating
down from the walls and are auctioned off during the muscular dystro-
phy drive.**$**

LODGING   The inn, open all year, has 6 rooms and 3
                         2-bedroom cottages; reserve well ahead (a
                         two-night minimum stay is required).**$**

RENTALS   None.

CONTACT   Cabbage Key, Box 200, Pineland, FL
                         33945 (283–2278).

CALADESI ISLAND

Area Code 813
LOCATION   Approx. 2 miles off Florida's Gulf Coast,
                         near Dunedin.

SIZE   3 miles by approx. ½ mile.

ACCESS   **Ferry:** From Honeymoon Island, which is ac-
                         cessible by causeway from Dunedin. The
                         ferry is operated by the Captain Anderson
Dinner Boat Co. (734–5263), which took over the ferry in May 1986,
calling it the *Caladesi Connection*. The boats are 2 40-foot catama-
rans. Service on a larger boat is scheduled to begin in the Spring of
1989 from Clearwater. **Air:** There is commercial service to Tampa or
St. Petersburg/Clearwater. **Private boat.**

HISTORY AND   The trip to Caladesi Island State Park from
DESCRIPTION   Honeymoon Island, aboard one of the can-
                         opied, open-air *Caladesi Connection* fer-
ries, takes about 20 minutes. The boat passes small green islands;
long-necked egrets and blue herons, pelicans, and sea gulls are visible en route. The island is rich in dunes, sea oats, exotic shells and
white sandy beaches; boardwalks have been built to protect the fragile
ecology of the island. There are bath houses and shaded pavilions.
Families often bring children over, and other visitors come for nature
study, castnetting for mullet, and boating. Shelling is popular (but no
live seashells may be removed). More than 2 miles of white sand
beach front on the Gulf of Mexico, and the bay side of Caladesi is a
mangrove swamp.

An Indian burial site on Caladesi excavated in the early 1900s bears
evidence that Indians lived on the island prior to the arrival of the
Spaniards in the early 1500s. The island remained unchanged, except
by nature, for several centuries, but in 1921, a hurricane split the
island, forming Hurricane Pass, which today separates Caladesi from
Honeymoon Island. In the late 1800s, Henry Scharrer came upon the
island on a stormy night and thought he had discovered paradise. He
built a house, lived on the island, and raised his daughter Myrtle
there; she rowed across St. Joseph Sound to go to school in Dunedin.
The chimney of the house he built is still visible in the interior of the
island.

Today the island draws visitors from as far away as England and
Germany. Many visitors come on private boats to enjoy the swimming,
beachcombing, and boardwalks. The island was saved in the 1960s
from the ravages of condominium developers and was acquired by the
state as a park.

POINTS OF INTEREST   A nature trail offers good views of coastal
                         strand plants, virgin south Florida slash
                         pine flatwoods, live oak hammocks, and a
mangrove swamp.

SIGHTSEEING TOURS   Interpretive programs and guided walks by
                         Park rangers are provided according to sea-
                         sonal demand.

PARKS, BEACHES AND   **Parks:** See Description section. Coolers
CAMPING   are permitted on the island, but no intoxi-
                         cants. **Beaches:** The beach is one of the
nicest in Pinellas County, with 2½ miles of sugar-fine sand; it is uncrowded, as a rule, since no vehicles are allowed on the island. **Camping:** This is a day-use state park; there are no overnight facilities, un-
less you stay on your boat at the marina or anchor out in the Gulf.

Caladesi Island

MARINAS   There is a marina on the bay side of the
                        island with 100 slips; at mean low tide the
                        approach depth is 4 feet; dockside depth 7
feet; electric power—no; restaurant within walking distance—no.
Docking space is available on a first-come, first-served basis. Boats
can be anchored offshore in the Gulf during calm weather.

RESTAURANTS   None, but there is a concession stand with
                        hot food and cold drinks.

LODGING   None.

RENTALS   None.

CONTACT   Caladesi Island State Park, #1 Causeway
                        Blvd., Dunedin, FL 33528 (443–5903).

CAYO COSTA STATE PARK

Area Code 813
LOCATION   On the Intracoastal Waterway, north of
                        North Captiva Island, on the south side of
                        Boca Grande Pass.

SIZE   6 miles long; width varies from 200 yards
                        to 1 mile.

ACCESS   *Ferry:* Cruise boat *Tropic Star* from Pine-
                        land Marina, Pine Island (283–0015), all
                        year, every morning at 9:45; there are also

less frequent boats from Boca Grande (Knight Brothers, 964–2484) and Punta Gorda (King Fisher Line, 639–0969). The Bocilla Island Club on Pine Island will arrange trips for guests. **Air:** There is commercial service to Fort Myers. **Private boat.**

HISTORY AND   Cayo Costa State Park, accessible by tour
DESCRIPTION   boat from Pine Island and Captiva, is one
                         of the largest undeveloped barrier islands
remaining in Florida. Dedicated to preserving Florida's natural beauty, it looks as it did 500 years ago, when the Spaniards first arrived. The only warm-blooded animals include birds, a few wild pigs, and a lone wild horse. The Johnson shoals yield shells and sand dollars at their finest. It is designated a game and bird refuge, and ospreys and bald eagles nest on the island. There is also a large colony of white pelicans wintering in the area each year. Loggerhead sea turtles nest on island beaches on summer nights.

The only inhabitants now are Lee County park rangers, though there was once a settlement. Their headquarters is on the east side of the key overlooking Pelican Bay.

POINTS OF INTEREST   There are miles of beaches and dunes.
                         Cayo Costa has an extensive mangrove
                         swamp, along with Australian pines, cab-
bage palm forests, and gumbo limbo hammocks. The islands are interesting botanically because of the mixture of native plants—some characteristic of temperate North America and others found in the West Indian tropics.

SIGHTSEEING TOURS   None, but some cruise boats, such as the
                         Tropic Star from Pine Island, call at other
                         islands also, such as Cabbage Key; if you
are staying on the island, you might, after your visit, have lunch on Cabbage Key.

PARKS, BEACHES AND   **Parks:** The entire island is a nature pre-
CAMPING   serve; there are some trails and board-
                         walks through the vegetation. **Beaches:**
There are miles of beach with fine white sand. **Camping:** There are campsites in a shady area on the Gulf side, one mile from the docks (tents only). Twelve rustic cabins are available on a reservation basis (966–3594, Monday through Friday, 8 A.M. to 5 P.M.). They are furnished with bare mattresses and have restroom facilities, picnic tables, and fireplaces. For holidays and winter weekends reserve well in advance.

MARINAS   On the Gulf side, docks are provided for day
                         use only. Overnight dockage is available
                         for campers and cabin occupants on the
                         bay side only.

RESTAURANTS	None; take food and drinks for the time you plan to be on the island (no intoxicating beverages allowed).
LODGING	There are 12 rustic cabins (see Camping section for details).
RENTALS.	None.
CONTACT	For general information: Cayo Costa State Park, Box 1150, Boca Grande, FL 33921 (964-0375). For cabin reservations call 966–3594.

CEDAR KEY

Area Code 904

LOCATION	Gulf of Mexico, 50 miles west of I–75 at Gainesville, 4 miles into Gulf.
SIZE	Cedar Key is the largest settlement, approximately 1,000, on the Cedar Keys, a group of about 100 tiny islands which form

a National Wildlife Refuge and Bird Sanctuary.

ACCESS	**Car:** Rt. 24 from Gainesville. **Air:** 2,400-foot lighted landing strip. **Private boat:** Public dock with slips.
HISTORY AND DESCRIPTION	"If the people of this country knew as much about Cedar Key as we do," wrote one Northwestern 19th-century visitor to the is-

land, "the place could not contain the number of those who would come here." A century later, Cedar Key is still fighting to maintain the ambience of a quiet turn-of-the-century island town. Second Street has weathered balconied storefronts and traffic is minimal. Within a few blocks in any direction you are very much aware of water, either at the town dock or rippling against the working boats pulled up in the Back Bayou anchorage.

Cedar Key was first settled in the 1840s, but gained importance when the railroad from Fernandina was completed in 1861. It was called the Venice of America. During the War Between the States supplies for the Confederacy were brought to the port by blockade runners. The town was captured by Federal forces in 1862. Lumbering flourished after the war, until the cedars, cypress, and pine were depleted in the manufacture of pencils; later, the seafood industry provided a livelihood for residents. The town was devastated at the end of the 19th century by a fierce hurricane, which destroyed most of the buildings. The chain of barrier islands is home to many migratory and shore birds, such as the white pelican, roseate spoonbill, and bald eagle.

Two ardent preservationists are Marcia Rogers, owner of the Historic Island Hotel, and Dorothy Tyson, a native of Britain who is President of the Cedar Key Historical Society. Both hope to retain the purity and simplicity of the little island community and prevent flavor-wrecking incursions by developers; "if we go down, we shall go down fighting," says Dorothy Tyson. Julie Stetzel, editor of the *Cedar Key Beacon*, says the island "is like Key West as it once was, with a flavor reminiscent of a New England fishing village. The world hasn't really found Cedar Key yet." A few emissaries from the world have done so, however, including writers and artists, some of whom exhibit in the island's small galleries. The town has a surprising number of non-native residents who, on brief visits, were seized by the notion of never leaving and found themselves house-hunting that very day. Many of the old homes and other buildings have been surveyed and found to be eligible for the National Historic Register.

POINTS OF INTEREST   The Cedar Key State Museum, Highway 24 and 2nd St. (closed Tues., Wed.), set in 18 acres of wilderness overlooking the Gulf of Mexico, has dioramas and panels illustrating the town's history, along with a famous shell collection assembled by St. Clair Whitman. The Cedar Key Historical Society Museum, 2nd and D Sts., has a large collection of early photos, articles, maps, and records of Cedar Key which give a memorable picture of its early development.

There are a number of uninhabited keys nearby, such as Atsena Otie Key, Way Key, Snake Key, Scale Key, and Rye Key (home of Hodgson's Mill, of John Muir fame); see Sightseeing section.

SIGHTSEEING TOURS   Island Hopper Scenic Cruises (Jim Kemp, 543-5889) offers trips around some of the uninhabited keys nearby. Guides are available for offshore fishing trips; call Abbie Nappier (543–5511), Hal Hodges (543–5756) or Bill and Anna Rae Roberts (each has a boat; 543/5690) or consult the Chamber of Commerce. Boat rentals are available at Cason's Hardware & Marine Supplies.

PARKS, BEACHES AND   **Parks:** The City Park, facing the Gulf of
CAMPING   Mexico, between 1st and 2nd Streets, offers picnic tables, a gazebo, a children's playground, and restrooms. The Cedar Keys are federally protected sanctuaries. Bird, North, Snake, Seahorse, Richards, Scale, Hickory, and Live Oak Keys are part of the refuge, which was established in 1929. The brown pelican and osprey nest here. Access is by boat only; the public may use the beaches between July and December. (For in-

formation, contact Refuge Manager, Rt. 1, Box 1193-C, Chiefland, FL 32326; 493–5238). Bicycles are for rent at Park Place, the Cedar Cove Motel and the Faraway Inn; there is moped rental at the Country Store. **Beaches:** There is a public bathing beach at the municipal park, and, as explained under **Parks,** the public may use the beaches in the Wildlife Refuge between July and December. **Camping:** There is camping at the Cedar Key RV and Trailer Park (543–5150) and at the Sunset Isle RV and Trailer Park (543–5375). Hunting, camping, and building fires are not allowed on the Keys which are part of the National Wildlife Refuge.

MARINAS   Cedar Municipal Dock (no telephone no.) has boat slips (first come, first served). There are strong currents here; be careful. 4 transient slips; maximum length 100 feet; approach depth 10 feet; dockside depth 14 feet; electric power—no; restaurant within walking distance—yes (there are several good seafood restaurants on a shopping street with boutiques).

RESTAURANTS   The Captain's Table, West Pier (543–5441); closed Mon., and Johnson's Brown Pelican (543-5428), both perched on wooden stilts, offer shady seating out over the water and specialize in seafood and palm salad, an interesting concoction native to Cedar Key.**$$**

The Cedar Cove Dining Room, on 2nd St. (543–5332), is known for its gourmet fare.**$$**

The Heron Restaurant, 2nd St. (543–5666), has a Victorian atmosphere and gourmet food.**$$**

The Historic Island Hotel (see Lodging) serves excellent natural food without preservatives; specialties include poppyseed bread and soft shell crabs. The dining room is graced with a poignant manatee doll sculpture and has a pleasant formal atmosphere.**$$**

LODGING   The Cedar Cove Motel and Marina, 2nd St. (543–5332), has a pool and allows pets.**$$**

The Cedar Inn, on 2nd St., Box 490 (543–5455), is a 2-story structure with airy rooms; homemade pastries and coffee are included in the rate.**$**

The Historic Island Hotel, 2nd St. (543–5111). The hotel was built in 1849 as a general store, and is the only building in Levy County on the National Register of Historic Buildings; it became a hotel in 1915. Marcia Rogers has owned it since 1980, and is striving to restore it to its original condition. She is a notary public, and has conducted many weddings here. The lobby has a homey quality, with carefully tended plants and comfortable furniture. An immense upper lobby characterizes the second floor, with doors on 4 sides, an historic wind chimney, a library in an alcove, a chess table almost insisting that you sit down beneath the shaded lamp and relax for a game at least, and 100-year-old murals with palm scenes Ms. Rogers hopes to restore. The beds are enfolded by immense mosquito netting canopies which impart a bridal feeling. Actor Richard Boone, stays in one of the front rooms adjacent to the wide veranda which wraps around the second floor. You may wish to enjoy the continental breakfast (included in the room rates, with hot muffins) out here, amid the hammock and swing and comfortable canvas sling chairs.**$$**

Island Place, 1st and C St. Box 687 (543–5307), has kitchen condos.**$$**

The Park Place Motel, 2nd at A St. Box 613 (543–5737), offers modern studio, efficiency, and loft units. Near the pier, it has balconies facing the Gulf.

RENTALS   The Faraway Inn Motel, Third and G. Sts. (543-5330), has rental cottages. Island Place and Park Place have modern condos for longer rentals. Rentals are also available at Seahorse Cottages (543-5310).

CONTACT   Cedar Key Area Chamber of Commerce, Box 610, Cedar Key 32625 (543–5600).

CLEARWATER BEACH

Area Code 813
LOCATION   2 miles west of Clearwater, which is 22 miles north of St. Petersburg and about the same distance west of Tampa.

SIZE   4 miles long.

ACCESS   *Car:* Causeway from Clearwater. *Air:* There is commercial air service to Tampa and St. Petersburg/Clearwater. **Private boat.**

HISTORY AND   The community is a corporate part of Clear-
DESCRIPTION   water, connected with its downtown section by a 2-mile palm-lined causeway across Clearwater Harbor. The island, however, is self-contained, with residential and business sections, hotels, motels, and restaurants. The beach has easy public access (but don't forget to feed the parking meter; the police are fanatical about this).

The city of Clearwater occupies the highest bluffs along Florida's coast, standing 30 to 75 feet above sea level. It was first visited in

1528 by Panfilo de Narvaez, who arrived with 5 ships, 40 horses, and 600 men. He was greeted by a large tribe of Timucuan Indians, which he drove out of the area. The Indians regained it, however, and held it until they were conquered in the Seminole Wars of 1835–42. The Timucuans had named the area "pocotopaug," or "clear water." Fort Harrison was built in 1841 on the bluffs overlooking the harbor. The area was rapidly settled, and the first newspaper, the *Clear Water Times*, was published in 1873. In 1880, Clearwater began to be developed as a resort community, when the first hotel, the Orange Bluff, was built. The town was incorporated in 1891, three years after the narrow-gauge Orange Belt Railroad came to the city en route to St. Petersburg. After the freeze of 1894–95, the railroad was taken over by Henry B. Plant, who later built the Belleview Biltmore hotel (*see* Lodging).

Clearwater Beach was originally known as Tate's Island, named after a young couple who lived there just before the turn of the century. Ernest Tate bought the 200-acre island in 1897 for $1.25 an acre, and sold it a few years later for $450 an acre, a bargain for the purchaser seldom equalled in the annals of real estate. A rickety wooden bridge to Clearwater Beach was built in 1916, nicknamed the "rickets bridge," but it soon became obsolete and was replaced by the present Garden Memorial Causeway in 1926. There are many vestiges of the early decades of the century here, such as Heilman's Beachcomber restaurant, dating from 1910. The Palm Pavilion, in the central beach area, has been in the family of Howard Hamilton a number of years. He has watched Clearwater Beach grow, he says, "from a little fishing community in the 1950s to quite a big place now." The area attracts many retired people, some of whom are shaky drivers, but it is also popular with young refugees from colder climates, who pounce on jobs in the beachfront restaurants and shops, taking in the sun and surf in their leisure time. The strand is graced by Big Pier 60, a long pier extending into the Gulf, ideal for fishing.

POINTS OF INTEREST   The Florida Aquarium and the Clearwater Marine Science Center, 249 Windward Passage, Clearwater Beach (447–0980); the center specializes in marine research and also rescues many sea animals.

It would take several weeks to make even brief visits to the many rich attractions of the surrounding area. Just a short list includes the Salvador Dali Museum in St. Petersburg (which has the world's largest collection of works by Dali); Busch Gardens in Tampa; Ybor City, in Tampa (founded by Cuban cigar makers and the heart of the city's Latin Quarter); the Ybor City State Museum; the Tampa Museum of Art; the Sunken Gardens in St. Petersburg, the Museum of Fine Arts of St. Petersburg, the Henry B. Plant Museum in Tampa; the Tampa Museum of Science and Industry, the Haas Museum Complex in St. Petersburg; and, in Largo, the Heritage Park and Museum, a 21-acre open-air museum showing the early history of Pinellas County. After visiting the region for a time, one subscribes to the theory of John Nesbitt, author of *Megatrends*, that Tampa will be one of the 10 top cities of opportunity in the near future.

SIGHTSEEING TOURS   The *Admiral* Dinner Boat, Clearwater Municipal Marina (462–2628), offers sightseeing, bird feeding, and dinner cruises on Clearwater Bay, with 2 decks for dining and another for viewing the sunsets and other sights.

Gray Line Water Tours, 401 2nd Ave. NE, St. Petersburg (823-8171), has a sternwheeler, *The Belle of St. Petersburg*, which cruises the Bay.

Captain Memo's Pirate Ship Cruises, Dock 3, Clearwater Municipal Marina (446–2587); the company offers day and champagne cruises. The ship sails through the Intracoastal Waterway into the Gulf of Mexico.

The *Flamingo*, at the Clearwater Municipal Marina (461–3113), has several narrated scenic cruises per day.

The *Starlite Princess*, located at Hamlin's Landing in Indian Rocks Beach (595–1212), is a 3-deck paddlewheel offering dinner cruises and charters.

There are a number of party yachts and fishing boats for charter at Clearwater and Clearwater Beach.

There are Gray Line bus tours from St. Petersburg (822-3577).

PARKS, BEACHES AND   **Parks:** Moccasin Lake Nature Park, 2750
CAMPING   Park Trail Lane, Clearwater, is a 50-acre park featuring a lake, upland forest, wetlands, and a nature trail. **Beaches:** Clearwater Beach is a beachlover's beach, provided you don't expect huge breakers. On the tranquil Gulf of Mexico, its 4-mile-long strand has sand fine enough for egg-timers; this section of Pinellas County has been aptly called "The Suncoast." **Camping:** There is no camping on Clearwater Beach, but the Chamber of Commerce will send a list of campgrounds in Tarpon Springs, Dunedin, Largo, and St. Petersburg.

MARINAS   Clearwater Municipal Marina, 25 Causeway (462-6954); this marina is almost a small city, with a post office, barber shop, and photo shop. There are 20 transient slips; maximum length 100 feet; approach depth 6 feet; dockside depth 10 feet; electric power—yes; restaurant within walking distance—yes. The marina is only about 300 yards from Clearwater's wide, appealing beach.

RESTAURANTS   Calico Jack's, 430 S. Gulfview Blvd., Clearwater Beach (442–4442) is a seafood restaurant with a panoramic view of fishing and sailboats on the Intracoastal Waterway; one of the most popular dishes is a shrimp and lobster brochette.**$$**

Heilman's Beachcomber, 447 Mandalay Ave. (442–4144), has a waterfall, beachcomber murals, and an interesting wine cellar. The seafood platter and prime rib are specialties. Established in 1910, it is a favorite with locals; Maine lobsters are flown in from Boston and meat comes from a special Philadelphia butcher. **$$**

Kapok Tree Restaurants, 923 McMullen Booth Rd., Clearwater (726-0504), though not on Clearwater Beach, is a landmark in the vicinity, with walk-through gardens, strolling minstrels, and sparkling chandeliers. There is a second Kapok Tree Restaurant at 5001 Duhme Rd., Madeira Beach.**$$**

The Pelican Restaurant and Lounge, 470 Mandalay Ave., Clearwater Beach (442–3151), has been on the beach for half a century; it has a light and airy Garden Room.**$$**

Siple's Garden Seat, 1234 Druid Rd., Clearwater (442–9681), though not on Clearwater Beach, is set in a garden overlooking the bay; it has very good food and unusual desserts. It dates from the 1920's.**$$**

LODGING   Adam's Mark/Caribbean Gulf Resort, 430 S. Gulfview Blvd. (800/231–5858), has rooms with balconies and suites; it is on the gulf.**$$$**

Aegean Sands, 421 S. Gulfview Blvd. (447–3464), has 1 and 2-bedroom efficiencies, with many balconies, and features lawn games.**$$**

Bel Crest Beach Condo-Motel, 706 Bayway Blvd. (442–4923) is on the bay and has boat rentals; 1 and 2-bedroom efficiencies are available daily and weekly.**$$**

One of the most historic hotels in the area is the Belleview Biltmore Resort and Spa, 25 Belleview Blvd., Belleair 33516 (442-6171), built on a bluff in Clearwater. Though not on the beach itself, the grand old Victorian hotel is listed on the National Registry of Historic Places as an Historic Site and is well worth visiting. It is the largest occupied wooden structure in the world. It was built between 1895 and 1896 by Henry Bradley Plant to house shippers and attract patrons to his group of Florida railroads. It became a favored winter retreat of railroad presidents, steel magnates, and other industrial barons; at one time, as many as 15 private railroad cars were parked on the special siding east of the hotel. There are 2 golf courses, along with a number of tennis courts. Within the hotel there are more than two miles of corridors, and at peak season, 3,000 meals are served daily.**$$$**

Clearwater Beach Hilton, 715 Gulfview Blvd. (800/HILTONS), has deluxe rooms and suites and is on the beach.**$$$**

Clearwater Beach has many motels, condo-motels, and inns. For a full list of lodgings, write the Chamber of Commerce.

RENTALS   Key Realty & Rentals, Inc., 1370 Gulf
                                     Blvd., Clearwater 33515 (595–7711).
                                     KeppieTours, 41 N. Ft. Harrison Ave.,
Clearwater 33515 (800/237–1486), is a travel agency which has
been in business since 1924. As a sideline, they offer sightseeing,
condo rentals, along with sightseeing, car rentals, and deep-sea fishing excursions. They handle properties along the coast from Clearwater Beach to Treasure Island.

A full list of realtors can be obtained from the Pinellas Suncoast
Tourist Development Council or the Chamber of Commerce.

CONTACT   Pinellas Suncoast Tourist Development
                                     Council, 2333 East Bay Dr., Suite 109A,
                                     Clearwater 34625 (530–6452), or the
Greater Clearwater Chamber of Commerce, 128 N. Osceola Ave.,
Clearwater 33517 (461–0011).

DOG ISLAND

Area Code 904
LOCATION   Approx. 5 miles from Carrabelle, which is
                                     50 miles south of Tallahassee.

SIZE   7½ miles long by about ½ mile at widest
                                     point; area is 1,800 acres.

ACCESS   *Ferry:* from Carrabelle (Captain Raymond
                                     Williams, Box 648, Carrabelle 32322;
                                     697–3434). *Air:* there is a 2,700-foot
grass airstrip for private planes. *Private boat.*

HISTORY AND   Dog Island is a long sliver of a barrier is-
DESCRIPTION   land, with about 100 private homes and
                                     about 14 full-time residents. The island
was purchased by Jeff Lewis, a Florida businessman, shortly after
World War II for $12,000. In the late 1970s, Lewis decided to sell the
island and was approached by a real estate consortium. It was saved
from luxury development (with a bridge and condominiums) by a de-
termined group of island residents who persuaded the Nature Conservancy to buy three-fourths of it as a preserve. The Conservancy, in
turn, sold 1,100 acres to the Cuyahoga Trust of Akron, Ohio, a non-
profit charitable trust dedicated to preserving the island in its natural
state. Today it has no commercial enterprises; it is said that the pier
is the only "grocery store." There are no telephones, radios, or television sets. A single road meanders about half the length of the island,
pausing at the private homes and at the inn.

More than 30 endangered and threatened animals, plants, and birds inhabit the island. Dan Tonsmeire, of the Pelican Inn, has called the easternmost point of Dog Island "the last resting place for birds on their long journey south." The sand dunes are a landmark for mariners; the terrain consists of marsh, forest, and beach, with live oaks and sand pines. The marshes on the bay side of the island serve as an interface between the sea and uplands, providing nutrients for the fish and crabs of the estuary which, in turn, provide food for the birds and mammals. Island life is often studied by scientists, such as Sam Johnston of Florida's Dept. of Environmental Regulation, who recently discovered the northernmost location of the black mangrove, growing in bonsai form. The island is peaceful and pristine; the coin of the realm is shells and the theater of lingering and uninterrupted sunsets the prevailing pastime.

POINTS OF INTEREST   On the western part of the island, dunes fringed with sand pine and live oak provide miniature "mountains" for exploration. After a morning of swimming and hiking around the island, most visitors retreat to the air conditioning of the Pelican Inn during the hot afternoons. There is varied wildlife on the island; a list of birds which may be spotted is available at the Pelican Inn.

SIGHTSEEING TOURS   None.

PARKS, BEACHES AND   **Parks:** Most of island is a wildlife preserve.
CAMPING   **Beaches:** The wide beaches are ideal for early morning walks and shell collecting. **Camping:** Tent camping is allowed with special permission.

MARINAS   None on the island, but just inside the hook of the west end of the island, you may anchor and explore the beaches. Carrabelle is the eastern terminus of the Gulf Coast Intracoastal Waterway, and a well-known boating center. There are several marinas here, including the Carrabelle Marina (697–2251); 5 transient slips; maximum length 100 feet; approach depth 10 feet; dockside depth 10 feet; electric power—yes; restaurant within walking distance—yes. Also there is the Carrabelle Villa & Marina (697–3375); 30 transient slips; maximum length 65 feet; approach depth 9 feet; dockside depth 9 feet; electric power—yes; restaurant within walking distance—yes.

RESTAURANTS   None; bring all food and drink.

LODGING   The Pelican Inn (Box 1351, Fairhope, AL 36532; 800/451–5294) has 8 small apartments with kitchen facilities, linens, private porches, and both ceiling fans and air conditioning. There are

daily, weekend, weekly, and monthly rates as well as mid-week pack-
ages. Five percent discount to Nature Conservancy members.**$$$**

RENTALS   None, unless arranged privately.

CONTACT   Dan Tonsmeire of the Pelican Inn (see
                         Lodgings); also the Carrabelle Area Cham-
                         ber of Commerce, Drawer DD, Carrabelle
32322 (697–2585).

FISHER ISLAND

Area Code 305
LOCATION   South of Miami Beach, near the MacArthur
                         Causeway from Miami.

SIZE   216 acres.

ACCESS   **Ferry:** Private ferries (the *Eagle*, the *Fla-
                         mingo*, and the *Pelican*) take guests on the
                         7-minute trip from MacArthur Causeway to
the island. **Air:** The island has a heliport and seaplane ramp. There is
commercial service to Miami. **Private boat.**

HISTORY AND   Fisher Island did not exist until about the
DESCRIPTION   turn of the century when authorities
                         dredged Government Cut from Biscayne
Bay through to the Atlantic Ocean and created the island. Miami's first
black millionaire, Dana Dorsey, purchased it in 1918; he sold it to a
developer, Carl Fisher, a friend of William Kissam Vanderbilt, Jr. In
1925, Vanderbilt traded his yacht *Eagle* for the entire island, a re-
markably astute real estate maneuver. He then built a $1.5 million
estate, with 7 marble fireplaces, oak and mahogany paneling (which
he acquired from one of Napoleon's homes in France), and a huge
kitchen. Other amenities included a hangar for his seaplane, a golf
course, an aviary, fish ponds, a swimming pool, and tennis courts.
After Vanderbilt's death, the island was owned by Edward S. Moore of
U.S. Steel, inventor Gar Wood, and the Richard Nixon-Bebe Robozo
investment organization. It was then sold to a partnership of Island
Developers Ltd. and Mutual Benefit Life Insurance Co., and is now
operated as a private club. It advertises "a level of service and privacy
unsurpassed in America," a claim which is likely unexaggerated. There
are private condominiums on the island, which is home to celebrities
such as Briton Freddy Laker. The club has had many distinguished
guests, among them Zsa-Zsa Gabor. Transportation on the island is
usually by golf cart. It has been said that guests are treated like "sul-

tans and princes," enjoying an opulent atmosphere which would have appealed to Fitzgerald's Jay Gatsby; they are driven about in a tropical paradise amid royal palms, all in a setting of rich Mediterranean architecture, with Roman-style sculptures and hidden porticos.

POINTS OF INTEREST   The Vanderbilt clubhouse (see History and Description), the gardens, and the aviary are the principal attractions.

SIGHTSEEING TOURS   There are no sightseeing tours on the island.

PARKS, BEACHES AND CAMPING   **Parks:** There are no parks as such, but the landscaping is meticulous; topiary soldiers, large rose, red, and orange bougainvillea, and other tropical plants contribute to the atmosphere, which has been likened to that of a botanical garden. There is a full-time consultant on birds who cares for the aviaries, which have Amazonian parrots, conures, toucans, and other rare birds. **Beaches:** There is a mile of private beach. **Camping:** No camping is allowed.

MARINAS   The marina (535–6071) has 86 transient slips; maximum length 140 ft.; approach depth 8 ft.; dockside depth 6 ft.; electric power—yes; restaurant within walking distance—yes. Residents and property owners keep boats here, and guests in black tie, sipping champagne, often arrive in private craft from the mainland, to be entertained aboard yachts, in the clubhouse, or in their hosts' condominiums.

Fisher Island

RESTAURANTS   Guests may choose between the club
                             house dining room, **$$$**, and the beach
                             club dining room, **$–$$**. The cuisine is re-
puted to be among the best in Miami, featuring dishes such as veni-
son in coriander sauce and roulade of poached salmon and sole with
minted wasabi cream.

ACCOMMODATIONS   There is accommodation in 1- and 2-
                             bedroom cottages, villas, and guest
                             suites.**$$$**

RENTALS   There are no rentals, but memberships in
                             the Fisher Island Club, which include its
                             privileges, are available.

CONTACT   The Fisher Island Club, 1 Fisher Island Dr.,
                             Fisher Island, FL 33109 (800/624–3251
                             or 535–6020).

FORT MYERS BEACH (ESTERO ISLAND)

Area Code 813
LOCATION   On the Gulf coast, about 15 miles south-
                             west of Fort Myers.

SIZE   7 miles by about 3 blocks.

ACCESS   ***Car:*** by bridge from the mainland. ***Air:***
                             There is commercial air service to Fort
                             Myers. ***Private boat.***

HISTORY AND   Fort Myers Beach has been called the
DESCRIPTION   "world's safest beach," with good reason
                             since there is no undertow, and there are
no steep drop-offs or deep holes. Certainly it is one of the most popular of those on the Gulf. Though resort and motel parking lots are
only for guests, there are enough residential areas where it is possible
to park the car on a side street and stroll along the beach. In addition,
there are 2 municipal beaches and 2 piers, including a 600-foot municipal pier. Lee County has more golf courses, it is said, than any-
where else in the nation; the Bay Beach Golf Club on Fort Myers Beach
is one of many in the area. Estero Island offers a wide range of lodging

in all price categories, and for easy beach access and safe swimming, it may be the island of choice for this locality. Easy side trips may be made to Sanibel and Captiva, which are close by.

POINTS OF INTEREST The Fort Myers Beach Pier, at the northern end of the island, stretches out amid specialty shops and outdoor cafes, attracting visitors as well as fishermen. The municipal pier, which appeals to freshwater fishermen, is on the Caloosahatchee River.

Mound Key, near Estero's southern tip, is a huge pile of emptied shells fashioned by the Calusa Indians more than 1,000 years ago.

In Fort Myers, the winter home of Thomas Edison is well worth seeing. The house is still lit by light bulbs made by Edison in 1912; they have been burning an average of 12 hours per day since they were installed in 1925.

Near Estero, on the mainland, on Rt. 41, is the Koreshan State Historic Area, former home of a religious sect led by Cyrus Reed Teed, which moved there from Chicago in 1894 in hopes of founding a New Jerusalem.

SIGHTSEEING TOURS There is a tram ride from Carl E. Johnson Park to Lover's Key (see Parks).

The Glass-Bottom Boat cruises around Estero, Sanibel, and Captiva Islands; it leaves from the Gulf Star Marina, 708 Fisherman's Wharf, Fort Myers Beach (463–2219).

The *Liberty Belle*, a replica of a Mississippi paddlewheeler, has luncheon and dinner cruises; it is located in front of Sheraton Harbour Place, Fort Myers (332–0511).

One of the nation's few sailing flotillas leaves from Estero Bay. It offers week-long boat tours led by a captained lead boat and stops at the various islands for meals (guests sleep aboard the boats). The company running the flotilla, Royal Palm Tours (489–0344) has recently entered the houseboat business, renting blue-water cruising houseboats by the day, week, or season.

Out-island cruises, as well as the famous shelling charters run by Capt. Mike Fuery, leave from the 'Tween Waters Inn on Captiva (472–3459).

Tall Ship Excursions offers sail excursions on the *Norfolk Rover* (463-SAIL).

There is a whale watcher river cruise leaving from the Ramada Inn on the River, Fort Myers, touring the Caloosahatchee River and its tropical foliage and going as far as Cabbage Key on some trips (2220 West First St., Fort Myers 33901; 332–4888).

Everglades jungle cruises leave from the Fort Myers Yacht Basin, 1300 Lee St. (334–7474); there are a number of 1- and 2-day cruises, as well as dinner cruises.

PARKS, BEACHES AND   **Parks:** Carl E. Johnson Park is at the south-
CAMPING   ern tip of Estero Island. A tractor-driven
                         tram transports visitors along a rustic
boardwalk, crossing over picturesque Oyster Bay and past mangrove
islets, to Lover's Key, an unspoiled (yet public) beach, so named because of the many private places along the tree-lined beach. It is seldom crowded except on weekends. Fort Myers Beach Park, adjacent
to the fishing pier, is more central; nearby there are jet ski, water ski,
parasail, windsurfer, and catamaran rentals. Close by there is a cozy
network of shops, cafes, and restaurants. **Beaches:** The palm-fringed
beach is wide and inviting, **Camping:** Red Coconut R.V. Park on the
Beach, 3001 Estero Blvd., Fort Myers Beach 33931 (463–9352).
There is also camping near the beach at San Carlos Blvd.; San Carlos
R.V. Park & Island, 1042 San Carlos Blvd., Fort Myers Beach 33931
(466–3133) and at the Gulf Air Travel Park, 17279 San Carlos Blvd.
SW, Fort Myers Beach (466–8100).

MARINAS   There is a shrimping fleet based at the Fort
                         Myers Beach marina, along with many
                         charter fishing boats. There are a number
of marinas; here is a sampling of those which welcome transient
boaters.
   Getaway Marina (466–3600); 24 transient slips; maximum length
100 feet; approach depth 8 feet; dockside depth 8–10 feet; electric
power—yes; restaurant within walking distance—yes.
   Moss Marine, Fort Myers Beach (463–6137); 30 transient slips;
maximum length 100 feet; approach depth 12 feet; dockside depth
10 feet; electric power—yes; restaurant within walking distance—
yes.
   Gulf Star Marina, Fisherman's Wharf (463–2219); no transient
slips, but will try to fit boaters in when space is available; maximum
length 40 feet; approach depth 8 feet; dockside depth 8 feet; electric
power—yes; restaurant within walking distance—yes (opened the
Bridge restaurant in 1988).

RESTAURANTS   The Mucky Duck, 2500 Estero Blvd. (463-
                         5519), is in a renovated Florida beach
                         house. The Swiss owner-chef serves local
seafood and steak; it has a pleasant informal atmosphere, but no
water view.**$$**
   The Pelican Restaurant (see Lodging) has cypress walls and a nau-
tical decor; the back wall is a series of large glass windows overlook-
ing the Gulf.**$$**
   The Snug Harbor Restaurant, 645 San Carlos (under the Sky Bridge;
463–4343), has a nautical decor and water view; it is known for its
fresh seafood, unloaded on docks by the restaurant. There is a dock
for pleasure boats.**$$**

LODGING   Island Winds, 6621 Estero Blvd. (463–
                               0688), is a high-rise with 100 kitchen
                               units, tennis courts, and lawn games; weekly
                               rates.**$$$**

Lani Kai Island Resort, 1400 Estero Blvd. (463–3111; US except FL
800/237–6133), has units with refrigerators, efficiencies with kitchens, and suites with balconies; there are lawn games and sailboat
rentals.**$$$**

The Outrigger Beach Resort, 6200 Estero Blvd., Fort Myers Beach
33931 (463–3131), is on a wide sandy beach overlooking the gulf.
There is an elevated deck with an unobstructed view of the beach and
large, pleasant rooms with balconies; there is a laundromat on the
premises as well as a coffee shop and restaurant.**$$**

The Pelican Restaurant and Inn, 3040 Estero Blvd., Fort Myers
Beach 33931 (463–6130). The Pelican began in the early 1900s as
a 2-story converted houseboat; the galley was the kitchen (with kero-
sene lamps). Owned by the Reasoner family for nearly 30 years, it has
survived storms and hurricanes. While it has since expanded, it retains the charm which originally marked it as a Fort Myers Beach in-
stitution. No pets are allowed and there are no telephones or pools;
the Pelican is an oasis of the "Old Florida" style of accommodation,
with potted geraniums, breeze porches, and cozy cottages.**$$**

The Pink Shell Family Resort, 275 Estero Blvd. (463–6181), may
appeal to families who long for something more old-fashioned than
the usual motel. It has cottages on stilts as well as motel rooms and
apartments; it is at the northern end of Estero Island, near the fishing
pier, and there is a boat ramp.**$$**

Pointe Estero, 6640 Estero Blvd. Fort Myers Beach 33931 (US except FL 800/237–8906; FL 800/282–8906), is a high-rise resort overlooking the gulf with 1- and 2-bedroom suites; there are daily, weekly,
and monthly rates.**$$$**

RENTALS   The Vacation Shoppe, Box 6046, 1661 Es-
                              tero Blvd., Fort Myers Beach, 33931 (US
                              except FL 800/237–7370; FL 800/282–
                              7097).

Red Coconut Realty, 3001 Estero Blvd., Fort Myers Beach, 33931
(463–7200); Kathy Nesbit Vacations, 7205 Estero Blvd., Fort Myers
Beach 33931 (463–4253).

ESI (Executive Services, Inc.), 1648 Periwinkle Way, Sanibel Island,
FL 33957 (US except FL 800/237–6002; FL 800/282–7137), has
some properties on Fort Myers Beach as well as 11 other islands. The
company handles weekly rentals of luxury condominiums and private
residences at various resorts; up to 6 renters at a time may share the
cost (no pets; no high school or college students unaccompanied by
adults).

There are many realtors in the area handling rentals; the Chamber
of Commerce will send a complete list.

CONTACT   Greater Fort Myers Beach Chamber of Com-
                               merce, 1661 Estero Blvd., Box 6109, Fort
                               Myers Beach, FL 33931 (800/782–9283).

GASPARILLA ISLAND

Area Code 813
LOCATION   Midway between Sarasota and Fort Myers
                               on the Southwest Gulf Coast.

SIZE   7 miles long; up to 1 mile wide.

ACCESS   *Car:* Over the Boca Grande causeway (Rt.
                               771 from Placida). *Air:* There is commer-
                               cial service to Fort Myers. *Private boat.*

HISTORY AND   "Boca Grande is the *old* Florida," say those
DESCRIPTION   who knew Florida before it was "discov-
                               ered" by developers. It is located on the
barrier island of Gasparilla, which was mentioned in Portuguese
chronicles as early as the mid–16th century. During the early 1900s,
affluent families (the Morgans, the Drexels, the Cabots, the Du Ponts,
the Crowninshields) from cities such as Philadelphia, Boston, Baltimore, and Wilmington, Delaware, traveled to Boca Grande by private
railroad car for the winter. J. P. Morgan died in Boca Grande, and John
Jacob Astor shot a shark here. Until 1958, the only way to reach the
island was by boat or by rail. At that time, after much discussion, a
causeway was built connecting the island to the mainland, rendering
obsolete the rail and ferry which once crossed the chasm of Lemon
Sound.
    According to legend, the buccaneer Jose Gaspar, after a quarrel
with the Spanish monarch, settled on Boca Grande, enjoying ware-
houses full of luxuries, a prison for female captives, and fruit and
vegetable gardens. His hacienda, High Town, was reputedly furnished
with books and tapestries. While Gaspar's retreat has not been docu-
mented, most historians do agree that there was a Spanish mission
here about 1565, built to convert the Calusa Indians. In 1894, Peter
Bradley, a Boston businessman, bought stock in the Peace River Phosphate Mining Co. He chose Boca Grande as a good site for storage
and shipping of the phosphate, but he needed a railway connection.
This was built with the aid of James Gifford, president of the Charlotte
Harbor and Northern Railroad. Bradley then decided to develop Boca
Grande as a resort, controlling sales and promoting the island among
the wealthier sportsmen of Boston and New York. The town was built,
with gracious boulevards lined with casuarina (Australian pine) and

banyan trees. Gilchrist Boulevard, wide and stately, is lined with some of the earliest beach homes. The Gasparilla Inn was completed in 1912, along with a casino, bathhouse, boat house, and marina. Affluent patrons then began coming down; the island even lured people away from Palm Beach, which was becoming overcrowded.

The village of Boca Grande has small, modest villas and houses, unlike the Newport, R.I. retreats built by wealthy industrialists, which, though called "cottages," were grand estates. The town is only about 4 by 5 blocks in area. Most of the original buildings have been restored, so that the ambiance of a 1920s resort has been preserved. Many long-established shops beckon, such as Hudson's Market, with its tiny carts, and Fugate's old-fashioned drugstore, run by the third generation of the family, where you can reserve the New York Times and purchase various sundries, such as stationery and boat shoes. Newer shops include Ariel Ltd. (for adults) or Ltl. Ariel (for children).

The social season in Boca Grande runs from about the middle of December through the middle of April; it is then followed by the tarpon fishing season. Barron G. Collier, a fisherman and early developer of the island, is reported to have prayed, "Lord, suffer me to catch a tarpon so large that even I, in speaking of it afterwards, shall have no need to lie."

The island is, at least at present, free of fast food take-outs, discos, and high-rise developments; it harks back to a richer yet simpler era. There are about 1,500 year-round residents, but a far larger population during the two Seasons (Social and Tarpon Fishing). Katherine Hepburn is a frequent visitor, and the Lévi-Strauss family has a home here. The Gasparilla Island Conservation and Improvement Association is devoted to preserving the island and to keeping out high-rise developments. So far they have succeeded; residents such as Bill Gillan, manager of the Lighthouse Hole restaurant, says, "Gasparilla is one of the most unique islands in the United States, and will continue to be a great island to live on for the next hundred years." Some additional developments are underway, however; permission has been granted for a 127-acre development, with 372 units, on the south end of the island, but they will be single-family units (Florida's Conservation and Recreational Lands Program bid but lost).

POINTS OF INTEREST   The Boca Grande Lighthouse, built in the 1890s, overlooks the Gulf in Boca Grande Lighthouse Park.

The Boca Grande Theatre, built in 1928, now houses specialty shops; local artist Patty Middleton has her gallery here.

The original railroad depot, at Park Ave. and 4th St., has a scenic bike path, donated by members of the Du Pont family; instead of tracks, railroad ties have been transformed into flower boxes.

SIGHTSEEING TOURS   None.

PARKS, BEACHES, AND   **Parks:** The Boca Grande Lighthouse Park
CAMPING   offers picnicking and a good site from
                                 which to watch the maritime traffic. Other
parks are the Boca Grande Community Park, with picnic and play
areas, multi-purpose courts, and a community building, and Boca
Grande Beach Park, on the Gulf, with picnic tables, barbecue grills,
and restrooms. **Beaches:** There are 2 public beaches at Boca Grande;
one has shelters. **Camping:** None.

MARINAS   Miller's Marina (964–2232); 25 transient
                                 slips; maximum length 100 feet; approach
                                 depth 6 feet; dockside depth 9 feet; elec-
tric power—yes; restaurant within walking distance—yes.
   Boca Grande Pass Marina (964–0232); 10 transient slips; maximum length 26 feet; approach depth 10 feet; dockside depth 7 feet;
electric power—no; restaurant within walking distance—no.
   Boca Grande Club Marina (964–0211); 15 transient slips; maximum length 90 feet; approach depth 6 feet; dockside depth 7 feet;
electric power—yes; restaurant within walking distance—yes.

RESTAURANTS   Reservations are advised at all restaurants
                                 during the winter season.
                                     The Gasparilla Inn (964–2201); make
reservations well in advance (see Lodging). This is the vintage hostelry
in town, and the food is superb, including such specialties as fresh
fish, pear bread pudding, and homemade ice cream. The Sunday buffet is justifiably famous, featuring lobster, baked Alaska, roast beef,
and other delicacies. Those staying elsewhere may dine here, pending
availability.**$$$**
   The Lighthouse Hole (964–0511) overlooks Miller's Marina and is
open for lunch and dinner; they specialize in seafood such as grouper
and red snapper right off the boat. In addition, there are special all-
you-can-eat shrimp nights.**$$**
   Loose Caboose Restaurant (964–0440), housed in the old train de-
pot, will fix boat lunches, picnics, etc.
   The Pink Elephant (964–0101), overlooking the yacht basin, is popular with boaters; closed Mondays and July 5 through October 15. This
Swiss-style chalet is very elegant, though dress is casual chic (even
polos and boat shoes are acceptable). No credit cards are ac-
cepted.**$$**
   Temptation (964–2610), an island institute and the town's main
watering hole, is popular with fishermen and a bastion of conserva-
tism (an old license plate above the bar says "Hoover for President").
The restaurant, offering New Orleans-style cuisine, has been written
up twice in *Gourmet* (once for a renowned crab dish), and reservations
for social season are sometimes made weeks in advance.**$$**
   The Theater Restaurant (964–0806), in the restored Theater Mall,

has recently opened. During the late 1920s and 1930s, audiences for new films would arrive by limousine. Closed Tuesdays.**$**

The Laff-a-Lott lounge has live entertainment and is especially popular on Friday and Saturday nights.

LODGING The Boca Grande Club (964–2211) is a private membership-only club which "invites inquiries about membership." You need to be sponsored by a member for a visit. There are separate villas and beach access. The Club has weekly and daily rates.**$$$**

The Gasparilla Inn (964–2201), a stately pale yellow structure with an imposing columned portico, is a landmark in Boca Grande and has been called "the center of historic grandeur in downtown Boca Grande." There is no clear sign, just a small notice on the front door: "Members & Guests Only." (People who own homes on the island are considered "members" and can use the beach and the golf course.) High tea marks afternoons here. The Inn is only open from December 15 through April 15 and during the Tarpon season, April 15 through June 20. It is owned by a descendant of the Du Pont family. Its many amenities include an 18-hole golf course and a croquet lawn. Rates include three meals.**$$$**

The Waterfront Motel, 11th and Bayou Dr., Boca Grande 33921 (964–2294), is about 30 years old and has spacious rooms, boat slips, a ramp, and a pool; they accept pets.**$$**

RENTALS Executive Services, Inc., 455 Periwinkle Way, Sanibel Island, FL 33957, will make reservations for condominium rentals at several Boca Grande resorts (US except FL 800/447–6002; FL 800/282–7137). Among them are Sea Oats of Boca Grande, with 87 condominiums, and Dunes of Boca, with 40 2-story town houses. Other realtors include Seale Family Realty (964–0333) and J. R. Harper Real Estate (964-0302). The Chamber of Commerce will send a full list.

CONTACT Lee County Visitor and Convention Bureau, Box 2445, Fort Myers, FL 33902–2445 (800/LEE-ISLE), or the Boca Grande Area Chamber of Commerce, Box 704, Boca Grande, FL 33921 (964–0568).

HONEYMOON ISLAND

Area Code 813
LOCATION Off the Gulf Coast at Dunedin.

SIZE 2,808 acres.

ACCESS   **Car:** Causeway (SR 586) from Dunedin. **Air:**
                              There is commercial service to Tampa and
                              St. Petersburg/Clearwater. **Private boat.**

HISTORY AND   Honeymoon Island is one of the chain of
DESCRIPTION   central Gulf coast barrier islands extending
                              from Anclote Key State Preserve, just north
of Honeymoon, southward to Cape Romano, off Collier County. The
narrow low-lying islands are separated from the mainland by shallow
saltwater sounds or bays. They act as a barrier, protecting the mainland against storms. The island was once the home of the Tocobaga
Indians, who were alarmed to note the Spanish expeditions, led by
Narvaez and de Soto, coming up the coast from Tampa Bay in the
1520s and 1530s. Disease brought by subsequent Spanish explorers
exterminated the Tocobaga Indians. The island was later named Sand
Island, and, by 1880, Hog Island. In 1921, a hurricane separated what
was then Hog Island and Caladesi Island and created Hurricane Pass.
In 1939 it was renamed Honeymoon Island by a New York developer,
who had bought it for $30,000. He constructed 50 palm-thatched
bungalows; honeymoons were advertised in *Life* and in newsreels, and
were used as prizes in contests sponsored by major northern department stores. During World War II, exhausted Cleveland defense plant
workers were flown in for recuperation. The cottages were eventually
destroyed by storms and beach erosion, but Honeymoon Island began
to be developed commercially in 1966.

By 1969, a massive dredging project had begun; a dredge pumped
1.5 million cubic yards of sand and limestone onto the southern corner of the island from 600 yards offshore. The intent was to elevate
the land and increase the area available for development. Condominiums were built on the south end, and road systems were laid out.
Concrete groins were installed along the beach and mosquito control
ditches dug. By 1970, however, major environmental studies had
demonstrated the importance of marine sea grass beds, mangroves,
and salt marshes to coastal fisheries, and the dredging and filling
were stopped. The fragility and dynamic nature of Florida's barrier islands had been recognized. By 1974, the Department of Natural Resources had acquired most of the Island. Today it is a recreation area
with rare osprey, over 208 species of plants and a wide variety of
shore birds.

POINTS OF INTEREST   The Caladesi Island ferry dock is a pleasant
                              stroll from the parking lot next to the en-
                              trance station. Along the island's northern
loop trail, one of the few remaining south Florida virgin slash pine
stands may be observed; these trees serve as nesting sites for the
threatened osprey.

SIGHTSEEING TOURS   None, but the trip to Caladesi Island is well
                          worth making.

PARKS, BEACHES AND   **Parks:** The park lands are managed to ap-
CAMPING   pear as they did when the first Europeans
                          arrived. Consumptive uses, including hunt-
ing, livestock grazing, and timber removal, are not permitted. This
park, and others like it, fulfill an important purpose as representative
examples of "Original Natural Florida." The park opens at 8:00 A.M.
and closes at sunset year-round. Surf and pass fishing may provide
catches of flounder, snook, redfish, trout, snapper, whiting, sheepshead and tarpon. **Beaches:** There are 4 miles of Gulf beaches, but the
island has had a bad erosion problem; it underwent renourishment in
1988. **Camping:** None, though there are bath houses and there is a
swimming beach.

MARINAS   None.

RESTAURANTS   None.

LODGING   None.

RENTALS   None.

CONTACT   Honeymoon Island State Recreation Area,
                          #1 Causeway Blvd., Dunedin, FL 33528
                          (734–4255).

KEY BISCAYNE

Area Code 305
LOCATION   In Biscayne Bay, 3½ miles east of Miami.

SIZE   5 miles by 1 mile.

ACCESS   **Car:** Via the Rickenbacker Causeway from
                          Miami. **Air:** There is commercial service to
                          Miami. **Private boat.**

HISTORY AND   The earliest known inhabitants of Key Bis-
DESCRIPTION   cayne were descendants of Asians; then
                          came Vizcayanos of the Tequesta mainland
tribe. John Cabot is the first known white visitor; he landed on the
island in 1497, naming it Cape of the End of April. Ponce de Leon
arrived in 1513 and renamed the island Santa Marta. Later the island

provided a haven from storms for treasure-laden galleons traveling from Cartagena to Spain. Southern Florida's first town was established here in 1838; during the 1800s, Key Biscayne was headquarters for a band of wreckers who lured ships onto the reefs and it became known for the many treasures from these ships. Commodore W. J. Matheson, a Wisconsin native, began developing Key Biscayne in the late 19th century; he imported birds, drained swamps, built roads, created yacht basins, and established a Malayan coconut plantation. By 1938, the island had 50 residents; by 1952 there were more than 3,000 (in the 1950s, small VA-financed homes were going for $10,000; today those same homes, or "villas," are nearly $200,000.) The island now has a population of over 6,000. It has been home to such celebrities as Jack Paar, Beverly Sills, and former President Richard Nixon. Tom Selleck, Goldie Hawn, and other stars have visited the island, which is a popular film location; the film crew of *Miami Vice* often frequents the area also. Although the island has several resort hotels, hundreds of acres are devoted to parks and fine beaches.

POINTS OF INTEREST   The Cape Florida Lighthouse, one of South Florida's oldest structures, is in the Cape Florida State Park at the southernmost tip of Key Biscayne. (The original lighthouse was built in 1825 but burned by Indians in 1846). A museum complex features a reconstructed keeper's home and office.

Planet Ocean (361–5786) is located on the Rickenbacker Causeway; this is an ocean exhibit and headquarters for the International Oceanographic Foundation. Visitors are introduced to the facility through the film *The Unlikely Planet*, produced by the same studio that did *2001: A Space Odyssey*.

The Seaquarium (361–5705), also on the Rickenbacker Causeway, has a large marine aquarium and 50 acres of gardens. It is the home of "Flipper," known to millions of Americans from his television and film performances, who can be seen on the top deck; he throws a special splash three times daily.

SIGHTSEEING TOURS   In Crandon Park, a narrow-gauge railroad provides a tour of the palm jungle.

In Miami, the *Island Queen* (379–5119) makes various cruises, including a Millionaires Row excursion; it leaves from Biscayne Blvd. and NE 5th St.

Other Miami tours include the Gold Coast Railroad (253–0063), American Sightseeing (871–4992), and Gray Line bus tours (573–0550; FL 800/432–1185).

PARKS, BEACHES AND   **Parks:** The Bill Baggs Cape Florida State
CAMPING   Park, on the southern tip, is wild and un-
                           developed, with a beautiful 1-mile beach.
There is a nature trail winding through several plant zones. Crandon

Park has 2 miles of ocean beach, a specially designed swimming facility for the handicapped, a children's playground, and a narrow-gauge railroad touring the palm tree jungle. The annual Superstars television show is filmed here each February. Calusa Park, bordering it, is home to Key Biscayne's Little Theater group. **Beaches:** In 1987–1988, Key Biscayne's beaches, which had suffered from erosion, were greatly widened over a 2.4 mile stretch between the lighthouse and the southern end of Crandon Park. **Camping:** Tent camping is allowed at Cape Florida park.

MARINAS   Crandon Park Marina (361–1281); 10 transient slips; maximum length 50 feet; approach depth 10 feet; dockside depth 10 feet; electric power—yes; restaurant within walking distance—yes.

Rickenbacker Marina (361–1900), located just off the Causeway at Virginia Key; 25 transient slips; maximum length 60 feet; approach depth 12 feet; dockside depth 6 feet; electric power—yes; restaurant within walking distance—yes.

RESTAURANTS   La Scala, at L'Esplanade Shopping Plaza, 951 Crandon Blvd. (361–2436), specializes in Northern Italian cuisine.**$$**

The Spoonbill Restaurant at the Key Biscayne Hotel (see Lodging) is known for its art deco decor and good food.**$$$**

The Two Dragons at the Sonesta Beach Hotel (see Lodging) has Chinese and Japanese menus.**$$**

LODGING   The Key Biscayne Hotel and Villas, 701 Ocean Dr. (361–5431; US except FL 800/ 327–7922), was originally a coconut plantation and now covers 17 acres. It has private villas with kitchens as well as rooms with balconies, whirlpools, saunas, and other amenities.**$$$**

The Sheraton Royal Biscayne, 555 Ocean Dr. (361–5775), is a large and luxurious establishment with a playground, offering lawn games, windsurfing, ten tennis courts, rental boats, aqua bikes, and screened balconies.**$$$**

The Silver Sands Oceanfront Motel, 301 Ocean Dr. (361–5441), one of the smaller establishments in the area, has a casual, friendly atmosphere. It has efficiencies and beach cottages as well as rental bicycles, and scuba diving equipment and instruction.**$$$**

The Sonesta Beach Hotel, 350 Ocean Dr. (361–2021), a Mayan-style building, has 10 acres of beach front and a special recreational children's program.**$$$**

RENTALS   Cervera Real Estate, Inc., 260 Crandon Blvd. #5, Key Biscayne (361–6600), handles rentals.

CONTACT   Key Biscayne Chamber of Commerce, 95
                               W. McIntire St., Key Biscayne, FL 33149
                               (361–5207).

KEY WEST

Area Code 305
LOCATION   Key West, on the final inhabited island in
                               the Florida Keys, is the southernmost city
                               in the continental U.S.

SIZE   4 miles by 2 miles.

ACCESS   *Car:* Via the Overseas Highway. *Air:* From
                               Miami, Fort Myers, Tampa, West Palm
                               Beach, and other Florida cities. *Private
boat.* Also by *cruise ship* (Norwegian Caribbean Line and Bahamas
Cruise Lines make Key West stops; also, the Bermuda Star Line makes
cruises from New Orleans which stop at Key West).

HISTORY AND   Key West is not named for its location; the
DESCRIPTION   name is actually a derivation of "Cayo
                               Hueso," or "Bone Island," the name Span-
ish explorers gave the island when they found it littered with bones.
   The population here is highly individualistic. In the 19th century,
Key West was a fishing and sponge-hunting center, a village-like
settlement which was also the headquarters for wreckers, smugglers,
and other entrepreneurs. Later, it was home to U.S. Navy personnel. A
stroll along some of the Old Town residential streets, especially Eaton
St., evokes the Key West of the 1800s; high-ceilinged wooden
houses, often ornately decorated with gingerbread fretwork, rise behind sidewalks cracked and raised by fiscus and jacaranda trees. Date
palms fringe the roofs of wide wrap-around porches, where, in the
warm evenings, people chat softly.
   Ernest Hemingway is reported to have said, "I like Key West because
people don't stare at me on the street," but it is doubtful that he, or
any celebrity, could go unrecognized in the cosmopolitan climate of
Key West today. In *To Have and Have Not*, Harry Morgan says pre-
sciently, "What they're trying to do is starve you Conchs out of here so
they can burn down the shacks and put up apartments and make this
a tourist town. That's what I hear. . . . after the poor people are
starved out and gone somewhere else to starve some more they're
going to come in and make it into a beauty spot for tourists." Owing
to vigilant preservation, the "shacks" and the majority of the 19th-
century houses have not been burned, but the prediction has in some
ways come true. Key West is not only a "beauty spot for tourists" but

the "poor people" have given way to theater people, international celebrities, wealthy businessmen, yachtsmen, politicians, designers, singers, and journalists, as well as ordinary tourists and college students on spring break. There is a strong aesthetic overlay; artists and photographers have flocked here, along with writers as diverse as Hemingway, Tennessee Williams, Robert Frost, Reynolds Price, Gore Vidal, and John Dos Passos. Other writers visit the island each year for the popular Key West Literary Seminars; past speakers have included Peter Taylor and Richard Wilbur. The island now has 2 thriving theaters, the Red Barn (small and with occasional domestic touches, such as a door latched with a bent teaspoon) and the Waterfront Playhouse. The Tennessee Williams Fine Arts Center is on adjacent Stock Island. A unifying event each day is Sunset, which brings on a popular dash to Mallory Square and the pier, as much to see the kilted bagpipers, jugglers, and crazy quilt of eccentrics as the sunset (which may in fact be blocked by a cruise boat which perversely sets out just as the crowds gather). Judgments are suspended in Key West, which peacefully accommodates many disparate groups, from working-class fishermen to gays, who in turn range from flamboyant extroverts to less visible business people. The latter have been responsible for much of the town's preservation effort. On Duval St., particularly, there is a startling mixture of people—gays who would be equally at home on Castro Street, in Provincetown, and on Fire Island, along with foreign tourists, college students in town for the partying, conservative groups of older people from the mid-West, and Spanish-speaking residents who have happily settled here. (It has been said that Key Westers live in northern Cuba rather than the southern U.S.) Prepare to pay more for food and lodging in Key West; food has to be imported, along with fuel (electricity is generated by oil), and water.

POINTS OF INTEREST   The Hemingway Home and Museum, 907 Whitehead St. (294–1575), a Registered National Historic Landmark, is probably the leading attraction; the name "Hemingway" can be heard among diverse groups of tourists along Key West streets, from Germans to French to Japanese. Hemingway bought the house in 1931 to house his second wife, Pauline, and sons Gregory and Patrick; it was here that he wrote *For Whom the Bell Tolls*, and *A Farewell to Arms*. The gracious yellow house is replete with much of Hemingway's furniture and memorabilia, along with dozens of 6-toed cats, descendants of Hemingway's own menagerie, reclining in nooks and crannies.

The Audubon House, 205 Whitehead St. (294–2116), is a restored 1830s house, once the home of the sea captain John Geiger; Audubon did not live here, but the house recreates the ambiance of the days when he visited the town. Many of his works are on display.

The Wrecker's House Museum, 322 Duval St. (294–9502), is the oldest Key West house, with a "conch" construction. Its exhibits depict the wrecking and salvage industry which once flourished on the Keys.

The Hemingway House, Key West

The Key West Aquarium, Wall & Whitehead Streets (296–2051), has shark feedings, a "Touch Tank," and daily tours.

The Dry Tortugas, 70 miles west of Key West, can lay claim to being the most remote and least known of Florida's nautical attractions (the name comes from their lack of fresh water and plethora of large sea turtles). Fort Jefferson was constructed, beginning in 1846, to defend this remote area. In 1865 Dr. Samuel Mudd, who had unwittingly set the leg of Lincoln's assassin, was unjustly imprisoned here (he was released but not absolved of guilt until 1979). The fort was abandoned in 1874 and became a naval base in 1898. The Tortugas are now under the auspices of the Fort Jefferson National Monument. For seaplane tours from Key West, see Sightseeing. The Tortugas are accessible by private boat (which should have ample food and water aboard for the round trip; none is available there).

SIGHTSEEING TOURS   The Conch Tour Train is actually several trains, appealing conveyances of open canvas-canopied cars which chug all over the island, pulled by simulated steam engines. These tours have been conducted since just after World War II (294–5161).

Old Town Trolleys are modeled after the San Francisco cable cars and are excellent for rainy weather sightseeing (296–6688).

The *Captain Nemo*, a glass-bottom boat, departs several times a day from the Galleon Marina on Front St. (294–8856).

The *Fireball*, No. 2 Duval St., is another glass-bottom sightseeing boat (296–6293).

The Key West Seaplane offers tours to Fort Jefferson (see Points of Interest); from above you can spot marine life, shipwrecks, and Mel Fisher's treasure site (294–6978).

Personalized tours of Key West are also available from a concern called Key West by the Sea; call 294–2335.

PARKS, BEACHES AND   **Parks and Beaches:** Key West is not known
CAMPING   for desirable parks or beaches; Smathers
Beach and Monroe County Beach are public, but disconcertingly full of dry, brittle sand, with big rocks underfoot offshore. **Camping:** No tent camping is allowed in Key West, but there is camping close by on Stock Island (Boyd's Key West Camping, Stock Island, Key West, FL 33040; 294–1465).

MARINAS   Key West is always crowded, even though there are numerous marinas; boaters are advised to make advance reservations. Among the closest to Old Town is the Galleon Marina (296–7711); 50 transient slips; maximum length 100 feet; approach depth 9 feet; dockside depth 9 feet; electric power—yes; restaurant within walking distance—yes. Two others are the new A & B Marina (294-2535); 20 transient slips; maximum length 100 feet; approach depth 20 feet; dockside depth 15 feet; electric power—yes; restaurant within walking distance—yes; and the City Marina (292–8161); 6 transient slips; maximum length 50 feet; approach depth 6 feet; dockside depth 6 feet; electric power—yes; restaurant within walking distance—yes.

RESTAURANTS   The Cafe des Artistes, 1007 Simonton St. (294–7100), specializes in seafood, and has a French menu.**$$**
Louie's Back Yard, 700 Waddell Ave. (294–1061), overlooking the water, has tables on terraces, bordered by manicured hedges and outdoor lights; for atmosphere, this is one of the most popular restaurants in Key West.**$$$**
Martha's, 1801 S. Roosevelt Blvd. (294–3466), offers outdoor dining overlooking the ocean.**$$**
The Pier House (see Lodging) has 3 restaurants and is known for its Sunday brunches.
Key West night life is always lively; it is said that the town has more bars than churches. Different bars appeal to different tastes, but visitors will not want to miss one of the oldest active bars in Florida, Capt. Tony's Saloon, 428 Greene St. The proprietor, Capt. Tony Terrazina, greets all guests personally. He ran for Mayor in 1985 and has been called "a dropout from a Hemingway novel." Tony's Saloon was the site of the first "Sloppy Joe's" bar, owned by Joe Russell. Between 1933 and 1937 it was frequented by Hemingway, who met his third wife, Martha Gellhorn, here in 1936. The bar appears as "Freddy's" in *To Have and Have Not* and his Harry Morgan stories and has also been frequented by such writers as Tennessee Williams and Truman Capote. In 1937 Russell moved Sloppy Joe's to larger quarters at the

corner of Greene and Duval; after the move Hemingway continued his patronage. Sloppy Joe's is a major sponsor of the July week-long Hemingway Days Festival.

LODGING Key West has dozens of motels, hotels, and guest houses; the Chamber of Commerce will send a complete list. Among those which are especially noteworthy are:

The Coconut Grove, 817 Fleming St. (296–5107), is a spacious guest house with gingerbread trim and balconies in Old Town; rates vary according to size and facilities and include a lavish breakfast. 4-nt. minimum.**$$–$$$**

The Holiday Inn La Concha, 430 Duval St. (296–2991), was the old La Concha Hotel, built in 1925, a landmark mentioned in Hemingway's *To Have and Have Not.* The rooftop bar has an excellent view.**$$$**

Pelican Landing Motel and Marina, 915 Eisenhower Dr. 33040 (296–7583), is an excellent choice for those who would rather be somewhat removed from the revelry and noise of Duval St. It is on the Gulf, with deluxe suites and balconies overlooking the marina.**$$$**

The Pier House, One Duval St., 33040 (US except FL 800/327-8340; FL 800/432–3414), is a vintage resort, with rooms varying in architecture and decor, expensive yet informal.**$$$**

The Reach, Simonton St. at the Ocean 33040 (296–5000), is a large luxurious pink complex with white porches and a good beach and its own fishing pier.**$$$**

The Santa Maria Motel, 1401 Simonton St. (296–5678), is a moderate and pleasant motel very near the ocean.**$$**

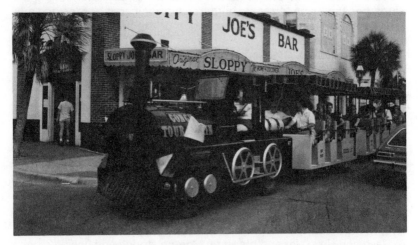

The Conch Tour Train in front of Sloppy Joe's Bar, Key West

RENTALS Property Management of Key West, Inc., 517 Eaton St., Key West 33040 (296–7744), handles homes and condos.

CONTACT Greater Key West Chamber of Commerce, 402 Wall St., Key West 33040 (294–2587). Visitors may also call for information from the Florida Keys and Key West Visitors Bureau (800/FLA-KEYS).

LOWER KEYS
SUNSHINE, BAHIA HONDA, BIG PINE KEY, BOCA CHICA KEY, AND OTHERS

Area Code 305

LOCATION The Lower Keys are the myriad islands between Vaca Key and Key West.

SIZE The Lower Keys extend from Key West at MM (Mile Marker; *see* explanation under History and Description) 1 to Sunshine Key at MM 40.

ACCESS *Car:* Over the Overseas Highway. *Air:* Commercial service to Key West; there is an airstrip on Summerland Key. *Private boat.*

HISTORY AND DESCRIPTION The section of the chain of islands called the Lower Keys is noted for its unspoiled tropical wilderness, exotic vegetation, and animal life not found elsewhere. It is here that the waters of Florida Bay merge into the blue-green Gulf of Mexico. The Mile Markers are a prominent feature of the Overseas Highway; they begin at 0 in Key West, and actually extend past Key Largo inland to Florida City (127); they are often the only address of an establishment. *Sunshine Key*, 75 acres, has a 400-site camping resort, with a complete array of services. The famous Seven Mile Bridge, the longest in Florida and worth a trip down the keys in itself, goes from Sunshine Key to Vaca Key. The next sizeable key is *Bahia Honda*, a State Recreation Area with 3 camping locations. Here the chain of islands broadens out to encompass many smaller islands, and the waters become extremely variegated. From this point to the Dry Tortugas, the islands are formed of Key West limestone, with mangrove tangles binding the soil of existing islands and building up new ones. *Big Pine Key* has tiny Key

The Seven Mile Bridge, Marathon

Deer, about the size of medium-sized dogs, which are protected by the government's National Key Deer Wildlife Refuge. Other keys in the group include No Name, Ramrod, Big Torch, Summerland, Cudjoe, Sugarloaf, Big Coppitt, and Boca Chica, as well as Stock Island, just before Key West. This was named for the cattle and pig holding pens which were once on the island. The drive through these keys is especially scenic just at sunset.

POINTS OF INTEREST   On Big Pine Key look for the Key Deer. The deer population has been endangered because visitors feed them junk food and attract them to the roadsides, where, unfortunately, they meet large dogs, fences, and cars. It is now a misdemeanor to feed the Key Deer.

The Perky Bat Tower on Sugarloaf Key is a monument to Richter C. Perky, who established a fishing camp on the island in the early part of the century. The camp was plagued by mosquitoes, and he built the tower to attract bats which were intended to dine on the mosquitoes. His venture proved futile, and it is said on the island that the mosquitoes actually consumed the bats.

Stock Island, just before Key West and all but merging with it, has the Tennessee Williams Fine Arts Center.

SIGHTSEEING TOURS   Stan Becker's Canoeing Nature Tours, Big Pine Key (872–2620), takes small groups on canoe excursions to view the scenery and wildlife. Capt. Buddy's Family Fun Trips, Big Pine Key (USA 3572), provides underwater cameras, refreshments, and equipment to explore the coral reefs. In addition, there are a number of charter fishing boats.

PARKS, BEACHES AND CAMPING

Parks: With Bahia Honda State Recreation Area and the National Key Deer Refuge, the Lower Keys have much to offer lovers of the outdoors. There is also the Coupon Bight State Aquatic Preserve on Looe Key, as well as the Looe Key National Marine Sanctuary, which offers good opportunities for divers and snorkelers to enjoy undersea gardens full of tropical fish. **Beaches:** Bahia Honda has a very good beach. **Camping:** Sunshine Key Camping Resort, Box 790, Sunshine Key, FL 33043 (872–2217).

MARINAS

Sunshine Key Marina/Camping Resort (872-2217); 2 transient slips; maximum length 45 feet; approach depth 7 feet; dockside depth 6 feet; electric power—yes; restaurant within walking distance—no.

Dolphin Marina, Little Torch Key (872–2685); 5 transient slips; maximum length 50 feet; approach depth 3 feet; dockside depth 10 feet; electric power—yes; restaurant within walking distance—no.

RESTAURANTS

The Baltimore Oyster House, MM 30.5, Big Pine Key (872–2314), specializes in seafood and will cook your catch.**$$**

The Cedar Inn, MM 31, Big Pine Key (872–4031), has alligator dinners and appetizers and daily fish specials.**$$**

Monte's, Summerland Key, has a rustic environment and a water view; a fish market is attached, and it is popular with local people seeking really fresh seafood.**$**

The No Name Pub, a "nice place if you can find it," is at the north end of Watson Blvd. on Big Pine Key. It has over 80 imported beers and serves chili and sandwiches.**$**

Sugar Loaf Lodge (see Lodging) has a pleasant restaurant.

LODGING

The Barnacle, Big Pine Key (872–3298), is a bed-and-breakfast run by the Cornell family.**$$**

Casa Grande, Big Pine Key (872–2878), is a bed-and-breakfast run by the Threlkeld family.**$$**

Little Palm Island, Rt. 4, Box 1036, Little Torch Key, 33042 (800/343–8567), is a private island which doubled for a South Pacific island in the filming of the movie *PT–109*. It recently opened as a resort. Presidents Teddy Roosevelt, Truman, and Eisenhower stayed at the old Great House, now a gourmet restaurant. Nestled among the palm trees are 18 thatched-roof huts containing 2 suites. It is a 15-min. boat ride from Little Torch Key; the staff will ferry you out. Rates include meals.**$$$**

Looe Key Reef Resort, Box 509, Ramrod Key 33043 (872–2215); this is an oceanside establishment offering dive trips, with a 24-hour liquor store on the premises.**$$**

Old Wooden Bridge Fishing Camp, Jim Oettle, Box 810, Big Pine Key, FL 33043 (872–2241), has modern cottages.**$$**

Parmer's Place, Box 445H, Big Pine Key 33043 (872–2157), is on Little Torch Key, a complex of waterfront cottages and apartments; there is also a boat launching ramp.**$-$$**

Sugar Loaf Lodge, Box 148S, Sugarloaf Key 33044 (745–3211), with an air strip, tennis courts, a porpoise pool, marina, grocery store, and motel rooms, is a complete resort community.**$$**

RENTALS   Raymond Real Estate, Box 913, Big Pine Key, FL 33043 (872–9116), handles seasonal rentals, as does Suncoast Unlimited, Drawer 383, Big Pine Key 33043 (872–2334). The Chamber of Commerce will send the names of other realtors.

CONTACT   Lower Keys Chamber of Commerce, Mile Marker 30, Big Pine Key 33043 (872–2411). Visitors may also call for information from the Florida Keys and Key West Visitors Bureau (800/FLA-KEYS).

MIDDLE KEYS
DUCK KEY, GRASSY KEY, KEY COLONY BEACH, VACA KEY (Marathon), AND OTHERS

Area Code 305

LOCATION   The Middle Keys are 12 islands extending between the Upper Keys and the Lower Keys.

SIZE   The Middle Keys stretch from Conch Key, just beyond MM (Mile Marker) 65 to Pigeon Key, just beyond Vaca Key at MM 45.

ACCESS   *Car:* Over the Overseas Highway. *Air:* There are flights to Marathon from Miami. *Private boat.*

HISTORY AND   **Conch Key,** below Long Key, is like a snug
DESCRIPTION   New England fishing village, with whitewashed cottages and fishing nets spread out to dry. **Duck Key** was the site of a failed industry which tried to make salt from sea water. **Grassy Key** is named for an early settler and not for its vegetation. It had long been rumored that pirates buried

treasure here, but they were unsubstantiated until 1911, when 61 gold pieces were unearthed in a goatskin bag. There are many trailer parks here. *Crawl Key* through *Vaca Key* (MM 56 to 47) contain Key Colony Beach, Marathon Shores, and part of Marathon. Crawl Key was named for the pens where large sea turtles were once kept until they were butchered for soup and steaks (forbidden today). *Fat Deer Key* has the only incorporated city in this area, *Key Colony Beach*; this was a mangrove swamp in 1954 and now has thriving businesses and accommodations.

Vaca Key, the largest island, was named by Spanish explorers for the cattle which once roamed the island. This is the most southern of the keys where water may be obtained by deep drilling. The commercial center, Marathon, is a busy town, traffic-choked but with appealing residential areas. The area includes Marathon Shores, Boot Key, Knight Key, and Hog Key. During construction of Flagler's railroad, workers were in the habit of celebrating in the labor camps, with the aid of liquor boats which made frequent calls. Key West churches sent "gospel boats" to hold nightly services and distribute religious tracts. There were ferries from Key West to Knight Key, and from No-Name Key to Marathon; the latter ran until 1937. *Pigeon Key* is actually side-stepped by the new Seven Mile Bridge, as it is under the old Seven Mile Bridge and only accessible from it. Here there are conch houses which are a favorite subject for artists and photographers. At MM 45, Pigeon Key marks the end of the Middle Keys.

POINTS OF INTEREST The Dolphin Research Center, at Grassy Key, offers the opportunity to play and swim with dolphins in exchange for a tax-deductible contribution to the Center (about $50).

The Zoovet Productions training facility is on the grounds of the Hawk's Cay Resort, Duck Key (Zoovet creates marine animal shows for attractions such as Busch Gardens in Tampa). Resort guests may observe the training at no cost; there is a fee of about $40 to swim with the dolphins.

SIGHTSEEING TOURS There are half-day sailboat trips and evening champagne cruises aboard the 31-foot cutter *Amantha*, sailing from Faro Blanco Marine Resort, MM 48, Marathon (743–2500). Also, there are many fishing and sailing charter boats available throughout the Middle Keys.

Kelsey's Flying Circus, MM 52 (Marathon Airport; 743–4222; information also at 800/759–3276), has open cockpit flights over the keys.

PARKS, BEACHES AND CAMPING **Parks and Beaches:** The Wanda Switlik Public Beach is at Sombrero, MM 50; the Marathon Chamber of Commerce Beach is at the end of 33rd St., MM 49. **Camping:** The Key RV Park, MM 50.5, has full hook-ups, boat ramps and dockage. There are several other RV parks as well; the Chamber of Commerce will send a list.

MARINAS   The Middle Keys have too many marinas to list. One attractive facility is the Faro Blanco Marine Resort, Marathon (743–9018), which is visible from some distance because of its historic red, white, and black lighthouse tower; 75 transient slips; maximum length 100 feet; approach depth 7 feet; dockside depth 12 feet; electric power—yes; restaurant within walking distance—yes. Another with many transient slips is the Marina at Hawk's Cay (743–9000); 38 transient slips; maximum length 100 feet; approach depth 6 feet; dockside depth 8 feet; electric power—yes; restaurant within walking distance—yes.

RESTAURANTS   *Vaca Key (Marathon)*: Kelsey's, overlooking the Faro Blanco Yacht Basin at MM 48 (743–9018) specializes in seafood.**$$**

Bacchus by the Sea, overlooking the Seven Mile Bridge (743-6106), has a good stuffed lobster dish and many other seafood dishes.**$$**

The Quay, 12650 Overseas Hwy., MM 54½ (289–1810), offers outdoor dining by the gulf and many seafood specialties.**$$**

Key Colony Beach: The Landing at Fantasy Harbor Marina, Key Colony Beach Causeway (743–0774), has good seafood and nightly chef's specials, **$**; another favorite with locals is the Beach House, 401 E. Ocean Dr. (743–3939).**$$**

LODGING   *Duck Key*: Hawk's Cay Resort and Marina, MM 61, Duck Key, FL 33050 (743–7000), is on the site of the remodeled Indies House, which dates from the 1960s. It has a pink and green facade reminiscent of the West Indies.**$$$** *Grassy Key*: The Rainbow Bend Fishing Club, MM 58 (289–1505), carries on the tradition of the famous early Keys fishing clubs and combines it with modern comfort. "We try to keep our guests quiet and comfortable all day," says the manager, and a Boston whaler for four hours per day, plus a free full breakfast, are included in the daily rates.**$$$** *Fat Deer Key (Key Colony Beach)*: Key Colony Beach Motel, 441 E. Ocean Dr. (289–0411), is a good choice for the Middle Keys.**$$** Another is the Key Colony Point, 1133 Ocean Dr., Key Colony Beach 33051 (743–7701), which has oceanfront condominiums and weekly rates.**$$$** *Vaca Key (Marathon)*: The Sombrero, 19 Sombrero Blvd. (800/433–8660), has balconies, picnic tables, a marina, and dockage.**$$-$$$** The Boot Key Seaport Resort, 1000 15th St., Marathon 33050 (743–4200), has floating staterooms in houseboat efficiency-style accommodations, as well as yacht dockage.**$$** The Hidden Harbor Resort, MM 48.5, 2396 Overseas Hwy., Marathon 33050 (743–5376), provides a free boat slip with each room.**$$**

RENTALS   There are many realtors in the Middle Keys;
                                       2 are Sarah's Island Realty, Box 1, Key Col-
                                       ony Beach 33051 (289–0999), and Cobia
Realty, Inc., 67 53rd St. Ocean, Marathon 33050 (743–6795), both
of which handle rentals. The Chambers of Commerce for the individual
keys will send a list of additional ones.

CONTACT   Key Colony Beach Chamber of Commerce,
                                       600 W. Ocean Dr., Key Colony Beach, FL
                                       33051 (289-1212), and the Greater Mara-
thon Chamber of Commerce, 3330 Overseas Highway, Marathon, FL
33050 (743–5417). Visitors may also call for information from the
Florida Keys and Key West Visitors Bureau (800/FLA-KEYS).

UPPER KEYS
KEY LARGO, TAVERNIER, PLANTATION KEY, WINDLEY KEY, UPPER MATECUMBE (*Islamorada*), LOWER MATECUMBE, INDIAN KEY, LIGNUMVITAE, AND LONG KEY

Area Code 305
LOCATION   Key Largo is 42 miles SW of Miami; the Up-
                                       per Keys extend west, ending with Long
                                       Key.

SIZE   The Upper Keys stretch from MM (Mile
                                       Marker) 112 to MM 65. They are less than
                                       2 miles wide.

ACCESS   *Car:* Via the Overseas Highway, U.S. 1. *Air:*
                                       There is commercial service to Miami. *Pri-
                                       vate boat.*

HISTORY AND   The Overseas Highway links 43 Florida
DESCRIPTION   Keys (which have been called "bodies of
                                       land surrounded by fishermen"); in addi-
tion, there are many others above and below the chain. They extend
west from the southeast tip of Florida, varying to a surprising extent
in character and features. Some of them, especially towards Miami,
are now afflicted with the same plastic and neon one finds on the
mainland, but many are protected parks. Others have been little developed, and visitors can still find secluded spots evoking the early
1800s, when colorful wreckers flourished, when no bridges linked the
islands, and when settlers were self-sufficient pioneers.

The Flagler Railway, completed to Key West in 1912 (a train ferry continued to Havana), introduced the era of tourism, as visitors could travel all the way to Key West in comfort. It was destroyed by a 1935 hurricane and the roadbed utilized in the Overseas Highway, completed in 1938. This begins at Key Largo and vaults over 42 bridges (the one at Marathon is 7 miles long), stretching all the way to Key West, which is 155 miles from Miami.

The intervening islands are usually grouped as the Upper, Middle, and Lower Keys, the latter being the closest to Key West. Key Largo, in the Upper Keys, and Marathon, in the Middle Keys, are the largest settlements.

Key Largo: The longest of the Upper Keys, Key Largo is distinguished in part as being the site where the Humphrey Bogart/Lauren Bacall movie of the same name was filmed in 1948. One of the film sites is now the Caribbean Club. Key Largo is more commercial than most of the other islands, but has a variety of activities and accommodations ranging from the rustic to the luxurious. Charter fishing boats abound.

Tavernier (pronounced Taverneer): This key, between MM 93 and MM 91, was named for an early 19th-century French pirate who was an associate of the pirate Jean Lafitte. *Islamorada* and the "Purple Isles": Islamorada is the centerpiece of the palm-fringed "Purple Isles," a group including Plantation, Windley, and Upper and Lower Matecumbe Keys, along with Indian Key and Lignumvitae (both offshore). Islamorada is the town on Upper Matecumbe Key. It is said to have been named by Spanish explorers after the *morada*, the heavy concentration of the violet sea snail, (*Janthina Janthina*). There is excellent diving here (you can take trips to nearby coral reefs) and the fishing is outstanding; the annual fishing tournaments are world-famous. In the 19th century, many wreckers made the Matecumbes their headquarters because of their central location. The waters were uncharted and filled with treacherous coral reefs; when the cry "Wreck ashore!" was heard, the "good news" was passed from key to key by signals blown on the conch horn. *Plantation Key* is named for the pineapple and banana plantations which once flourished here. *Long Key*, at MM 68 and 69, was Zane Grey's favorite fishing spot and one of the creeks here is now named for him. The Long Key Fishing Club was built by Henry Flagler.

Two nearby keys have colorful pasts. Indian Key, a Historical Site, is where Dr. Henry Perrine, a pioneer tropical-plant researcher, was killed by Seminole Indians during a raid in 1840. A salvage center was created here in the 1830s by the renowned wrecker Jacob Housman; he escaped the massacre, but his buildings were burned. Lignumvitae Key State Park, 2 miles south of Islamorada, is a 280-acre island with stone fences, and pieces of carved wood and wrought iron—the ruins of what is believed to have been a Spanish village. There are wildflowers, sea lavender, and virgin tropical hammock. The island is managed by the Florida Department of the Interior.

POINTS OF INTEREST *Key Largo:* The boat used in the classic Bogart-Hepburn film *The African Queen* is in drydock at MM 100, and the Caribbean Club sits on the site where the Bogart film *Key Largo* was made. *Plantation Key* is noted for the Museum of Sunken Treasure, a collection of artifacts from shipwrecks. (The Upper Keys had about 18 shipwrecks; one of the most notable, the *San Pedro*, is slated to become a state park.) *Upper Matecumbe (Islamorada):* The Hurricane Memorial, MM 81.5, is dedicated to the memory of the World War I veterans who died in the 1935 hurricane while working on the Overseas Highway. Islamorada also has the Underwater Coral Gardens; one of these, which may be reached by boat, has the wreck of the *Herrera*, a Spanish galleon. The Theater of the Sea, a dolphin show at MM 84.5, is a popular attraction.

SIGHTSEEING TOURS The Florida Park Service runs tours to Indian Key and Lignumvitae Key year-round; contact Long Key State Recreation Area (664–4815).

There are glass-bottomed boat tours of the submerged part of John Pennekamp Coral Reef State Park, well worth taking (for reservations, call the Coral Reef Park Co., Inc., 451–1621).

PARKS, BEACHES AND CAMPING *Parks: Key Largo:* This is the home of the John Pennekamp Coral Reef State Park, the first underwater preserve in the country, which includes a living coral reef and 150 square miles of protected Florida waters. Also located here are the Harry Harris County Park at MM 92.5 and the Cow Pens Bird Preserve. *Islamorada* has a county park at MM 73. *Indian Key* and *Lignumvitae Key* (see History and Description) may be visited, but only 50 people are allowed on the latter at one time. Access is limited to the state park tours (see Sightseeing Tours), private boats and charter boats available at nearby marinas. At *Long Key* is the Long Key State Park at MM 67.6. **Beaches:** Because of the 1935 hurricane, there are no extensive public beaches on the Upper Keys, but motels and hotels have nourished some private beaches. There are small beaches at the Harry Harris Park in Key Largo and the John Pennecamp Park. **Camping:** Key Largo Kampground, Box 118-A, Key Largo 33037 (451–1431); Calusa Camp Resort, MM 101, Key Largo, FL 33037 (451–0232).

MARINAS There are dozens of marinas in the Upper Keys. Those with ample slips for transient boats are Gilbert's Motel and Marina, Key Largo (451–1133); 30 transient slips; maximum length 100 feet; approach depth 9 feet; dockside depth 9 feet; electric power—yes; restaurant within walking distance—yes; and the Holiday Isle Resort, Islamorada (664–2321); 35 transient slips; maximum length 100 feet;

approach depth 5 feet; dockside depth 8 feet; electric power—yes; restaurant within walking distance—yes.

RESTAURANTS   *Key Largo*: Alabama Jack's, Card Sound
                                  Rd., Key Largo (248–8741), is known for
                                  its crab cakes and conch fritters.**$**

Cafe Key Largo, MM 97 at the Sheraton Key Largo Resort (*see* Lodging), has a popular Sunday champagne brunch.**$$**

The Italian Fisherman, MM 104, next door to the Caribbean Club of Humphrey Bogart fame, has a good reputation with local residents.**$$**

Shiver's Bar B Q, MM 102.5, at Key Largo, advertises the "sweetest corn on the cob you ever ate"; other specialties are chocolate chip cheese cake and key lime pie.

For breakfast or lunch, try the Tropical Cafe, MM 90.5, on the water just south of Tavernier Creek (852–3251); they specialize in crepes, Belgian waffles, and salads (closes at 3:00 P.M.).**$**

Islamorada: Cheeca Lodge Dining Room, Islamorada (*see* Lodging), is a semicircular room with excellent views and freshly-caught seafood.**$$**

The Conch, MM 83, Islamorada (664–4590), specializes in seafood platters and key lime pie.**$$**

Erik's Floating Restaurant, MM 85.5, Islamorada (664–9141), is a 100-foot houseboat with an excellent view and fresh seafood.**$$**

The Green Turtle Inn, MM 81.5, Islamorada (664–9031), has been a landmark on the Keys since 1947, does its own baking and has a pleasant atmosphere.**$$**

The Plantation Yacht Harbor Resort, 87000 Overseas Hwy. (852–2381), is at a marina, overlooking the wharf; the restaurant does its own baking and specializes in seafood.**$$**

Plantation Key: The Marker 88 Restaurant, Plantation Key (852–9315), is a gourmet restaurant overlooking the Gulf; reservations recommended.**$$**

LODGING   There are dozens of motels and resorts in
                                  the Upper Keys, chiefly at Key Largo and Is-
                                  lamorada. A complete list, with prices, will
be sent by the Chambers of Commerce. A few of them are:

Key Largo: Gilbert's Resort and Marina, MM 107.5-B, 107900 Overseas Hwy., Key Largo 33037 (451–1133), has a full-service marina and jet-skiing.**$$**

Kona Kai Resort, MM 97.8, 97802 S. Overseas Hwy., Key Largo 33037 (852–4629), is on the Gulf, and has tennis and a jacuzzi.**$$**

Marina Del Mar Resort and Marina, MM 99, 527 Caribbean Dr., Key Largo 33037 (US except FL 800/451–3483; FL 800/253–3483), is on a canal overlooking the marina.**$$$**

Sheraton Key Largo Resort, MM 97, 97000 S. Overseas Hwy., Key Largo 33037 (852–5553), oceanside waterfront, with a beach and some rooms with refrigerators.**$$$**

Islamorada: Barefoot Pointe Club, MM 80.5, 80581 Old Hwy., Islamorada 33036 (664–8632), has sailing, a pool/aquarium, and cottages with hammocks.**$$$**

Cheeca Lodge, MM 82, Box 527, Islamorada 33036 (US except FL 800/327–2888; FL 664–4651), is a prestigious resort with golf course, beach, pool, and an ocean view restaurant. President George Bush, Jack Parr, and Ted Williams have all vacationed here to fish for tarpon, marlin, and sailfish. It was founded as a private club in 1960 and opened to the public in 1973. If you happen to have a helicopter, there is a helipad next to the tennis courts.**$$$**

Pelican Cove Resort, 84457 Overseas Highway (MM 84.5), Islamorada, FL 33036 (800/445–4690), is on the Atlantic, and every room has its own balcony. There is a fresh-water pool and a jacuzzi, along with a private beach, boat ramp, and dock.**$$$**

Ragged Edge Resort, MM 86.5, 243 Treasure Harbor, Islamorada 33036 (852–5389), is oceanside and has a fishing pier.**$$**

Tropical Reef Resort, MM 85.5, 84977 Overseas Hwy., Islamorada 33036 (664–8881), on the ocean, has lawns and some screened porches, a boat ramp, and dockage.**$$**

RENTALS   Many real estate agents in the Upper Keys handle vacation houses and condominiums. Two are Freelancers, Ltd., Inc. Vacation Rental, MM 103, 10300 Overseas Hwy. (451–0349), and Freewheeler Vacations, Inc., Box 1634, Islamorada 33036 (664–2075). For a full list of agents, write the Chambers of Commerce.

CONTACT   Key Largo Chamber of Commerce, MM 106, Key Largo, 33037 (451–1414); Islamorada Chamber of Commerce, MM 82.5, Islamorada 33036 (664–4503). Visitors may also call for information from the Florida Keys and Key West Visitors Bureau (800/FLA-KEYS).

LONGBOAT KEY / LIDO BEACH

Area Code 813

LOCATION   West of Sarasota; the southern half is in Sarasota County and the northern half is in Manatee County.

SIZE   10.8 miles long; between 100 yards and ½ mile wide.

ACCESS   *Car:* Rt. 780 from Sarasota; Rt. 789 from
                              Anna Maria Island. *Air:* There is commer-
                              cial service to Sarasota. *Private boat.*

HISTORY AND   The island was the vacation land of the
DESCRIPTION   Timucuan and Calusa Indians for hundreds
                              of years. The explorer Hernando de Soto is
thought to have visited here in 1539 with his scout, Juan Anasco; they
were in a "longboat" as it went through the north pass. Thomas Mann,
a Civil War veteran, settled here after the war with his grown sons. In
1891 he was awarded 144 acres as a homestead grant and he sold
his land for about $500 at the turn of the century. Gradually, in the
early 1900s, homes were built on the north end of Longboat Key and
extended to the south end, where, in the 1920s, John Ringling bought
hundreds of acres. He planted Australian pines along Ringling Boulevard, now called Gulf of Mexico drive. During World War II part of the
island was a target range for Army Air Force planes. During the 1960s
and 1970s, development reached a crescendo; the first condominium
built was Longboat Key Towers and very few tracts of over a few acres
remain undeveloped.

The population fluctuates widely. It is estimated that in March the
8,100 dwelling units, accommodating 2 persons per unit, are 95 percent filled, but in September the occupancy in some condominiums
falls to 20 percent. Population estimates range from 8,000 to
25,000, with no accurate measure yet devised. Tourism is the main-
stay of the economy; both families and conventions are booked
throughout the year.

The drive along Longboat Key is a beautiful one, past elegantly
landscaped resorts and homes (there are, in fact, as many landscaping and lawn care services on the island as there are grocery stores).
The tangle of native trees includes mangrove, buttonwood, pine, and
sea grapes; there are bayous and canals.

POINTS OF INTEREST   The Longboat Key Art Center, 6860 Long-
                              boat Dr. S. (383–2345), boasts 3 galler-
                              ies, a craft sales shop, and arts and crafts
studios. It was founded in 1952; Grace Yerkes and Lora Whitney were
the driving forces behind the effort. The Longboat Key Historical Society has amassed considerable memorabilia and is searching for a
permanent home.

The Longboat Key Recreation center, 4040 Gulf of Mexico Dr., begun in 1948 under the leadership of Patty Cobb, offers children a variety of pursuits, ranging from peanut hunts to bike hikes and planetarium visits.

Sarasota has many attractions. Perhaps the most prominent is the
Ringling Museums, a 68-acre cultural complex on the estate of the
late John Ringling.

SIGHTSEEING TOURS   None on the island, but the cruise ship *Le Barge* (366–6116) is docked at Marina Jack in Sarasota. Narrated cruises of Sarasota Bay are given, along with special cruises featuring live entertainment and meals. The *Marina Jack II* Dinner Boat (366–9255), offering dinner cruises, also leaves from Marina Jack; this is a 100-foot double-decked sternwheeler. (For cruises from Cortez, see Anna Maria Island entry).

PARKS, BEACHES AND   **Parks:** There are none on the island.
CAMPING   **Beaches:** Public access to the beaches is not as easy as on the island's neighbor to the north, Anna Maria Island. Though there are 13 public access areas, there has not been sufficient land in public ownership to build parking lots; vehicular parking is currently limited to about 50 cars. However, if you are staying in one of the inns or private homes, the secluded strands are splendid. **Camping:** There are campgrounds in Bradenton and Sarasota.

MARINAS   Fields' Buccaneer Inn, Sleepy Lagoon Yacht Harbor, 595 Dream Island Road (Harbourmaster 383–4468); 20 transient slips; maximum length 70 feet; approach depth 5 feet; dockside depth 6 feet; electric power—yes; restaurant within walking distance—yes. Welcomes transient boaters; reservations recommended.
Cannons Marina and Beach Houses, 6051 Gulf of Mexico Dr. (383-1311); 5 transient slips; maximum length 25 feet; approach depth 5 feet; dockside depth 5 feet; electric power—no; restaurant within walking distance—no.
Longboat Key Club / Harbourside Moorings, 2800 Harbourside Dr. (383–8383); 25 transient slips; maximum length 100 feet; approach depth 6 feet; dockside depth 15 feet; electric power—yes; restaurant within walking distance—yes.

RESTAURANTS   *Longboat Key:* Abbondanza!, 23 Ave. of the Flowers (located in a shopping complex) is a busy but pleasant deli with a variety of bagels and other food, open from "8:00 A.M. till . . ."**$**
Colony (see Lodging), noted for Sunday brunch, has outdoor dining overlooking the Gulf. Two dining rooms; **$$** and **$$$**.
The Crest Dining Room, Holiday Inn Longboat Key (see Lodging), has a good seafood buffet Friday night.**$$**
Fields' Buccaneer Inn, 615 Dream Island Rd. (383–1101), next to the Harbour Villa Club, has a nautical atmosphere and is on the Intracoastal Waterway; the restaurant has won magazine awards.**$$**
Lido Beach: Cafe l'Europe, 431 Harding Circle (388–4315),features continental cuisine in interesting atmosphere.**$$**

Charley's Crab, 420 Harding Circle (388–3964),offers sidewalk cafe-style dining.**$$**

LODGING   *Longboat Key*: Beach Castle, 5310 Gulf of Mexico Dr. (383-2639), has both gulf and bay sections; this is an apartment motel with 19 units.**$$$**

Colony Beach and Tennis Resort, 1620 Gulf of Mexico Dr. (383-6464), has private patios and balconies on the Gulf, 232 units.**$$$**

Harbour Villa Club at the Buccaneer, 615 Dream Island Rd. (lodging reservations 383–9544), has suites with balconies on the Intracoastal Waterway, 38 dock-front villa residences.**$$$**

Holiday Inn Longboat Key, 4949 Gulf of Mexico Dr. (383–3771), has a glass-enclosed courtyard and offers miniature golf; 146 rooms.**$$$**

Longboat Key Club, 301 Gulf of Mexico Dr. (383–8821), with extensively landscaped grounds on the Gulf, 221 units.**$$$**

Longboat Key Hilton Inn, 4711 Gulf of Mexico Dr. (383–2451), is also on the Gulf, 102 units.**$$$**

Lido Beach: Azure Tides Resort, 1330 Ben Franklin Dr., Box 2896, Sarasota, FL 33577 (388–2101), has 34 units, nicely decorated; 1- and 2-bedroom suites.**$$$**

Harley Sandcastle, 1540 Ben Franklin Dr., Sarasota 33577 (388-2181), is a resort on a private beach and has efficiencies.**$$$**

RENTALS   Longboat Accommodations, Inc., 4030 Gulf of Mexico Dr., Longboat Key, FL 33548 (383–9505); Wedebrock Real Estate Co., 5620 Gulf of Mexico Dr., Longboat Key, FL 34228 (383–5543); White Sails Realty, 5610 Gulf of Mexico Dr., Longboat Key, FL 34228 (383–3718). There are many other realtors; a complete list is available on request from the Chamber of Commerce.

CONTACT   Longboat Key Chamber of Commerce, Box 188, Longboat Key, FL 33548 (383–1212).

MARCO ISLAND

Area Code 813
LOCATION   On the Gulf Coast, 16 miles south of Naples; 104 miles west of Miami.

SIZE   6 miles by 4 miles.

ACCESS   *Car:* Two bridges from the mainland. *Air:*
                           The island has a small airstrip. Nearest
                           commercial airports are Naples and Fort
Myers; the Jetport Express bus runs from the latter, a 50-minute drive.
Private boat.

HISTORY AND   Marco Island is the northernmost and larg-
DESCRIPTION   est of the Ten Thousand Islands chain. The
                           Spaniards originally named it La Isla de
San Marco, for the Christian evangelist St. Mark; the name was grad-
ually shortened to San Marco Island and then to Marco Island. The
Calusa Indians are the first known inhabitants.

The era of modern development (some people would call it unre-
stricted growth) began in the mid–1960s, and there are now about
10,000 year-round residents, a population which increases to more
than 25,000 in the winter season. The island has been transformed
from a quiet fishing mecca into a top tourist resort, and can no longer
qualify as a quiet hideaway (though it still has only 3 traffic lights).
There are high-rise hotels and numerous condominiums, whose clien-
tele has demanded and attracted boutiques and elegant restaurants
(fond wintering grandmothers will find no shortage of dresses made
by Florence Eiseman and Sarah Louise of England).

POINTS OF INTEREST   Indian Hill is the highest point on the is-
                           land, rising 58 feet above sea level. It was
                           created by Calusa Indian women who, over
many centuries, harvested mussels, clams, oysters, and other shellfish in nearby waters and made shell mounds in order to raise their
homes above the wet, boggy, soil.

Old Marco Village is the island's most historic section; here a ferry
once connected the island with the mainland, and children attended
the Marco Village School. The school is now gone, but the 1882 home
of Captain Bill Collier, who founded the Village, still stands. William
D. Collier, the captain's son, was digging on the property in 1985 and
discovered some unfamiliar objects. He called in archaeologists from
the University of Pennsylvania, whose excavation yielded more than
1500 Indian artifacts—Florida's richest discovery of carved and
painted ceremonial objects. Among them are the Key Marco cat, at-
tributed to Amazon Indians and now at the Smithsonian. Goodland is
an unpretentious fishing village on the southeastern tip of the island,
on a small peninsula just off San Marco Drive. It is a 15-minute drive
from the resort area, over a shell road lined with mangroves. Residents here fish commercially, charter boats, and guide fishing parties.
A marina/lodge and two other marinas provide good meals, gas, and
dockage, and the museum displays a collection of shells and artifacts
made by the Calusas which were preserved in the mulch of the mangrove swamps.

The four Isles of Capri are across Marco Pass from Old Marco, accessible by Routes 951 and 952. Visitors may drive from one island to the next along Capri Boulevard, catching some of the peacefulness which distinguishes them from the surrounding area. The islands were originally a fishing community. In the 1950s, L. L. "Doc" Loach purchased them and removed mangroves, shells, and sand in order to build canals and establish stable land areas. Today several thousand residents live there, enjoying the tranquil setting. The Isles of Capri retain the quiet, unhurried atmosphere of a small town, one of the few waterfront communities left in Southwest Florida to do so.

SIGHTSEEING TOURS   The narrated 90-minute Trolley Tour of Marco Island (394–1229) has several pick-up points, including a number of the hotels and malls.

The *Rosie O'Shea* (394–7531), a paddlewheeler, makes sightseeing and dinner cruises from O'Shea's Restaurant, 1081 Bald Eagle Dr.

Sunshine Tours (642–5413) offers fishing and shelling tours aboard pontoon boats.

Island Nature Cruises, aboard the *Island Princess*, leave from the Port of the Islands Resort, on Rt. 41, about 20 minutes from Marco Island, at the edge of the Everglades. The cruises through the Everglades are narrated by Capt. Al Godfrey, who is an expert on the vegetation patterns and the native wildlife (US except FL 800/237–4173; FL 800/282–3011).

PARKS, BEACHES AND   *Parks:* The island has no parks, but Collier
CAMPING   Seminole State Park is nearby, just off Rt. 41. *Beaches:* Tigertail is the island's only public beach; it is in a natural state, with dunes, sea oats, and sunsets rivalling those in Key West. *Camping:* There is camping at Collier Seminole State Park. There are two trailer parks at Goodland (the Drop Anchor, 394–3202) and the Mar-Good RV Park (394–6383).

MARINAS   Port of the Islands Marina (394–3101) is a 500-acre waterfront resort with direct access to the 10,000 islands and the Gulf; there are 10 transient slips; maximum length 50 feet; approach depth 7 feet; dockside depth 8 feet; electric power—yes; restaurant within walking distance—yes. Coon Key Pass Marina (Goodland; 394–2797); 5 transient slips; maximum length 32 feet; approach depth 8 feet; dockside depth 4 feet; electric power—yes; restaurant within walking distance—yes. O'Shea's Restaurant (394–7531); 10 transient slips; maximum length 75 feet; approach depth 10 feet; dockside depth 10 feet; electric power—yes; restaurant within walking distance—yes.

RESTAURANTS The Blue Heron Inn, 387 Capri Blvd. (394–6248), in Isles of Capri, has won an award as one of the 10 Best Restaurants in Southwest Florida (no credit cards).**$$$**

The Olde Marco Inn, 100 Palm Ave. (394–3131), has long been a favorite gathering place for islanders and visitors. It was built by William Collier in 1883 to house sportsmen who arrived at the island by yacht in the 1880s and 1890s. It is one of Florida's oldest inns, and today has 6 dining rooms, ranging from a Victorian veranda to an elegant paneled room with Audubon prints. In 1896, its rooms went for $2 and its one bathroom was mentioned by Ripley in his "Believe It Or Not" column as the world's only 2-story outhouse.**$$**

O'Shea's Restaurant & Lounge, 1081 Bald Eagle Dr. (394–7531), features fish and beef specialties (see Sightseeing Tours for paddle-wheeler operating from here).**$$**

LODGING The Boat House at the Olde Marco Inn, 100 Palm Ave. (394–3131), is a modern structure on the waterfront with rooms and docking facilities.**$$$**

The Eagle's Nest Beach Resort, 410 S. Collier Blvd., 33937 (US except FL 800/237–8906; FL 800/282–8906); the Marco Bay Resort, 1001 North Barfield Dr., Marco Island, FL 33937 (US except FL 800/282–0661; FL 800/282–6833), an all-suite hotel overlooking the bay; the Marco Beach Hilton, 560 S. Collier Blvd., 33937 (800/445–8667); and Marriott's Marco Island Resort, 400 S. Collier Blvd., 33937 (800/438–4373), are all on the beach and are in the **$$$** category.

The Port of the Islands Resort is just 20 minutes away on Rt. 41, at the edge of the Everglades National Park. In his book on notable fishing and hunting lodges in North America, outdoorsman and author A. J. McClane described it as "a grand oasis of luxury rising out of nowhere." It was built in the early 1960s, but 2 decades later it had declined to the point that a bear was reportedly living in the kitchen and alligators had taken over the swimming pool. In 1980, it was purchased and renovated by naturalist W. D. Ray of California, who also owns the elegant Balboa Bay Club in Newport Beach, California. Port of the Islands is decorated in Spanish "Old Florida" style with murals of Florida wildlife. It is on the edge of the Everglades, and its harbor is actually a manatee sanctuary; if you are lucky, you will glimpse the gentle creatures swimming about. There is much wildlife, including numerous bird species. The resort is popular with sportsmen and boaters, and in addition to the resort and marina, has an RV-park and a 3,500-foot airstrip for visitors.**$$**

RENTALS Island Rentals, Inc., 1110 N. Collier Blvd., Marco Island (394–8262), handles seasonal rentals. Marco Rentals, Inc., 960 N.

Collier Blvd. (800/257–6021), handles condominium and house rentals by the week, month, or year.

CONTACT   Marco Island Area Chamber of Commerce, 1102 N. Collier Blvd., Box 913, Marco Island, FL 33969 (394–7549).

MERRITT ISLAND

Area Code 407
LOCATION   On Florida's East Coast, between the mainland and Cape Canaveral.

SIZE   40 miles long; 6 miles wide.

ACCESS   **Car:** By bridges from the mainland. **Air:** There is commercial service to Melbourne. **Private boat.**

HISTORY AND   The past 3 decades have wrought many
DESCRIPTION   changes in Merritt Island, which is now the
                                home of the Kennedy Space Center, one of
Florida's top tourist attractions. The island, along with Cocoa Beach and Cape Canaveral, plus Rockledge, Titusville, and Cocoa, on the mainland, are known collectively as the Space Coast. Merritt island was named for an early settler to whom Spain granted the entire island about 1800. Sandy terrain is typical of the northern section, where the Merritt Island National Wildlife Refuge is located, but toward the south there are stands of Caribbean pine and small citrus orchards. Terns, white herons, and other birds feed in the lagoons and grassy ponds in the southern part of the island, which is divided into two tongues of land by Newfound Harbor. East of Merritt Island, the government has set aside the Canaveral National Seashore.

POINTS OF INTEREST   Spaceport USA, at the Kennedy Space Center, presents the sights, sounds, colors,
                                and drama of NASA's space program with
robots, lectures, films, exhibits, and an art gallery. "The Dream is Alive," shown at the IMAX theater, which has a 5½ story screen, gives an introduction to America's space program. (See Sightseeing for bus tours of the Kennedy Space Center.)

Cape Canaveral Air Force Station is located to the east of Merritt Island. On Sundays, as a rule, you may drive your own car around the Station (to check ahead for launches, call the number given under Sightseeing for bus tours). The Merritt Island moon-launch site is also of interest.

Port Canaveral, to the east of the island, is home to a deep-sea fishing fleet and to Premier Cruise Lines, whose ships make trips to the Bahamas, Caribbean, and other destinations.

SIGHTSEEING TOURS At Spaceport USA, double-decker buses leave the Visitors' Center continuously from 9:45 A.M. until 2 hours before dark, every day but Christmas, for tours of Kennedy Space Center and Cape Canaveral Air Force Station (for details call 800/432–2153 in Florida; locally call 452–2121).

The *Scandinavian Sky* makes 1-day SeaEscape cruises from Port Canaveral (379–0000; FL 800/432–0900). They run Monday-Thursday.

At nearby Cocoa Beach, the *Little River Queen* leaves from Gatsby's Dockside for cruises of the islands and residential areas of Cocoa Beach (783–2380).

Merritt Island Air Service, Inc., 900 Airport Rd., Merritt Island (453–2222), will arrange charter air tours.

PARKS, BEACHES AND **Parks:** The Merritt Island National Wildlife
CAMPING Refuge (867–8667) is a marshy area—a haven for deer, sea turtles, alligators, and eagles. North of the island is the Canaveral National Seashore (867–2805), which adjoins the Kennedy Space Center. It occupies 57,000 acres of undeveloped beach, dunes, and wetlands. **Beaches:** There are public beaches at either end of the National Seashore (but no linking road); Apollo is at the north, and Playalinda at the south. They are desolate, but there are small visitors' centers at both ends. **Camping:** Tingley's Campground, Rt. 2, Box 180, Barge Canal, Merritt Island 32952 (452–0504).

MARINAS Tingley's Marina, Merritt Island (452–0504); 30 transient slips; maximum length 40 feet; approach depth 12 feet; dockside depth 12 feet; electric power—yes; restaurant within walking distance—yes. Banana River Marine, Banana River, Merritt Island (452-8622); 2 transient slips; maximum length 60 feet; approach depth 5 feet; dockside depth 6 feet; electric power—yes; restaurant within walking distance—no. Indian Cove Marina, Merritt Island (452–8540); 3 transient slips; maximum length 65 feet; approach depth 5 feet; dockside depth 6 feet; electric power—yes; restaurant within walking distance—no.

RESTAURANTS Bernard's Surf, 2 S. Atlantic Ave., Cocoa Beach (783–2401), a famous Space Coast restaurant, features exotic foods (such as chocolate-covered ants and alligator appetizers), but is also known for excellent steak and seafood.**$$**

Captain Ed's Seafood, 401 Bridge House, Cape Canaveral (783-1580), is extremely popular because of its fresh seafood; one of the largest scallop processing plants in the country is 2 blocks away, and fishing boats unload their catch nearby. It is on an inlet off the ocean, with excellent views of the commercial vessels and pleasure boats; if the shuttle is going up, there is a ringside seat.**$$**

The Olive Garden, 205 E. Merritt Island Causeway (459–0306) is an Italian restaurant.**$**

The Pier House, 401 Meade Ave., Cocoa Beach (783–7549), is at the end of Canaveral pier, which extends out over the ocean; it is a popular spot because of the view. The broiled seafood platter is a specialty.**$$**

LODGING   Holiday Inn Merritt Island, 260 E. Merritt Island Causeway, 32952 (452–7711).**$**

There are many motels in the nearby community of Cocoa Beach; the Chamber of Commerce will send a full list. One pleasant establishment is the Polaris Beach Resort Inn, 5600 N. Atlantic Ave., Cocoa Beach 32931 (800/962–0028 or 783–7621), with a private beach and lawn games.

RENTALS   Heritage Real Estate, 130 Canaveral Plaza, Cocoa Beach, FL 32931 (for Merritt Island-call 453–3400) and JoAnn P. Davis, 1980 N. Atlantic Ave., Cocoa Beach 32931 (783–0120) handle rentals.

CONTACT   Cocoa Beach Greater Chamber of Commerce, Merritt Island, FL 32952 (452–4390).

PINE ISLAND

Area Code 813
LOCATION   West of Fort Myers.

SIZE   17 miles by 2 miles (at its widest point).

ACCESS   *Car:* By bridge from Matlacha. *Air:* There is commercial service to Fort Myers. *Private boat.*

HISTORY AND   Pine Island is something of an anomaly on
DESCRIPTION   the Gulf Coast, and especially in Lee County: a rustic island where every amenity can be found but which is relatively free of the hordes of tourists who frequent many Gulf coast retreats. The houses visible from the rural

road are modest; the island is mostly a residential and fisherman's island. Developments such as the Bocilla Island Club at Bokeelia have been accomplished deftly and without detriment to the surroundings. There are no parking problems and there is more water and sand than asphalt. Fortunately, the island cannot become a paved-over resort, as there is a maximum height restriction of 38 feet.

It is thought that the first tourist on the Lee Island Coast was Ponce de Leon, who deposited his stone marker on Pine Island in 1513 and was later mortally wounded in nearby waters by a Calusa Indian arrow. The sport of tarpon fishing began in these waters around the turn of the century; the great tarpon make a long trek from as far away as Nova Scotia and South America to spawn in the warm Gulf waters from May to September. Many knowledgeable sports fishermen claim that, along with Boca Grande Pass, Pine Island Sound is the best area for tarpon fishing.

The island is actually a combination of 5 small communities. Matlacha (pronounced Mat-La-Shay) is at the bridge (often called the "fishingest bridge in the world") that provides access to the island. At any hour of the day or night, you may find, posted on the bridge catwalks, fishermen from a variety of locales using everything from cane poles and worms to elaborate artificial bait.

Bokeelia is at the northern end of the island, where the waters of Charlotte Harbor, Boca Grande Pass, and Pine Island Sound meet. It is from here that you can get boats to Cabbage Key, Cayo Costa, and Useppa. Boca Grande Pass is famous for its silver tarpon. Bokeelia was first settled about 1904 by the Henry Martin family, who built the first store on the island (the building is still in use).

St. James City, at the southern end of Pine Island, was settled in 1887 by a group of wealthy New Englanders who built homes of spruce

Pine Island

and white pine shipped from Maine. The grand San Carlos Hotel, built in 1886, was a landmark visited by Henry Ford, Thomas Edison, and other notables; it burned in 1905. Before the railroad was extended to Palm Beach, St. James City was one of the most popular resorts in south Florida. It later deteriorated, and was purchased by a sisal hemp company which tried unsuccessfully to manufacture rope. Steamers from Fort Myers once stopped here to take passengers to various resorts.

Pine Island Center was originally known as Tom's Town, for Tom Phillips, who planned it during the 1940s. Pineland, the fifth community, is noted for the historic Calusa Indian mounds; they inhabited the island in the 1700s, a century in which the entire civilization mysteriously vanished.

POINTS OF INTEREST   At Pineland, the small park has a marker remembering the Calusa civilization. Pine Island Sound, which runs about 15 miles from just above Sanibel to the mouth of Charlotte Harbor at Boca Grande Pass, is dotted with small islands and protected from the open Gulf by a string of barrier islands. Many of the islands are part of the Pine Island National Wildlife Refuge, closed to public access to prevent disturbances to nesting birds. The Sound is one of Florida's aquatic preserves. The first of these was established in Estero Bay, near Fort Myers Beach, in 1966, and there are now 40, most of them along the state's coastline.

At Pine Island Center, on Russell Rd., the Museum of the Islands displays historical artifacts. The museum, recently opened, was the dream of Pine Islanders Jim Bone, Elaine Jordan, and Mike Shevlin.

SIGHTSEEING TOURS   The Bocilla Island Club (see Lodging) arranges sightseeing cruises for guests to Cayo Costa State Park and Cabbage Key.

The *Tropic Star*, docked at Pineland (Box 569, Bokeelia, FL 33922; 283–0015), makes day cruises to the State Park at Cayo Costa and to Cabbage Key; guests may return the same day or stay overnight, camping or renting cabins at the park, or else lodge at the inn at Cabbage Key (by advance arrangement with the inn).

Capt. Bill Cyzewski, Box 561, Bokeelia, FL 33932 (283–0106), arranges beachcombing, shelling, fishing, and sightseeing expeditions, as well as trips to out-island restaurants; he also runs a day and night water taxi if you wish to dine on an outer island, such as Cabbage Key.

Island naturalists give tours of bird life, Indian mounds, mangrove areas, and eagles' nests along the Intracoastal Waterway. Make reservations through the Pine Island Chamber of Commerce (see Contact).

See Fort Myers Beach and Sanibel/Captiva sections for other sightseeing cruises in the area.

PARKS, BEACHES AND   **Parks:** The Matlacha Community Park has
CAMPING   a community building with play areas, picnic areas, restrooms, and a boat ramp; this
is just over the bridge from Pine Island. Phillips Park, with a public
pool, tennis courts, and play area, is in Pine Island Center. Tropical
Point, with a boat ramp and beach area is four miles south of Pine
Island Center. No pets are allowed in the parks. **Beaches:** There is a
beach at Tropical Point and another at Bokeelia. **Camping:** Camping
is offered at Lakewood Travel Resort, 5120 Stringfellow Rd., St.
James City 33956 (283-2415), on the southern end of Pine Island,
and at Cherry Estates RV Park, 3039 York Rd., St. James City 33956
(283–1144), as well as at the Pink Citrus, 15061 Stringfellow Rd.
NW, Bokeelia, FL 33922 (283-0346). A complete list of camping
places is available from the Greater Pine Island Chamber of Commerce (see Contact). There is camping at Cayo Costa State Park (see
that entry).

MARINAS   Bocilla Island Club (283–7070) has a
ship's store, fishing pier, and clubhouse;
several transient slips but no live-aboard
boaters are allowed; maximum length 34 feet; approach depth 3 feet;
dockside depth 5 feet; electric power—yes; restaurant within walking
distance—yes.

Pineland Marina, Bokeelia (283–0015) has a campground with full
hook-ups (no laundry or shower).

Four Winds Marina, Stringfellow Rd. (283–0250); 15 transient
slips; maximum length 35 feet; approach depth 4 feet; dockside
depth 4 feet; electric power—no; restaurant within walking distance—no.

RESTAURANTS   The Dock, Stringfellow Rd. (Pine Island
Shopping Center) 283–0005), in St. James
City, is a family-style restaurant with home-
cooked meals.**$**

The Porthole Restaurant at 10880 Stringfellow Rd., Bokeelia (283-
5333), is popular with local people, who enjoy the steamed shrimp
and fried clam sandwiches; there is nightly entertainment.**$**

Sandy Hook Crab House, 4893 Pine Island Rd., Matlacha (283–
0113), has an antique nautical atmosphere, and overlooks Matlacha
Pass. It is popular with local people as well as with visitors.**$$**

LODGING   Beachouse Motel, Box 467, Bocilla Lane
(283-4303), has furnished one-bedroom
apartments and a private 260-foot pier.**$$**

The Bocilla Island Club, Box 700, Bokeelia, FL (283–7070), overlooking Jug Creek, which leads into Pine Island Sound, is an ideal
place to stay. It has timbered townhouse condominiums, set among

palms, flowering hibiscus, and mahoe trees. Trellised boardwalks lead to the pool, tennis courts, and a marina; the units have 2 private bedrooms, 2 full baths plus a half-bath, washers and dryers, covered parking, screened porches and fully equipped kitchens. Beside the beachfront units is a private pier stretching 400 feet into Charlotte Harbor. Units rent by the week, month, or season.**$$$**

Lime Tree Lodge, 16000 Buccaneer, Bokeelia 33922 (283–1609), is on the waterfront; it has 1-bedroom apartments and 1-room efficiencies, renting by the day, week, or month.**$**

Malu-Lani Motel, Box 28, Bocilla Lane (283–1795), on the waterfront with a dock, has furnished 1-bedroom apartments.**$**

For a complete list of accommodations, write the Chamber of Commerce.

RENTALS   Shady Nook Cottages (William Cyzewski, 283-0106), on Main St., are furnished 1-bedroom units. Einer Holman (Samoa Dr. off Russell Rd., 481–2260) is a house on stilts, on a canal. It is furnished with 2 bedrooms and rents by the month or season (no children or pets allowed). Greider Realty, Box 10, St. James City 33956 (283–1044) handles rentals also.

CONTACT   Greater Pine Island Chamber of Commerce, Box 525, Pine Island Rd., Matlacha, FL 33909 (283-0888).

ST. GEORGE ISLAND

Area Code 904
LOCATION   4 miles south of Eastpoint, which is about 50 miles southwest of Tallahassee and 7 miles east of Apalachicola.

SIZE   28 miles long by ½ to 1 mile wide.

ACCESS   **Car:** Toll bridge from Eastpoint. **Air:** There is a 3,800-foot paved air strip. **Private boat.**

HISTORY AND   St. George is one of Florida's largest bar-
DESCRIPTION   rier islands, with sand dunes, sea oats, and wide beaches. Thanks to diligence on the part of the 400 year-round residents of St. George, it is one of the few islands in the state left relatively untouched by developers; there are no wall-to-wall high rises and building has been carried out with

the goals of preserving the island's natural beauty and preventing pollution and erosion. To many homeowners, it is a private "Shangri-la." There are abundant shells along the wild and primitive beaches. This island has a small commercial area along with beach cottages and homes, and a small group of condominiums and townhouses.

Three other barrier islands in the vicinity, none of which may be reached by car, are Little St. George, St. Vincent, and Dog Island (*see* separate entry). Little St. George Island is just across Sike's Cut, on the west end of St. George. It is the site of the Cape St. George Lighthouse, built in 1833, which is still a beacon for mariners and is visible from many miles away. The island is uninhabited and owned by the state; it is only accessible by private boat. St. Vincent Island is a 12,358-acre National Wildlife Refuge; it also is uninhabited and accessible only by private boat. St. George Island has its own magazine, *St. George*, which publishes the work of island poets and brings visitors up to date on activity of the island's galleries and other businesses.

The entire Apalachicola Bay area is a haven for boat lovers. Carrabelle, which marks the eastern end of the Gulf Intracoastal Waterway, is a favorite gathering spot for yachtsmen before they make the Gulf crossing. Representative boats range from brawny tugs, homebuilt barges, shrimpers, and workboats to ketches, yachts, and sloops.

POINTS OF INTEREST   Nearby, in Carrabelle, there is "the" drugstore, a throwback to the 1940s and 1950s, with a marble soda fountain and huge dips of ice cream. Apalachicola has the John Gorrie State Museum, a memorial to Dr. John Gorrie, who built the first ice-making machine to cool the rooms of yellow fever victims.

Eastpoint is a fishing village, with row after row of oyster and seafood houses. The "world's most succulent oyster" is said to come from Apalachicola Bay, where nearly 90 percent of Florida's oysters are harvested.

SIGHTSEEING TOURS   None.

PARKS, BEACHES AND   **Parks:** The Dr. Julian G. Bruce State Park,
CAMPING   at the end of SR 300, is a protected bird sanctuary. It features beautiful beaches, boardwalks, and observation decks. **Beaches:** There are beautiful public beaches on the island. **Camping:** There are camping facilities at the state park.

MARINAS   At Apalachicola, there is the Rainbow Motel and Marina (653–8139); 23 transient slips; maximum length 100 feet; approach depth 12 feet; dockside depth 12 feet; electric power—yes; restaurant within walking distance—yes. Also, Miller Marine Service (653–8139), 10 transient slips; maximum length 100 feet; approach depth 12 feet; dockside depth 20 feet; electric power—yes; restaurant within walking distance—yes. (*See also* Carrabelle Marina and Carrabelle Villa and Marina, listed under Dog Island).

RESTAURANTS   The Happy Pelican, St. George Island, run by Buddy and Mary Nell Crawford (670–9993), serves sandwiches and steaks.**$**

The Islander, St. George Island (670–2335), serves very good seafood.**$**

The St. George Inn (see Lodging) has a good restaurant with a well-known chef and a pleasant ambiance.**$**

In Apalachicola, the Gibson House (653–2191) is a handsome and popular restored inn, originally built in 1907; it serves breakfast, lunch, and dinner.**$**

The Pot of Gold at the Rainbow Motel (see Lodging) overlooks the river and has a popular oyster bar; seafood platters are a specialty.**$**

LODGING   The Buccaneer Inn, St. George Island, Eastpoint 32328 (670–2585), a recently built chain motel, has comfortable rooms.**$**

The Rainbow Motel and Marina, Apalachicola (653–8139) overlooks the water.**$**

The St. George Inn, Box 222, St. George Island, Eastpoint 32328 (670–2903), in a white building with blue shutters just over the causeway, has a Victorian style reminiscent of the early 1900s and has acquired a following since its opening.**$**

RENTALS   Several realtors handle rentals: Resort Realty, St. George Island, Eastpoint 32328 (670–2666); Alice D. Collins Realty, Inc., Box 16, St. George Island, Eastpoint 32328 (670–2758; US except FL 800/423–7418).

CONTACT   Apalachicola Bay Chamber of Commerce, 128 Market St., Apalachicola, FL 32320 (653–9419).

ST. PETERSBURG BEACHES:

SAND KEY *(which includes Indian Rocks Beach and Madeira Beach)*, TREASURE ISLAND, ST. PETERSBURG BEACH *(or Long Key)*, MULLET KEY *(site of Fort DeSoto Park)*

Area Code 813

LOCATION   West of Clearwater/St. Petersburg, on the Gulf Coast.

SIZE   The islands span approximately 24 miles along the Gulf Coast.

ACCESS   **Car:** Via several causeways from the mainland (the greater Clearwater/St. Petersburg area). **Air:** There is commercial service to Tampa and St. Petersburg/Clearwater. **Private boat.**

HISTORY AND   The 4 islands are strung along below Clear-
DESCRIPTION   water Beach and above Anna Maria Island. They are all part of the "Pinellas Suncoast" (as is Clearwater Beach; see separate entry). The Pinellas Peninsula was discovered in 1528 when Panfilo de Narvaez, searching for gold and slaves, sailed into Boca Ciega Bay and landed in northwest St. Petersburg. The Spaniards found many Timucuan Indian mound builders, but permanent settlement was not to come about for three centuries. The first white settler was Count Odet Philippe, a French navy surgeon who escaped from France and settled in South Carolina; he then went to the Pinellas Suncoast in the 1830s and cultivated Florida's first grapefruit grove; he wrote about a "heaven on earth" when he first settled here. Like Brighton, England, the area owed its early popularity to having received a medical stamp of approval. At an April, 1885 meeting of the American Medical Association in New Orleans, Dr. W. C. Van Bibber of Baltimore presented the results of a 10-year study for the establishment of a "world health city." He concluded that "Point Pinellas," with its superb winter climate, was the ideal location. The report was widely publicized, as doctors were at that time prescribing visits to hot springs and seaside spas as cures for varied ailments. "Point Pinellas," from the Spanish phrase "punta pinal" or "point of pines," now attracts as many as 3 million visitors per year.

The area is still ideal for escaping from the cold, but during the winter season the traffic along Gulf Blvd. may be bumper-to-bumper. It is not always clear where one community ends and another begins, as the entire stretch is built up, but the blue Gulf is always close by, visible between buildings and down the short streets. From January to

April, prices are highest; budget-minded visitors may prefer to come
between May and January to avoid the crowds and take advantage of
off-season rates. At almost any time, visitors can find accommodations in a wide price range.

Sand Key is the island just below Clearwater Beach. It includes *Indian Rocks Beach*, which in turn is made up of 7 communities (Belleair
Bluffs, Belleair Beach, Indian Rocks Beach, Indian Shores, North Redington Beach, Redington Shores, and Redington Beach). It has a year-
round population of just over 11,000. Although the strand is not as
wide as Clearwater Beach, the Redington Pier attracts many fishermen. At the lower end of Sand Key is *Madeira Beach*, which is known
for its outstanding fishing. Madeira Beach has over 5,000 year-round
residents and about 2½ miles of strand.

Treasure Island: This island is about 3.5 miles long and has about
7,000 year-round residents. There are three municipal beaches, including Sunset Beach and St. Petersburg Municipal Beach. Treasure
Island was named by early settlers when they heard rumors of treasure
being buried on the island (none has been found). The strand is wide,
and the island as a whole has long been known for its fishing. In 1915,
Whiteford Harrell's Coney Island Hotel was built (a 25-room, 3-story
structure for which the lumber was barged down from Cedar Key). As
a resort, Treasure Island grew slowly until 1948, when James Harrison
built the Sands Motel; after that, the community burgeoned. The island has an active Recreation Department which plans many activities; one of the most festive events is "Pirate Days," held in late June
and early July, which includes a pirate "invasion."

St. Petersburg Beach: This 7½-mile-long beach has several fishing
piers and noted resort hotels; the resort community is, technically,
located on Long Key.

Mullet Key (Fort DeSoto Park): Fort DeSoto Park is made up of 5
islands or keys connected by roads: Madelaine Key, St. Jean Key, St.
Christopher Key, Bonne Fortune Key, and the main island, Mullet Key;
they total 900 acres with almost 3 miles of beach approved for swimming. It is interesting that one of the area's earliest settlements was
on Mullet Key, which is now protected. During the early 1800s, Capt.
William Bunce operated a fish farm on Mullet Key with about 300 Indians and Spaniards. Fort DeSoto was built on Mullet Key in 1898 to
protect Tampa Bay during the Spanish American War. The fort is listed
in the National Register of Historic Places and counts Robert E. Lee
among its distinguished visitors.

POINTS OF INTEREST   *Indian Rocks Beach*: At Indian Shores, Tiki
                              Gardens is reminiscent of Polynesia, with
                              shops, gardens, adventure trail, and res-
taurants. The Suncoast Seabird Sanctuary is also located in Indian
Shores; it is a refuge for injured and crippled birds and more than 500
species may be seen here. Hamlin's Landing, 401 2nd St. East, is a
new complex on the Intracoastal Waterway, built in Victorian style,
offering shopping and dining.

Redington Long Pier, Indian Rocks Beach

Madeira Beach: At the lower end of the island by John's Pass (which goes between the Gulf of Mexico and Boca Ciega Bay), there is John's Pass Village and Boardwalk, a complex patterned after an authentic turn-of-the-century Florida fishing village, complete with weathered woods and angled buildings built on stilts; it contains a variety of specialty shops and seafood restaurants.

Treasure Island: The 1986 Guinness record for the World's Largest Sand Castle is held by Treasure Island.

St. Petersburg Beach: The London Wax Museum, 5505 Gulf Blvd., is of interest.

In nearby St. Petersburg there are the Salvador Dali Museum (which has the world's largest collection of works by Dali), the Sunken Gardens, the Museum of Fine Arts, and the Haas Museum Complex; and in Largo there is the Heritage Park and Museum, a 21-acre open-air museum showing the early history of Pinellas County. (See the Clearwater Beach section for other attractions in Clearwater and Tampa).

SIGHTSEEING TOURS The *Capt. Anderson* Dinner Boat, St. Pete Beach Causeway (360–2619) offers both dinner cruises and sightseeing tours.

The *Starlite Princess*, located at Hamlin's Landing in Indian Rocks Beach (595–1212), is a 3-deck paddlewheel offering dinner cruises and charters.

Gray Line Water Tours, 401 2nd Ave. NE, St. Petersburg (823-8171), has a sternwheeler, *The Belle of St. Petersburg*, which cruises the Bay. (See the Clearwater Beach section for cruises from Clearwater and Clearwater Beach).

There are Gray Line bus tours from St. Petersburg (822–3577).

PARKS, BEACHES AND   **Parks:** Fort DeSoto Park, 407 S. Garden
CAMPING   Ave. (*see* History and Description section),
                                 and also Upham Park on St. Pete Beach.
There is tennis at Egan Park, Lazarillo Park, and Vina del Mar Park on
Vina del Mar Island, adjacent to the beach. **Beaches:** Even in season,
the miles of beaches can accommodate a good many people without
seeming crowded; just don't look for the high crashing waves which
characterize the northern Atlantic beaches. **Camping:** St. Christopher
and St. Jean Key, in Fort DeSoto Park, are approved for camping.
There are separate sections for tent camping and self-contained units
up to 30 feet long, with water, picnic tables, electricity, 2 dump stations, laundry, and a store; there are 235 sites. All reservations are
on a pay-in-advance cash only basis. Exact change is required for reservations made at the St. Petersburg office (545 1st Ave. North, Room
63, St. Petersburg, FL; 866–2662). Campers Cove, 12750 N. 118th
Ave., Indian Rocks (595–5722), has campsites. The Chamber of Commerce will send a list of campgrounds and trailer parks in the St. Pete
Beach area, as well as in Tarpon Springs, Seminole, Dunedin, Largo,
and St. Petersburg. Some are restricted to adults.

MARINAS   At Indian Rocks Beach there is Hamlin's
                                 Landing Marina (596–9788); 15 transient
                                 slips; maximum length 60 feet; approach
depth 7 feet; dockside depth 5 feet; electric power—yes; restaurant
within walking distance—yes. On the Pinellas Bayway, southeast of
St. Petersburg Beach (on Tierra Verde Island), there is the Tierra Verde
Marina (866–0255); 12 transient slips; maximum length 100 feet;
approach depth 18 feet; dockside depth 10 feet; electric power—yes;
restaurant within walking distance—yes. The Isla del Sol Marina, on
the Isla del Sol (867–3625), is also across from St. Petersburg
Beach; 12 transient slips; maximum length 30 feet; approach depth
15 feet; dockside depth 20 feet; electric power—yes; restaurant
within walking distance—yes. Madeira Beach Municipal Marina, not
far from the Madeira Beach Chamber of Commerce (393–9177); 10
transient slips; maximum length 50 feet; approach depth 6 feet; dockside depth 10 feet; electric power—yes; restaurant within walking distance—yes.

RESTAURANTS   The Suncoast has over 1,600 restaurants
                                 offering everything from gourmet to bare-
                                 foot dining. *Indian Rocks Beach:* Le Pom-
pano, 19325 Gulf Blvd., Indian Shores (596–0333), has a continental
menu, specializing in bouillabaisse; it has a fireplace, waterfront dining, and antiques. It was founded in 1973 by French chef Michel
Denis, who won the Gold Medal for cold duckling in the worldwide
Culinary Competition held in England.**$$** The Wine Cellar, 17307 Gulf
Blvd., N. Redington Beach (393–3491), has a European decor with
antiques and specializes in beef Wellington.**$$** Trader Frank's, in the

Tiki Gardens shopping complex (595–2587), has an outdoor peacock bar and seafood, along with a Far-Eastern and American menu.**$** *Madeira Beach*: The Captain's Galley, 660 Blackhawk Rd., Madeira Beach (392–9094) overlooks the marina and specializes in seafood and steak.**$** The Kapok Tree Restaurant, 5001 Duhme Rd. (398–2132), is a branch of the well-known restaurant at Clearwater Beach; it has an attractive garden setting.**$$**

Treasure Island: Restaurants here include Captain Kosmakos, 9610 Gulf Blvd. (367–3743), offering waterfront dining and free hors d'oeuvres during happy hour (**$**) and the Careless Navigator, 11595 Gulf Blvd. (367–2797), which has a treasure chest for children and a nautical decor.**$** The Kingfish, 12789 Kingfish Dr. (360–0881), at John's Pass, has been famous for many years; it specializes in fresh seafood.**$**

St. Petersburg Beach: The King Charles Room, at the Don CeSar resort (see Lodging), is famous for its food, including lobster medallions; the restaurant offers formal dining, accompanied by a harpist.**$$$** The Palm Court, at the TradeWinds (see Lodging) is known for its Italian cuisine and good service.**$$**

Fort DeSoto State Park: There is a cafeteria here.

LODGING

The Suncoast is dotted with over 500 motels, 79 hotels, and 85 rental condominiums. A complete listing is available from the Chamber of Commerce. Many of the establishments have rooms with full kitchens; others have suites and 1- and 2-bedroom apartments as well as motel rooms.

Indian Rocks Beach: Alpaugh's Gulf Beach Motel Apts., 68 Gulf Blvd. 33535 (595–2589), **$$**; El Morocco Resort Motel, 16333 Gulf Blvd., Redington Beach 33708 (391–1675), **$$**; Far Horizons, 17248 Gulf Blvd., North Redington Beach 33708 (393–8791).**$$**

Madeira Beach: Holiday Inn, 15208 Gulf Blvd. 33708 (392–2275).**$$$** The Shoreline, 14200 Gulf Blvd. 33708 (397–6641), has accommodations ranging from motel rooms to penthouse apartments (no children allowed).**$$$**

Treasure Island: There are over 2,500 units here, ranging widely in size and quality. Among the better known are the Bilmar Beach Resort, 10650 Gulf Blvd. 33706 (800/826–9724), **$$**; Land's End Resort, 7500 Bayshore Dr. 33706 (800/382–8883), **$$$**; the Quality Inn-Trail's End Resort Motel, 11500 Gulf Blvd. 33706 (360–5541), **$$**; and condo units at Island Inn Shores, 9980 Gulf Blvd. 33706 (367–1296),**$$-$$$**.

St. Petersburg Beach: A famous landmark for many years on St. Pete's is the Don CeSar Resort, 3400 Gulf Blvd., 33706 (800/237-8987), **$$$**. Opened during the 1920s, it is on the National Register of Historic Places and is as much of a Suncoast institution as the Belleview Biltmore in Clearwater. The huge pink rococo palace, with over 200 rooms and many suites, dominates the beach. F. Scott Fitzgerald stayed here often during the 1920s and 1930s, and many other celebrities have also been intrigued by its decor and interesting heritage. Other hotels here include the the Breckenridge Resort Hotel, 5700 Gulf Blvd. 33706 (US except FL 800/828–3371; FL 800/392–5700),**$$$**; the Colonial Gateway Inn, 6300 Gulf Blvd. 33706 (US except FL 800/237-8918; FL 800/282–5245),**$$**; the Dolphin Beach Resort, 4900 Gulf Blvd. 33706 (800/237–8916),**$$**; the Sandpiper Beach Resort, 6000 Gulf Blvd. 33706 (US except FL 800/237–0707; FL 800/287–5553),**$$$**; and the Trade Winds Beach Resort, 5400 Gulf Blvd. (US except FL 800/237-7700; FL 800/282–1263),**$$$**.

Fort DeSoto State Park: None.

RENTALS   St. Pete Beach Rentals, 1615 Gulf Blvd. (367- 7818). KeppieTours, 41 N. Ft. Harrison Ave., Clearwater, FL 33515 (800/237–1486), is a travel agency which has been in business since 1924. They offer condo rentals as a sideline, along with sightseeing, car rentals, and deep-sea fishing excursions. They handle properties along the coast from Clearwater Beach to Treasure Island.

A full list of realtors can be obtained from the Pinellas Suncoast Tourist Development Council or the Chamber of Commerce.

CONTACT   Pinellas Suncoast Tourist Development Council, 2333 East Bay Dr., Suite 109A, Clearwater, FL 34625 (530–6452). Individual Chambers of Commerce: Indian Rocks Beach, 105 Fifth Ave., Indian Rocks Beach, FL 33535 (595–4575); Madeira Beach, 501 150th Ave., Madeira Beach, FL 33708 (391–7373); Treasure Island, 152 108th Ave., Treasure Island, FL 33706 (367–4529); St. Petersburg Beach, 6990 Gulf Blvd., St. Petersburg Beach, FL 33706 (360–6957).

SANIBEL/CAPTIVA

Area Code 813

LOCATION   Southwest of Fort Myers, 6 miles from Punta Rassa.

SIZE   Sanibel is 12 miles long by 2 miles wide; Captiva, adjacent to it and reached via a short causeway over Blind Pass, is 5 miles by ½ mile.

ACCESS   ***Car:*** By toll causeway from the mainland. ***Air:*** There is commercial service to Fort Myers. ***Private boat.***

HISTORY AND
DESCRIPTION

On Sanibel, people are fond of the old saying, "If God ever retired, He'd come to live
on Sanibel." It is also said that many resi-
dents, once they've arrived, yearn to bomb the causeway and fend off
further settlers—and certainly the lines of cars waiting to get on the
island, especially during the high season, give force to both points of
view. Sanibel and her sister island, Captiva, together with North Captiva and Cayo Costa, form a shallow crescent. Because the currents
come in at an angle to this configuration, the islands receive what are
said to be the world's most prolific deposits of shells (more than 400
species have been found here). On Sanibel, the crouched shell-
collecting posture is called the "Sanibel Stoop." The best time to look
shells is after a storm, at low tide, but don't be surprised to find shell-
collectors combing the beaches at 4 A.M. by flashlight. In early March
there is a Shell Fair attracting thousands of people. The foreground of
a lush carpeting of shells, and the background of the seemingly infi-
nite stretch of beach, bordered by sea grape and Australian pines,
hovered over by roseate spoonbills, comic anhingas, and judicious
pelicans, argue strongly for bifocals.

Residents have worked hard to preserve Sanibel's idyllic and unspoiled ambiance. For most of this century, the island was reached by
ferry from Punta Rassa (one early WPA guide cites tolls of $1 for the
car and driver and $.35 for passengers). In 1963, a causeway was
built, which islanders fought bitterly all the way to the Florida Supreme
Court. Convinced that Lee County was pursuing a policy of uncon-
trolled development, residents of Sanibel managed to secede from

The "Sanibel Stoop," Sanibel Island

the county and incorporate as a city. Captiva was left out, as that island needed county funds to combat erosion. After many struggles, Sanibel residents finally had a comprehensive land-use plan approved in 1976, allowing for about 8,000 living units, and serving a projected population of 12,000 year-round residents and 6,000 visitors. While nothing could prevent completion of projects already begun, arresting development has largely preserved this treasure of an island, with its lush foliage, extensive beaches, and gleaming shells. The era of the traffic light has yet to come. The small shopping centers are tastefully constructed, with wooden boardwalks winding amid palms; there is nothing garish. The homes, hidden behind hedges, sea grape, and Australian pines, reflect the Florida of the pre-tourist era. No high-rises have been permitted, and signs are strictly regulated. Only the newspaper machines, lined up before the little cafes where the early-rising visitors sip coffee, hint that there are people here from all over the country, from New York to Chicago to Texas. The fact that there are 2 weeklies, the *Island Reporter* and the *Sanibel-Captiva Islander*, is an index of the intellectual vitality which pervades the island.

Public parking is limited on the island and firmly enforced; many visitors choose to tour by bicycle, which is far more efficient when the single twisting roads are choked by cars. There are special bicycle paths.

Sanibel was named by Jose Gaspar after Santa Isabella. Captiva's earliest inhabitants were the Calusa Indians; they left shell mounds, whose remains are still visible.

POINTS OF INTEREST   The Sanibel Lighthouse, on its southern tip, has been a landmark since 1884, when the entire island was a nature preserve.
The Island Historical Museum, Dunlop Road, has beaded woodwork and artifacts of early settlers.

SIGHTSEEING TOURS   During the winter season, starting about Nov. 1, Jim Anholt runs an excellent nar-rated trolley tour (472–6374).
Island Cruises (472–5463) runs cruises from the 'Tween Waters Marina on Captiva to Cabbage Key. Capt. Mike Fuery of Island Cruises also conducts famous shelling charters to promising beaches and sandbars, where no offshore reef breaks up the shells. He walks the beach with his charter customers, pointing out rare finds. Cruises also run from South Seas Plantation to Cabbage Key.

PARKS, BEACHES AND   **Parks and Beaches:** The J. N. "Ding" Dar-
CAMPING   ling National Wildlife Refuge (472–1100) is a 5,000-acre wilderness preserve which occupies nearly half of the island of Sanibel. Here there are many rare bird species, and if you have a telephoto lens, bring it along; huge alligators bask indolently in sunlight just off the roadside by the water. There are nature trails, a 5-mile scenic drive, and winding canoe

trails. The 2 islands have 17 miles of beach full of shells, but be warned that parking is quite limited. Bowman's Beach is a spacious bit of strand without hotels or houses on the northwestern tip of Sanibel and Lighthouse Beach is on the southern end. The Sanibel-Captiva Conservation Foundation (472–2329) has a 240-acre tract with nature trails; there are both guided and self-guided tours available. *Camping:* Backpacking and camping on the beach are not allowed on Sanibel or Captiva. There is 1 trailer park, Periwinkle Trailer Park, 1119 Periwinkle Way (472–1433), which is nicely landscaped, carefully maintained, and booked far ahead. No long-haired males allowed (once an outraged long-haired male M.D. was turned away and wrote the *Island Reporter*, charging discrimination).

MARINAS There are few landings on Sanibel, but passengers may be off-loaded on to the pier near the lighthouse at the southern end (boats may not tie up here, however). Sanibel Island Marina (472–2723); 20 transient slips; maximum length 70 feet; approach depth 6 feet; dockside depth 6 feet; electric power—yes; restaurant within walking distance—yes. South Seas Plantation (472–5111); 30 transient slips; maximum length 100 feet; approach depth 6 feet; dockside depth 9 feet; electric power—yes; restaurant within walking distance—yes. 'Tween Waters Marina (472–5161); 20 transient slips; maximum length 50 feet; approach depth 4 feet; dockside depth 7 feet; electric power—yes; restaurant within walking distance—yes.

RESTAURANTS Sanibel and Captiva abound in interesting restaurants. The Bubble Room, Captiva Road (472–5558), is decorated in eccentric and appealing 1940s furnishings, and the food is served by waitresses in Girl Scout uniforms; come early as it is usually crowded.**$$**

Sanibel's J. N. "Ding" Darling National Wildlife Refuge

The F & B Oyster Company, 2163 Periwinkle Way (472–5276), is known for its seafood.**$$**

The King's Crown (**$$**) and Chadwick's (**$$**), both at South Seas Plantation on Captiva (see Lodging), are known for their fine food. Chadwick's is a Florida-style frame house that has a popular Sunday champagne brunch, as does the Old Captiva House at the 'Tween Waters Inn (see Lodging;**$$**).

The Lighthouse Café, 362 Periwinkle Way (472–0303), is a delightful place for breakfast (served until 3:00 P.M.); it is decorated with colorful pennants and has had recipes requested by *Gourmet*.**$**

The Thistle Lodge at Casa Ybel (see Lodging) is an island favorite, a pretty Victorian-style building patterned after a New Orleans Garden District restaurant with turrets and frosted cut glass; the jambalaya and the gin fizzes are excellent.**$$**

The Timbers, 975 Rabbit Rd., Sanibel (472–3128), adjoining a fresh fish market, is good for seafood. The restaurant does not serve lunch.**$$**

LODGING   There are many condominiums, hotels, and motels on both Sanibel and Captiva Islands. The Chamber of Commerce, just over the bridge, maintains a list of vacancies, so prospective visitors can tell at once whether there are any accommodations available.

Casa Ybel Resort, 2255 West Gulf Dr., Sanibel Island 33957 (US except FL 800/237–8906; FL 800/282–8906), is a contemporary resort "village" with high-peaked wide-porched condos, modeled after old Florida Gulf houses, set amid palm trees and flowering shrubs on the southernmost point of the island. It has time-share condos available, with a back yard facing the lapping surf.**$$$**

The Moorings, 800 E. Gulf Dr., Sanibel Island, FL 33957 (US except FL 800/237–5144; 472–4119), has efficiency units, lawn games, and screened porches.**$$$**

The Shalimar, 2818 Gulf Dr., Sanibel, FL 33957 (472–1353), is a more moderate establishment with screened porches, balconies, and lawn games; it is on the beach.**$$**

The South Seas Plantation, Box 194, Captiva Island, 33924 (US except FL 800/237–3102; FL 800/282–3402), covers 330 acres and was an 1856 plantation. It has a private beach, a children's recreational program, 16 pools, marina, 22 Laykold courts, and one of Steve Colgate's Offshore Sailing Schools.**$$$**

Song of the Sea, 863 East Gulf Dr., Sanibel Island, FL 33957 (472–2220), is a pleasant waterfront establishment with efficiencies, golf, and shuffleboard.**$$$**

Sundial Beach & Tennis Resort, 1246 Middle Gulf Dr., Sanibel, FL 33957 (US except FL 800/237–4184; FL 800/282–3405), has condo units and a supervised children's program.**$$$**

The 'Tween Waters Inn, Box 249, Captiva Island, FL 33924 (US except FL 800/223–5865; FL 800/282–7560), dates back to the early 1900s. Among its famous guests were the Charles Lindberghs and the

Pulitzer Prize-winning editorial cartoonist and pioneer conservationist J. N. "Ding" Darling. Today, portions of the old inn have been preserved in a modern complex of motel units and cottages.**$$$**

RENTALS   Priscilla Murphy Realty, 1619 Periwinkle Way, Sanibel, FL 33957 (472–1511; US except FL 800/237-6008) and John Naumann Associates, 2427 Periwinkle Way, Sanibel, FL 33957 (472–3121; US except FL 800/282–0360) both handle vacation rentals.

CONTACT   The Chamber of Commerce, Box 166, Sanibel, FL 33957 (472–3232).

SANTA ROSA ISLAND
(Pensacola Beach and Navarre Beach); PERDIDO KEY

Area Code 904
LOCATION   In Florida's Panhandle, on the Gulf of Mexico, 5 miles south of Pensacola.

SIZE   Santa Rosa Island is 50 miles long and about ½ mile wide at its widest point; Perdido Key is approximately 7 miles long and about ½ mile wide.

ACCESS   *Car:* From the mainland; Rt. 87 goes to Navarre Beach; Rt. 110 to Pensacola Beach; Rt. 292 goes to Perdido Key Beach. *Air:* Several commercial airlines serve Pensacola. *Private boat.*

HISTORY AND   Santa Rosa Island is one of the barrier is-
DESCRIPTION   lands that protects the mainland of Florida. Pensacola Beach has high-rise luxury hotels and condominiums, along with many new shops and restaurants. The Gulf Pier is a popular fishing spot.

Navarre Beach is a small community east of Pensacola Beach; it is about 4 miles long by 2 miles wide. It has escaped intensive commercial development; only half of the 4-mile beach has been developed. To the west is a 12-mile section of the Gulf Islands National Seashore and to the east is a segment of beach owned by Eglin Air Force Base.

Perdido Key Beach, a separate island west of Santa Rosa, was for centuries known only to Spanish explorers and pirates. In 1693 the Spanish explorer Carlos Siquenza sought a new settlement with a seaport, and discovered Perdido Key. On his charts, he found the large shallow water bay between Spanish-ruled Pensacola and French-dominated Mobile, and visually confirmed its presence, but he could not explore it because it was inaccessible to large sailing vessels. French and Spanish navigators hoped to make the Bay a natural boundary between the 2 settlements, but failed; instead, the name "Perdido," or "lost," was given to this body of water. Later, Jean Lafitte and other Gulf Coast pirates frequented Perdido Bay. Fort McRae, at the eastern end of Perdido Key Beach, was occupied by Confederate forces during the Civil War; they exchanged cannon duels with Union forces in Fort Pickens, across Pensacola Pass. The remains of Fort McRae have been spotted by skin divers. Perdido Key Beach has recently been developed as a resort with luxury condominiums.

POINTS OF INTEREST   Fort Pickens, at the western end of Santa Rosa Island, Pensacola Beach, is part of the Gulf Islands National Seashore.
In Pensacola itself, don't miss Seville Square, a complex with several museums and historic houses; the Pensacola Museum of Art is also well worth visiting. Portions of the Naval Air Station may also be visited. Pensacola was once the port of a large red snapper fleet, which used fishing smacks brought from Gloucester, Massachusetts. One of these vessels remains, saved for restoration.

SIGHTSEEING TOURS   The rangers at Fort Pickens give tours; also, in Pensacola, a company called Right This Way (944–1700) does pre-arranged group tours of the area, including one of Santa Rosa Island.

PARKS, BEACHES AND   **Parks:** Gulf Islands National Seashore, **CAMPING**   bracketing Pensacola Beach to the west and east, has a picnic pavilion, an amphitheater with nature films, a Dune Nature Trail, and daily activities. Big Lagoon State Park is just a mile from Perdido Key on the Gulf Beach Highway. **Beaches:** There are extensive beaches on the island; the sand here is 99 percent quartz, giving it the consistency of fine sugar. **Camping:** Permitted at the National Seashore and at Big Lagoon State Park.

MARINAS   There are ample facilities here for repair of boats. There are numerous marinas on Santa Rosa Island. The Moorings of Pensacola Beach, in Little Sabine Bay, south of Bob Sikes Bridge (932–0305), has a restaurant specializing in seafood dishes (they will prepare meals to go for fishing trips); 10 transient slips; maximum length 65 feet; approach depth 7 feet; dockside depth 7 feet; electric power—yes; restaurant within walking distance—yes. The Marina (932-5700) has 10 transient slips; maximum length 100 feet; approach depth 6 feet; dockside depth 14 feet; electric power—yes; restaurant within walking distance—yes.

At Perdido Key Beach, there is the Oyster Bar Restaurant and Marina (492–0192); 15 transient slips; maximum length 100 feet; approach depth 14 feet; dockside depth 10 feet; electric power—yes; restaurant within walking distance—yes.

RESTAURANTS   *Pensacola Beach:* Butler's, 27 Via De Luna (932–6537), is the oldest family restaurant on Pensacola Beach, with such specialties as buttermilk biscuits.**$** The Moorings Restaurant, 655 Pensacola Beach Blvd. (934-3606; *see* Marinas), has a tropical atmosphere and overlooks Little Sabine Bay; it has good sunset views.**$$** *Navarre Beach:* The Tropics at the Holiday Inn (939–2321), is the main restaurant on this section of the island.**$** *Perdido Key Beach:* The Original Point Restaurant, 14340 Innerarity Pt. Rd. (492–3577), has many seafood specialties, including charbroiled shrimp.**$** The Oyster Bar, 13700 River Rd., on the Intracoastal Waterway (492–0192), has a good view of the dolphins and boats on the waterway.**$** Gulf Shores, Alabama, has many restaurants and people often drive along the Gulf to dine there.

LODGING   *Pensacola Beach:* Dunes Motel, 333 Fort Pickens Rd. (932–3536); senior citizen discounts.**$–$$** Five Flags Motel, 299 Fort Pickens Rd. (932–3586) has all rooms facing the Gulf.**$** Holiday Inn, 165 Fort Pickens Rd. 32561 (800/HOLIDAY).**$$** Mai Kai Motel, 731 Pensacola Beach Blvd. (932–3502), is near the fishing pier.**$** There are other motels here also; the Chamber of Commerce will send a list.

Navarre Beach: Holiday Inn, 8375 Gulf Blvd. (800/HOLIDAY), has indoor and outdoor pools, theater, game room.**$$**

Perdido Key Beach: There are a number of condominiums here, some of which rent for the day: Sandy Key Condominium, 13575 Perdido Key Dr., 38507; 3-nt. min. (492–3084) **$$$**; Sea Spray Resort Condominium, 16287 Perdido Key Dr., 38507; 3-nt. min. (800/824–2231) **$$$**; and Perdido Towers, 16785 Perdido Key Dr., 38507 (492–2809) **$$$**. Further up the island, about 8 miles east of Gulf Shores, in Alabama, there is the Perdido Beach Hilton, Hwy. 182, Orange Beach, AL 36561 (800/634-8001) **$$$**.

RENTALS   Many realtors handle vacation rentals; the Chamber of Commerce will send a brochure. Among those who handle condominiums and cottages are: *Pensacola Beach:* Pensacola Beach Realty, 649 Pensacola Beach Blvd. (800/874–9243); *Navarre Beach:* Gulf Properties Realty, 8477 Gulf Blvd. (800/821–8790); *Perdido Key Beach:* Century 21, Leib & Assoc. Realty, 14113 Perdido Key Dr. (800/553–1223).

CONTACT   Pensacola Area Chamber of Commerce,
                                                1401 E. Gregory St., Pensacola 32501 (US
                                                except FL 800/874–1234; FL 800/343–
                                                4321).

SIESTA KEY

Area Code 813
LOCATION   4 miles from downtown Sarasota.

SIZE   6 miles long and 1 mile wide at its widest.

ACCESS   *Car:* Via bridge from Sarasota. *Air:* There is
                                                commercial service to Sarasota and
                                                Tampa. *Private boat.*

HISTORY AND   Siesta Key is a violin-shaped island with an
DESCRIPTION   outstanding beach which has been praised
                                                and promoted for many years. In 1907,
Harry L. Higel and Captain Louis Roberts began advertising it as "the
prettiest spot on the world." Crescent Beach was rated by *National
Geographic* magazine as one of the world's top beaches, ranking with
the French Riviera and Waikiki. Samples of sand from Siesta Key won
first place in the 1987 Manatee County, Florida, "International White
Sand Contest." The full-time population is about 12,000 (augmented
in winter by temporary residents from Canada, the northern parts of
the U.S., and other places with colder climates). Vacationers number
about 100,000 annually. Writers and artists congregate on the island,
which is slender and heavily wooded, with many large private estates
and deluxe condominiums; over 20 miles of canals meander through
the residential areas.

POINTS OF INTEREST   Sarasota, nearby, has many attractions,
                                                most notably the Ringling Museums, a 68-
                                                acre cultural complex on the estate of the
late John Ringling.

SIGHTSEEING TOURS   None on the island, but the cruise ship *Le
                                                Barge* (366–6116) is docked at Marina
                                                Jack in Sarasota and gives narrated cruises
of Sarasota Bay, along with special cruises featuring live entertain-
ment and meals. The *Marina Jack II* Dinner Boat (366–9255), offering
dinner cruises, also leaves from Marina Jack; this is a 100-foot
double-decked sternwheeler.

PARKS, BEACHES AND   **Parks and Beaches:** Most of Siesta Key's
CAMPING   8.8 miles of Gulf coastline is sandy beach.
The largest beach is Siesta Public Beach,
with park facilities. Crescent Beach is south, and Turtle Beach is located at the southern tip of the island. **Camping:** No camping is allowed on the island.

MARINAS   Midnight Pass Marina (349–9449); 3 transient slips; maximum length 42 feet; approach depth 4 feet; dockside depth 4 feet;
electric power-yes; restaurant within walking distance—yes.

RESTAURANTS   Magic Moment, 5831 Midnight Pass Rd.
(349-9494); has a tableside magic show
and a magic shop, and an entrance with
fountains and bridges.**$$**
The Inn Between, 431 Beach Rd. (349–7117), specializes in veal
and duck with peaches.**$$**

LODGING   Siesta Key has over 5,000 units available;
full information is obtainable from the
Chamber of Commerce.
Surfrider Beach Apartments, 6400 Midnight Pass Rd., Sarasota
34242 (349–2121), has a pool, beach, and kitchen cottage units.**$$**
Tropical Shores, 6717 Sarasota Circle, Sarasota 34242 (349-
3330); this has kitchen units and is on the beach; it has both daily
and weekly rates.**$**

RENTALS   Carolyn Root, Schlott Real Estate, 5145
Ocean Blvd., Sarasota, FL 34242 (349–
5650) and Helen Anderson, 6021 Midnight
Pass Rd., Sarasota, FL 34242 (349–4840), handle condominium and
villa rentals.

CONTACT   Siesta Key Chamber of Commerce, 5263
Ocean Blvd., Box 35400, Siesta Key, FL
34242 (349-3800).

USEPPA

Area Code 813
LOCATION   At the north end of Pine Island Sound, east
of the Intracoastal Waterway.

SIZE   100 acres.

ACCESS   Useppa Island Club boat; guests are picked
                              up at the Four Winds Marina in Bokeelia.
                              Private boat.

HISTORY AND   Useppa Island has an intriguing history. In
DESCRIPTION   the late 1700s, a Spanish pirate, Jose
                              Gaspar, was said to inhabit the area, es-
tablishing headquarters on Sanibel. He reportedly jailed his captives
on Captiva, burying his booty on Gasparilla, and installing his special
prize, the Mexican princess Joseffa de Mayorga, on Useppa. Legend
has it that he quarreled with her, beheaded her, and was then haunted
by her ghost until, later, he chose to drown himself in chains rather
than submit to capture by an American naval sloop. In the local dia-
lect, "Joseffa" became "Useppa."

In 1912, the publisher Barron Collier purchased the island for the
luxury of doing absolutely nothing. He turned the existing inn into an
elite resort, added his own 2-story mansion, and rented out rooms and
cottages to the day's upper-class tarpon fishermen, housing such dig-
nitaries as Teddy Roosevelt and Herbert Hoover. In the 1920s and
1930s, Vanderbilts, Rockefellers, and Rothschilds were among the
notables who visited Useppa. Old photos from Collier's original Izaak
Walton Fishing Club decorate the inn; sepia-toned anglers hold up
their prized catches. Collier died in 1939, and for a time the island
was virtually abandoned. The U.S. Government had even considered
using it as a base for planning the Bay of Pigs invasion.

It was purchased in 1976 by Garfield Beckstead and his partner Bob
Taylor. Recounting his initial visit, Beckstead said: "Within 2 hours I
had fallen in love with it. What I couldn't understand was why such a
beautiful place was totally out of service." They began to "pull the
past" out of Useppa, rebuilding the cottages erected by Barron Collier

Useppa Island

in 1912 for his tarpon-fishing friends. His mansion now serves as the clubhouse and restaurant, and newer buildings have been added, preserving a quiet sophistication and pleasant ambiance. The island has been recreated as a sort of Eden, with a flavor of the South Seas; there are luxury accommodations, a beach, swimming pool, tennis court, and small golf course. It is run as a private club, but nonmembers may come and stay on an "investigatory visit" prior to joining; interested parties may contact the Membership Director, Bob Sumwalt, and he will make arrangements.

POINTS OF INTEREST There is a 16-by–16 foot chessboard with 3-foot chesspieces. The "Pink Promenade" is a shaded pink walk, built in the early 1900s of sand and crushed shells and excavated in 1976 from beneath 10 feet of vegetative debris. Today it winds through thick groves of palmetto, and banyan trees with hanging aerial roots; royal poinciana also grace the landscape. There are herons, snowy egrets, and swooping white pelicans.

SIGHTSEEING TOURS None.

PARKS, BEACHES AND CAMPING There are no parks or camping, but guests may enjoy the fine white beach.

MARINAS Useppa Island Club (283–1061); 22 transient slips; maximum length 120 feet; approach depth 9 feet; dockside depth 9 feet; electric power-yes; restaurant within walking distance—yes. This is a private club, but those who have made prior arrangements are welcome.

RESTAURANTS Prior arrangements must be made to dine at the Club.

LODGING The "bungalows" are actually luxuriously furnished 3-story townhouses, with screened porches, hanging swings, and ceiling fans.**$$$**

RENTALS None (accommodations are let through the Useppa Island Club).

CONTACT Useppa Island Club, Box 640, Bokeelia, FL 33922 (283–1061).

GEORGIA

Georgia, the largest state east of the Mississippi, has had a varied and colorful past, with a history spanning more than 300 years, especially among the islands of the coast, which have seen Indian dugouts, Spanish galleons, pirate ships, millionaires' yachts, and working fishing boats. Georgia's islands have been peopled by Indians, Spanish missionaries, traders, Scottish highlanders, poets, planters, slaves, and millionaires; today, they are a top vacation destination. The state was initially settled along the coast. Hernando de Soto's 1540 expedition brought the first Europeans, and Spain established Franciscan missions on St. Simons and Jekyll Islands and tried to establish colonies. Jean Ribaut, a French Huguenot, sailed up the coast in 1562 and pronounced the region the "fairest, fruitfullest, and pleasantest" he had ever seen. In 1733, General James Oglethorpe arrived with the first colonists and founded the Georgia colony on behalf of a private group of English trustees; he named the state for King George II of England, established Savannah, and made a settlement on the island of St. Simons. The barrier islands sheltered the early colonists and constituted a bulwark against the Spanish forces until the Spanish were conquered in 1742, and the colony became a largely agricultural community.

The famous Sea Islands, off the 100-mile-long Atlantic coast, are separated from the mainland by channels, lagoons, and inlets. The coastal islands are characterized by fine shell-strewn beaches and appealing scenery, with moss-draped live oaks, camellias, stretches of woods and misty marshes, blossoming oleanders, and fragrant magnolias. Darien is the mainland gateway to Sapelo, Brunswick to the "Golden Isles" of Jekyll, St. Simons, Little St. Simons, and Sea Island, and St. Marys to Cumberland. Vigilant preservation efforts are now underway on most of the islands, particularly Sapelo, which is under the protection of the Georgia Department of Natural Resources, and Cumberland, managed by the National Park Service. On privately owned Little St. Simons, there is a policy of careful wildlife management and there are quarters for a limited number of paying guests. On the other islands, visitors will find top resorts, excellent golf courses, and good restaurants, mixed with cherished historic sites and structures.

The Scottish naturalist John Muir, who walked through Georgia enroute to Florida in 1868, wrote, "of the people of the States that I have now passed, I best like the Georgians. . . . they have a most charmingly cordial way of saying to strangers, as they proceed on their journey, 'I wish you well, sir.'" Visitors today will find the same hospitable welcome.

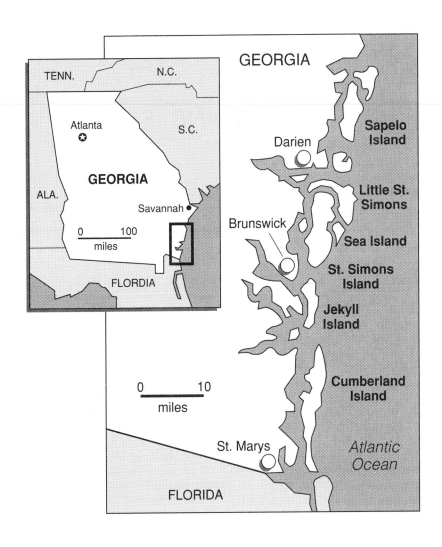

GEORGIA

CUMBERLAND ISLAND
NATIONAL SEASHORE

Area Code 912

LOCATION   Off Georgia's mainland, just above the Florida border, between Brunswick and St. Marys.

SIZE   16 miles x 3 miles.

ACCESS   ***Ferry:*** The only access is by boat; no cars or pets are permitted. The ferry departs from the Visitor Center at St. Marys; once a month there is a run to Plum Orchard mansion. Reservations for the ferry are necessary; contact the National Park Service.

HISTORY AND   Cumberland Island was inhabited by the
DESCRIPTION   Missoe Indians as early as 4,000 years ago. In 1566, the Spanish governor of Florida ordered construction of a fort. In 1736, the island was renamed Cumberland by Gen. James Oglethorpe, founder of the English colony of Georgia; the English built a hunting lodge, Dungeness. In 1783, Gen. Nathanael Greene purchased a large acreage on the island; his widow married Phineas Miller and built a second Dungeness, a 4-story tabby mansion now known as Greene Dungeness, which was destroyed by fire after the Civil War. Thomas Carnegie, brother of Andrew, purchased the Dungeness property and built a third mansion, known as Carnegie Dungeness, now in ruins because of a fire during the 1950s (the ruins are unstable and closed).

In 1898, Plum Orchard was built by the Carnegie family on the banks of the Brick Hill River midway up the island from the Dungeness ruins. It has been restored by the Park Service. Once a month tours are made to the Plum Orchard mansion (the first Wednesday of each month June-August, and the first Sunday during the remainder of the year). This trip includes a tour of the house.

Today, 85 percent of the island is part of the Seashore; visitors are asked to respect the rights of the private inhabitants. Present legislation, according to K. O. Morgan, Superintendent of the Cumberland Island National Seashore, precludes restoring the mansion as a hotel or commercial venture; it mandates preservation of the seashore in its primitive state, and forbids any construction which would be incompatible with the preservation of the unique flora and fauna now on the

Ruins of Dungeness Mansion, Cumberland Island

island. Herds of horses graze in the marshes, and loggerhead turtles come ashore to lay eggs. This is an island tailor-made for nature lovers.

Only 300 visitors per day are allowed. You should carry food, drinks, suntan lotion, insect repellent, walking shoes, rain gear, film, and sunglasses. Salt water fishing is permitted, as is swimming, but there is no lifeguard. In winter there are deer drives; participants are decided by lottery (consult the National Park Service).

The Dungeness-Grayfield Inn's ferry operated up to the 1960s. In 1974, the ferry service began again with a boat called the *Marineland,* which was used until the *Cumberland Queen* made her first trip in 1976.

POINTS OF INTEREST   The Carnegie mansions are the principal sites of interest (*see* History and Description).

SIGHTSEEING TOURS   There are walking and driving safaris conducted by the Greyfield Inn staff for guests of the inn.

PARKS, BEACHES AND   **Parks:** Most of the island is part of the
CAMPING   Cumberland National Seashore. **Beaches:** There are 16 miles of white sand beach and rows of sand dunes as high as 40 feet; visitors may swim, but are warned not to miss the ferry back. **Camping:** Restricted camping is allowed up to 7 days at developed and primitive backcountry sites; reservations must be made in advance by telephone or in person.

MARINAS   There are no marinas and no facilities for docking private boats at this time.

RESTAURANTS There are no restaurants on the island, except for guests at the Greyfield Inn (all meals are included in the room rate). The public may dine here in groups of 4 or less provided the Inn has 7 days advance notice.

LODGING The Greyfield Inn, Drawer B, Fernandina Beach, FL 32034 (904/261–6408), is a rambling, turn-of-the century plantation built by Thomas Carnegie; his descendants still own and operate the inn. There is a white-columned front porch with swings adorned with cushions. The living room has antiques and a fireplace; aperitifs are served each night on an honor-bar basis. Guests are invited to make use of the small library and view the collection of memorabilia and photographs. Some of the rooms have shared baths and are sparsely furnished; most guests come for the beauty of the island and its wildlife, not for luxurious accommodations. The inn provides boat service from Fernandina Beach for $15 per person, per round-trip, or will pick up guests at the Park Service dock for $15 per couple round-trip.**$$$**

RENTALS There are no rentals.

CONTACT Superintendent, Cumberland Island National Seashore, Box 806, St. Marys, Ga., 31558 (for information, call 882–4336 Mon.–Fri. 8–4:30; for reservations, call 882–4335 Mon.–Fri. 10–2:00). See Lodging for Greyfield Inn contact.

JEKYLL ISLAND

Area Code 912
LOCATION Off the Georgia coast, southeast of Brunswick.

SIZE 5,600 acres of highlands; 10,000 acres of marshland.

ACCESS **Car:** Via Hwy. 50 from Brunswick. **Air:** There is commercial service to Jacksonville, Florida, 60 miles away. You can also fly from Atlanta to Glynco Jet Port, 15 miles from Jekyll. The island has its own airport with a 3,700-foot runway. **Private boat.**

HISTORY AND DESCRIPTION Indian settlements dating back to 2,500 B.C. have been found on Jekyll Island; the island was a favorite hunting and fishing ground. In 1562, French Huguenots came to the island and called it

"Ile de la Somme." They were followed by Spanish Jesuit friars in 1566; Spain had claimed the semi-tropical coastal islands of Georgia as the "Golden Isles of Guale." The English wrested the island from the Spanish. In 1736, an outpost was established here under Captain William Horton. One story is that General James Oglethorpe named the island, at that time, for his friend Sir Joseph Jekyll. This legend is disputed by coastal folk, however, who say that a 17th-century supply station for pirates and buccaneers was operated by a Frenchman named Jacques; the name deteriorated into Jekyl and then Jekyll. In 1858, the last slave ship, the *Wanderer*, unloaded her slaves on Jekyll. In 1886 the Jekyll Island Club was organized; it was composed of 50 of the most prominent social and financial leaders in the country, including the Morgans, Drexels, Astors, Vanderbilts, Tiffanys, Pulitzers, Rockefellers, and Goulds. They purchased the island from John Eugene du Bignon for $125,000, intending to establish a hunting resort and exclusive club. The *New York Times*, on April 4, 1886, predicted that the Jekyll Island Club was going to be the "'swell' club, the *crème de la crème* of all, inasmuch as many of the members are intending to erect cottages and make it their winter Newport." Unlike Newport, however, it was to be a secluded haven from the demands of their business and social lives. There was an atmosphere of camaraderie, with communal activities, including meals, parties, and sporting contests. Each season battalions of servants were imported from Northern hotels; the club kitchen had a fry cook, pastry chef, roast cook, oysterman, dessert chef, and many others. Among the notable transactions which occurred on Jekyll were the drafting of the Federal Reserve Act in 1914. It was here that the first transcontinental telephone call was made in 1915. Here George F. Baker became friends with Bishop William Lawrence, Chairman of the Harvard Fellows; Baker later built the Harvard Business School. In the early part of the century, it was said that Jekyll Island Club members represented one-sixth of the world's wealth and that no uninvited or unwanted person visited the island for the next 56 years. Gradually the members grew old and their children favored more stylish resorts. In 1942, with gas rationing and rumors of German U-boats just offshore, the remaining residents left the island, abandoning the structures which had sustained the club in its heyday.

In 1947 the State of Georgia purchased the island for $675,000 and declared it a State Park, saving it from ruin. A causeway was built by the State, linking Jekyll with the mainland and making it accessible to thousands of Georgians and out-of-state visitors for the first time. Commercialism is controlled, however; only one-third of the island can be developed; the hotels and houses which have since been built are mainly on the beach side of the island, away from the historic section. The Clubhouse itself was rescued in 1986 by a Georgian architect, Larry Evans, who secured investors and began an **$18** million restoration. What could not be salvaged was reconstructed with the help of old blueprints and photographs; paint was chipped, plantation shutters were reproduced, and the original Queen Anne furniture was du-

The Clubhouse, Jekyll Island

plicated with custom-made reproductions. The 5-story entry hall, which had been replaced by an elevator shaft, was reconstructed spindle by spindle. Silver hurricane lamps now grace the Grand Dining Room. The island wharf was painstakingly reconstructed from photographs.

POINTS OF INTEREST   The Museum Orientation Center is in the rehabilitated club stables on Stable Road; it has decorative arts, historical photographs, and documents related to the Club era as well as a slide show giving the history of the island. The tram tours leave from here. The Jekyll Island Club Historic District consists of a number of historic buildings, including the 1887 Clubhouse and ten of the original 15 residences. Mistletoe (1901), Crane (1916), and Indian Mound, the McKay-Rockefeller cottage (1892) are open for tours. All are on the National Register of Historic Places. Also included are Faith Chapel (1904) and the Jekyll Clubhouse Library and Villa Marianna.

The Horton House is on the northwest side of the island. This is a 2-story ruin; there are tours twice weekly of what remains of the 1738 outpost and plantation (tickets are obtainable at the Jekyll Island Club Stables). Nearby is the du Bignon cemetery, named for the owner of the island prior to the millionaires.

SIGHTSEEING TOURS   The Jekyll Island Historic District tram tours leave from the Museum Orientation Center on Stable Road. They last 90 minutes and stop at selected cottages (US except GA 800/841–6586; GA 800/ 342–1042).

Island Images Tours gives van tours of the entire island (635– 2727).

Various cruises are available at the turn-of-the-century restored Jekyll Island Club Wharf (635–2891).

PARKS, BEACHES AND   **Parks:** Most of the island is a state park;
CAMPING   only one-third of it can be developed. Over 20 miles of paved bicycle and jogging trails wreathe the island, winding around tree trunks, through palmettos, over streams, and onto the beach. An 11-acre water park features serpentine and speed slides, a wave pool and lazy river, and a children's activity pool (summer only). **Beaches:** There are 10 miles of white sand beach; they are uncrowded and wide. **Camping:** There is year-round camping at the Jekyll Island Campground (635–3021) and at the Cherokee Campground, Beachview Dr. (635–2592).

MARINAS   Jekyll Island Marina (635–2891); 6 transient slips; maximum length 80 feet; approach depth 12 feet; dockside depth 6 feet; electric power—yes; restaurant within walking distance—yes.

RESTAURANTS   Blackbeard's Restaurant (635–3522) is on the oceanfront; it has a wooden, nautical decor; the specialties are seafood, steaks, and prime ribs. It has an ocean view and a patio deck.**$$**

The Grand Dining Room at the Jekyll Island Club/Hotel (*see* Lodging) has Southern specialties, such as crab cakes and Key lime pie, as well as new American dishes (grilled duck breast with warm fruit sauce). It is worth dining here just to see the splendid restoration. The Café Solterra is a less formal deli-style bakery and restaurant off the back veranda.**$$**

St. Andrew's Landing at the Jekyll Island Inn (*see* Lodging) has a nautical decor and views of the ocean or pool.**$$**

Crane Cottage, on the Jekyll Island Historic District Tour

LODGING   Jekyll Island has several hotels with over
                               1,500 rooms. The Jekyll Island Club, 371
                               Riverview Dr., Jekyll Island, GA 31520
(635–2600; US except GA 800/228–9822; GA 800/843–5355), has
been painstakingly restored to its former grandeur as the Jekyll Island
Clubhouse. The quarters are spacious and elegant; many rooms have
porches, high-post beds, and original fireplaces edged in antique
tiles. There are four golf courses and a tennis complex also. It is a
Radisson Resort.**$$$**

The Jekyll Inn, 975 North Beachview Dr., Jekyll Island 31520 (635–
2531; GA 800/342–6638)—this is the island's largest oceanfront re-
sort with over 200 rooms and 70 villas.**$$**

The Quality Inn-Buccaneer, 85 Beachview Dr., Jekyll Island 31520
(635–2261), is one of the older motels, but is located on the ocean
with pleasant rooms.**$$**

Villas by the Sea Resort Hotel and Conference Center, 1175 N.
Beachview Dr., Jekyll Island 31520 (US except GA 800/841–6262; GA
800/342–6872) offers 1-, 2-, and 3-bedroom villas set back beneath
live oaks and has boardwalks leading to the beach.**$$-$$$**

There are several other motels, including a Comfort Inn (635-2211),
a Days Inn (635–3319), a Holiday Inn (635–3311; GA 800/238-
8000), and a Ramada Inn (635–2111).

RENTALS   Two realtors on the island handle house
                               rentals—Parker-Kaufman (635–2512) and
                               Jekyll Realty (635–3301).

CONTACT   Jekyll Island Convention & Visitors Bureau,
                               901 Jekyll Island Causeway, Jekyll Island,
                               GA 31520 (US except Georgia 800/841–
6586; GA 800/342–1042).

LITTLE ST. SIMONS

Area Code 912
LOCATION   North end of St. Simons Island, near Bruns-
                               wick, Georgia.

SIZE   10,000 acres.

ACCESS   ***Ferry:*** From St. Simons along the Hampton
                               River; a map to the dock from which the
                               ferry to Little St. Simons departs is pro-
vided with the reservation. The trip takes about 20 minutes. ***Air:*** There
is air taxi service from Jacksonville, Savannah, and Brunswick and
commercial service to Jacksonville (70 miles) or Savannah (80 miles).
McKinnon Airport on St. Simons can handle corporate or charter

planes. There is commuter service to Glynco Jetport in Brunswick, where you may make arrangements to be met. *Private boat:* By prior arrangement only, you may dock at Little Saint Simons, but there is no marina.

HISTORY AND
DESCRIPTION

Thousands of years ago, when the ocean receded from the ancient dune systems, Little St. Simons was born. The first inhabitants were the Guale Indians, whose 1,000-year-old ruins can still be seen. Later, Little St. Simons was part of the estate of the famous English actress Fanny Kemble after her marriage to Pierce Butler. Her book condemning slavery touched off a furor throughout the country just before the Civil War. Over the years, Little St. Simons has had numerous famous visitors, ranging from Aaron Burr in 1804 to Jimmy Carter and Walter Mondale in 1976. The island has been privately owned since 1903; the owners have preserved it as a family retreat. They are now accepting a limited number of guests, usually not more than 15 or 20, with a maximum of 24. The island is so little known that even the waitresses on St. Simons have been known to deny its existence, but many of the guests are repeat visitors.

The island is home to a great deal of wildlife, including deer, alligators, and loggerhead sea turtles. Island naturalists enjoy talking with guests about the birds (you can watch them from the marsh tower at dawn) and various island fauna, including loggerhead sea turtles.

POINTS OF INTEREST

There are a few ruins on the island, along with nature trails.

SIGHTSEEING TOURS

Naturalist-led explorations, fishing, and boating are included in the rates.

PARKS, BEACHES AND
CAMPING

Parks: There are no formal parks on the island. *Beaches:* The beach, which is undeveloped, is over 6 miles long. *Camping:* No camping is allowed.

MARINAS

There are no marinas, but, by prior arrangement only, boaters may dock at the island.

RESTAURANTS

Three traditional Southern meals a day are included in the rates.They are served in 2 rustic dining rooms and dinners may include fresh fish and crabs caught by guests. Picnics are provided if desired. By prior arrangement only, guests may come over for the day from St. Simons and have lunch.

LODGING

There is accommodation in the Main Lodge, in bungalows, and in cedar houses (with 4 bedrooms, a comfortable panelled

Hunting Lodge on Little St. Simons Island

living room with fireplace, and a screened porch and deck). In the evening guests are invited to the Main Lodge for aperitifs; there is an honor bar. Rates include the ferry to and from St. Simons, dinner wines, hors d'oeuvres, fishing boats, canoes, beach umbrellas, and horseback riding. Other guest activities include shell collecting, fishing, seining, and gigging (for bass, shrimp, flounder and other fish), swimming, or just sitting on the porch, reading and talking, in the time-honored Southern tradition.**$$$**

RENTALS	None
CONTACT	Debbie McIntyre, Little St. Simons Island, Box 1078, St. Simons Island, GA 31522 (638–7472).

ST. SIMONS ISLAND

Area Code 912

LOCATION	Just off Georgia's mainland, east of Brunswick.
SIZE	14 miles by 2 miles (about the size of Manhattan).

ACCESS   *Car:* Golden Isles Parkway from Brunswick.
                                    Air: There is commercial service to Jack-
                                    sonville (70 miles) or Savannah (80 miles).
McKinnon Airport on St. Simons can handle corporate or charter
planes. There is commuter service to Glynco Jetport in Brunswick. *Private boat.*

HISTORY AND   St. Simon's is a 5-mile drive from the main-
DESCRIPTION   land across the golden "marshes of Glynn"
                                    immortalized by Sidney Lanier. With a pop-
ulation of about 6,500, the island is an interesting blend of historical
sites, elegant residential communities, and wilderness. There are
winding rural roads with intriguing shops set back off the road where
you can buy Icelandic sweaters, handmade quilts, folk art sculptures,
Steiff animals, and Reuge music boxes. There are live oaks described
by Lanier as "Glooms of the live-oaks, beautiful-braided and woven."
Before a church was built at Frederica, John and Charles Wesley
preached under the oaks of St. Simons. Other famous people asso-
ciated with the island include Fanny Kemble Butler, who wrote anti-
slavery letters at the Hampton Plantation, and Aaron Burr, who sought
refuge here after his duel with Alexander Hamilton. Timber cut on the
island was used in the construction of the *U.S.S. Constitution.* The
island is the only one of Georgia's Golden Isles that has never been
privately owned; it was long inhabited and has actually been under 5
flags: Spanish, French, British, U.S., and Confederate. During the
18th century, plantations were built; one of the most magnificent,
Hamilton, had a sawmill which cut many of the island's splendid old
oaks. It is now a conference center for the Methodist Church. Gradually the island became a popular summer resort; some of the lumber
executives remained on the island year-round, and regular boat service was established to the mainland aboard the *Ruby.* Later, visitors
arrived aboard the *Emmaline* and the *Hessie* (who have now given their
names to a seafood restaurant) and were met by horse-drawn surreys.
At one time, a donkey-drawn trolley carried summer visitors to their
hotels, boarding houses, and beach cottages. A steam engine replaced the donkeys, and the causeway was built in 1924.

POINTS OF INTEREST   Fort Frederica National Monument is one of
                                   the few pre-Revolutionary shrines in the
                                   United States; it was one of the largest
forts ever built by the British in this country. Oglethorpe used the fort
in his invasion of Florida. Still remaining are contours of the ancient
earthen breastworks and the grassy slope of the old moat which out-
lined the 18th-century fortified town. Tabby ruins are all that remain
of Frederica (tabby is a rock-hard mixture of lime, shells, water, and
gravel or stones, and water). Recognizing its historical significance,
the Georgia chapter of the Colonial Dames of America bought the Fort
ruins in 1903; the site was added to the parks system in 1945. The

Fort Frederica, Built in 1736

National Park Service markers make it possible to visualize the town as it once was, and the visitor center has exhibits and a film dealing with its life and history.

Christ Church, Frederica, was established in 1736; Charles Wesley was the first priest here. Local writer Eugenia Price based her novel *The Beloved Invader* on his life.

The Coastal Museum of History, 101 12th St. (638–4666), is in a restored lighthouse keeper's cottage built in 1872. The museum has exhibits showing the island's history; good views of the island can be had from the adjacent lighthouse.

St. Simons Lighthouse, built in 1872, replaced an 1808 structure; Confederate troops had destroyed it in 1862 to prevent it from guiding Union invaders to the island.

Gascoigne Bluff was the location for the headquarters of British ships after 1736.

The Fishing Pier has been a focal point of social and recreational activity ever since the days of ferry boat transportation between St. Simons and the mainland. People often gather here on balmy evenings to stroll and watch the sunset.

SIGHTSEEING TOURS   Island Tours offers daily 2-hour tours of the island from St. Simons Pier Village (638–1585). It is also possible to make day trips to Little St. Simons Island by prior arrangement (call 638–7472).

PARKS, BEACHES AND   **Parks:** There are no parks as such, but it is
CAMPING   interesting to wander among the ruins of Fort Frederica (see Points of Interest).
Beaches: The beaches here are often edged by towering live oaks. Sidney Lanier captured their flavor: "the shimmering band/Of the sand beach fastens the fringe of the marsh to the folds of the land." The oceanfront expanse is often called the "King and Prince beach," after the hotel (see Lodging). **Camping:** None on the island, but in Brunswick there is the Blythe Island Regional Park and Campground, Rt. 6, Box 224, Brunswick 31520 (264–4406 or 267–7460).

MARINAS   Golden Isles Marina (638–8633); 35 transient slips; maximum length 100 feet; approach depth 20 feet; dockside depth 20 feet; electric power—yes; restaurant within walking distance—yes.

RESTAURANTS   Alfonza's Olde Plantation Supper Club, Harrington Lane (638–9883), has steak and seafood, and does its own baking.**$$**

Blanche's Courtyard Seafood Restaurant, 440 Kings Way, near the Pier Village (638–3030), has a Bayou Victorian atmosphere and features an array of seafood, including crabs, fish, shrimp and oysters. The restaurant specializes in broiling seafood dishes and also has homemade breads and desserts.**$$**

Emmeline & Hessie Seafood Restaurant, 100 Marina Dr. (638–9084), is a popular riverfront restaurant at the Golden Isles Marina Village.**$$**

The Fourth of May, 3415 Frederica Rd. (638–5444), is an interesting gourmet restaurant owned by Florence Anderson, Judy Cheshire, and Jody Custer, whose birthdays are all on May 4. It offers 5-course formal dinners Thursday through Saturday; the menu and decorations change each month. Prices include red wine, white wine, champagne, and demi-tasse. Reservations are requested well in advance.**$$$**

Frederica House, 3611 Frederica Rd. (638–6789), built of aged cedar and cypress, has a unique rustic setting and is frequently where houseguests are wined and dined by the local people. The pit-cooked barbeque chicken and ribs are famous.**$$**

The Delegal Room at the King and Prince (see Lodging) offers

St. Simons Lighthouse

oceanfront dining (**$$**); the Tavern has more casual meals in an oceanfront setting.**$**

LODGING   The King and Prince Beach Hotel and Oceanfront Villas, Box 798, St. Simons Island, GA (800/342-0212), has beachfront rooms and 2- and 3-bedroom oceanfront villas. This is the most venerable establishment on the island, and the one with the best oceanfront view; it is attractively built in a sprawling hacienda style with a red roof.**$$-$$$**

The Queen's Court, 437 Kings Way (638–8459), is a motel with shaded grounds.**$**

The Riverwatch Inn, 1 Marina Dr. (638–4092), is at Golden Isles Marina Village; there are gift and specialty shops here as well as a pleasant view of the marina.**$$**

The Sea Gate Inn, 1014 Ocean Blvd., St. Simons Island 31522 (638–8661), has balconies overlooking the ocean and bedrooms, efficiencies, and suites.**$$**

Sea Palms Golf and Tennis Resort, 5445 Frederica Rd. (US except GA 800/841–6268; GA 800/282–1226), is a deluxe resort with golf, tennis, rooms, and kitchen villas; it has a children's recreation program in the summer.**$$$**

RENTALS   Glenn Lewis and Associates, 106 Redfern Village, St. Simons Island 31522 (638–8229), handles short- and long-term rentals.

Trupp-McGinty Realtors, Retreat Village, St. Simons Island 31522 (638–8600; GA 800/533–2679), also offers short-and long-term rentals and condominium units.

CONTACT   Chamber of Commerce, Neptune Park, St. Simons Island, GA 31522 (638–9014).

SAPELO ISLAND

Area Code 912
LOCATION   Off the coast of Georgia, northeast of Darien.

SIZE   Approximately 3 miles by 12 miles.

ACCESS   ***Ferry:*** The *Sapelo Queen* from Darien (25 mins.; Darien McIntosh County Local Welcome Center, 105 Fort King George Dr., Hwy. 17 at Darien River Bridge; 437–4192) or McIntosh County Chamber of Commerce (*see* Contact). *The* ferry runs Wednesday, Friday, and Saturday mornings and the trip includes a tour; there are all-day trips on the last Tuesday of each month from March through October. *Air:* There is commercial service to Savannah. *Private boat.*

HISTORY AND   Sapelo is one of the barrier islands off the
DESCRIPTION   coast of Georgia; it is managed by the
                              Georgia Department of Natural Resources.
The first Europeans arrived in the early 1500s. In 1760, the British Crown bought the island from the Indian Princess Mary Musgrove. In 1802, Thomas Spalding bought the island and began the ante-bellum plantation era with extensive Sea Island cotton and sugar operations; he built a tabby house which now serves as a Conference Center for the University of Georgia Marine Institute. It was also owned by millionaires Howard Coffin and Richard J. Reynolds; Reynolds formed the Sapelo Island Research Foundation, Inc., in 1950. There is a home here used by former President Jimmy Carter as a retreat. Today there are about 400 acres of private property on the island in a community called Hog Hammock, which has about 76 permanent residents. The State of Georgia purchased the northern three-quarters of Sapelo from Reynolds' widow in 1969, and in 1976 the Department of Natural Resources purchased the southern end of the island.

POINTS OF INTEREST   The University of Georgia Marine Research
                              Institute is included on the tour; visitors
                              will also see tabby ruins, the community of
Hog Hammock, dunes, and marsh ecosystems.

SIGHTSEEING TOURS   Tours are conducted by the Georgia De-
                              partment of Natural Resources and in-
                              cluded with the boat trip (*see* Points of In-
                              terest).

PARKS, BEACHES AND   *Parks:* There are no formal parks. *Beaches:*
CAMPING   Sapelo offers many miles of pristine beach
                              on the Atlantic Ocean. A pavilion is pro-
vided for a picnic lunch, and a bath house for changing. There is fishing from the surf, pier, or in tidal creeks, but no fishing equipment or bait is sold or rented on the island. *Camping:* The Department of Natural Resources has a primitive campground next to the beach, mainly used by groups. Reservations are necessary.

MARINAS   There are no marinas or public docking fa-
                              cilities (except for one or two very small
                              boats), but mariners may anchor out in the
                              river.

RESTAURANTS   The Weekender (see Lodging) has a limited
                                   catering service. Meals may be prepared by
                                   guests in the common kitchenette, or, if
advance notice is given, the Weekender staff will prepare a pit bar-b-
que lunch. You may bring provisions to the island. B. J.'s Confection-
ery, the local general store, has dry and canned goods.

LODGING   The Weekender, Hog Hammock Commu-
                                   nity, Sapelo Island, GA 31327 (485–
                                   2277), has 4 bedrooms, each with private
bath, and a 3-bedroom apartment, all rented by the day, week, or
month. There is a common kitchenette. The facility, nestled amidst
towering pines and majestic oaks, is owned and operated by Nancy
and Ceaser Banks, permanent residents of the island. They used to
live on St. Simons Island, but moved back to Sapelo, Ceaser's home.
Sapelo, says Nancy, is "really a unique place. We loved it here so
much we decided to provide a place where people could stay and enjoy
it as much as we do." It took 2 years to build the inn, which opened in
May of 1988. Guests must call the Weekender well in advance, as the
Department of Natural Resources requires 24 hours notice in order to
request passenger space on the ferry.**$**

RENTALS   Apartment at the Weekender (see Lodg-
                                   ing).

CONTACT   McIntosh County Chamber of Commerce,
                                   Box 1497, Darien, GA 31305 (437–6684
                                   or 437–4192).

SEA ISLAND

LOCATION   Off the coast of Georgia, near Brunswick;
Area code 912   approximately 70 miles north of Jackson-
                                   ville, Florida, and 70 miles south of Sa-
                                   vannah.

SIZE   5 miles by about ¾ mile at widest point.

ACCESS   *Car:* By causeway from St. Simons. *Air:*
                                   There is commercial service to Jacksonville
                                   or Savannah. McKinnon Airport on St. Si-
mons can handle corporate or charter planes. There is commuter service to Glynco Jetport in Brunswick. Shuttle service to the Cloister from
Glynco or McKinnon can be arranged with advance notice.

**HISTORY AND
DESCRIPTION**

Long Island, the 5-mile strip of beach and woodland that lies along St. Simons' outer edge, has long been known to naturalists and others (the famous English geologist Sir Charles Lyell found 30 varieties of shells here in 1846). However, it was undeveloped and not really appreciated when, in 1926, it was purchased by industrialist Howard E. Coffin, who renamed it "Sea Island." Coffin has been described as being of "that early school of automobile pioneers, a lusty, gusty, group of self-reliant visionary men who did not know the meaning of 'It can't be done.'" Envisioning an exclusive resort on the island, he formed the Sea Island Company, built a causeway from St. Simons, and began construction. His dream was fully realized in the Cloister.

The first section of the hotel, designed by renowned architect Addison Mizner, was opened in 1928, but the resort has been enlarged frequently over the years, always in a manner faithful to the original Mediterranean style. The main hotel and River House, the earliest buildings, have tiled roofs, beamed ceilings, and stucco walls. More recent additions reflect the deep eaves and rooflines of the Caribbean. Brick exteriors are used in some structures, and all are a form of masonry. A cottage colony shares the island with the hotel; there are about 500 private residences here, many of which are available for vacation rentals. The hotel operates a large Beach Club with 2 oceanfront pools, 2 golf clubs with 54 holes, a gun club with 3 skeet ranges, a tennis club with 18 courts, docks with many types of boats, a biking center, and an orchestra for nightly dancing. After Coffin's death in 1937, the Sea Island Company passed into the hands of Alfred W. Jones, and is still owned by the Jones family.

The Cloister is a deluxe resort, set amid gardens and lush foliage, with a wide range of amenities and activities. Honeymooners flock here from all over the South; they are often the children and grandchildren of former honeymooners who later return with their families.

The Cloister Motor Entrance, Sea
Island

It is difficult to imagine a better hotel for children, as there are special hostesses for day and evening children's recreational programs. In August, 3-day Cloister Cotillion courses teach pre-teens ballroom poise and confidence; they conclude with a full-course dinner, properly served in the Cloister dining room, where the young people practice what they have learned. There are also baby-sitters for hire. There are special packages also for various holidays.

Among the island's greatest charms are its live oaks, with branches overgrown with delicate fern tracery. Many famous visitors have stayed here over the years. Sarah Churchill, daughter of Sir Winston, became engaged here and was married nearby at the home of Alfred W. Jones, then the president of the Sea Island Company. President Calvin Coolidge helped open the resort, and other presidents have visited, including Dwight Eisenhower, Gerald Ford, and Jimmy Carter.

POINTS OF INTEREST   Constitution Oak (the same species that furnished timber for *the U.S.S. Constitution*) was planted by Calvin Coolidge in 1928. Two other famous oaks are Oglethorpe Oak, planted in 1931, a gift from the owners of the old Oglethorpe estate in England, and Queen's Oak, planted in 1952 by Juliana, Queen of the Netherlands.

SIGHTSEEING TOURS   The Cloister has jeep train tours along the beach.

PARKS, BEACHES AND   **Parks:** There are no formal parks, but there
CAMPING   are splendid gardens throughout the Cloister property. **Beaches:** The beach is 5 miles long. **Camping:** There is no camping.

MARINAS   There are no marinas, but the Cloister rents small boats.

RESTAURANTS   The Cloister Dining Room (638–5111), renowned for its excellent food and service, is happy to admit the public by reservation. All meals are included in the rates for guests staying at the Cloister.**$$$**

LODGING   The Cloister (*see* Contact) is one of the country's most luxurious resorts; its history has been congruent with that of the island for over half a century (*see* History and Description).**$$$**

RENTALS   Many of the 500 cottages on the island can
                               be rented; contact Sea Island Cottage
                               Rentals, Box 351, Sea Island, GA 31561
(638–5112).

CONTACT   The Cloister, Sea Island, GA 31561 (800/
                               SEA-ISLAND).

Horseback Riding on the Beach, Sea Island

KENTUCKY

The rugged Cumberland mountains, sealing the Kentucky wilderness off from Virginia, stymied early explorers who wished to move west into Kentucky, but Dr. Thomas Walker discovered the Cumberland Gap in 1750, and in 1769 Daniel Boone and a Virginia trader, John Finley, led a party through the gap.

With its islands, rim of striated cliffs, and green hills, Lake Cumberland has a romantic European ambiance. Formed in 1950, when the Wolf Creek Dam was built, it is one of the 10 largest man-made lakes in the world, although in many ways it looks as though it is still waiting to be explored. General Burnside State Park is on an island in one of the eastern branches of the lake, near Burnside. This is the only town on Lake Cumberland. Boone National Forest, with hiking trails, camping areas, the Natural Arch, and Yahoo Falls is nearby, as is the new Big South Fork National River and Recreation Area.

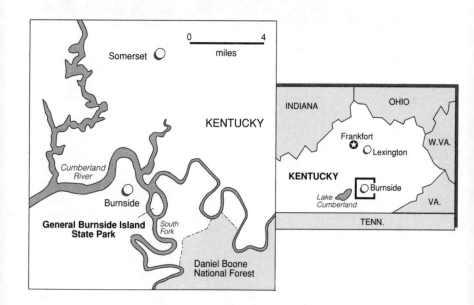

KENTUCKY

GENERAL BURNSIDE
ISLAND STATE PARK

Area Code 606

LOCATION	In Lake Cumberland, in Pulaski County, 8 miles south of Somerset.
SIZE	430 acres.
ACCESS	*Car:* Via Hwy. 27. *Air:* There is an airport at Somerset.
HISTORY AND DESCRIPTION	Lake Cumberland was formed when Wolf Creek Dam was built across the Cumberland River (about 10 miles southwest of

Jamestown and 12 miles north of Albany). The lake is in the foothills of the Cumberland mountains, which offer pleasant vistas across the water. The island is a high and rugged point of land; in the 1800s it was calld Point Isabel (legend has it that a maiden named Isabel, disappointed in love, threw herself over the bluff to her death). A detachment of General Ambrose E. Burnside's army was stationed on the island and his lookouts commanded the whole countryside. Later, the island's name was changed in his honor.

During the later 19th century, Burnside, the end of the navigation channel on the Cumberland River, made the island an important shipping point; steamboats stopped here, and there were many hotels to serve travellers who stopped in Burnside to await connections elsewhere. The growth of truck transportation began to eclipse the town's importance, and in 1950 the mammoth Wolf Creek Dam was built, impounding the waters of the Cumberland River 101 miles upstream, thus covering Burnside. The government relocated all the homes, but many historic structures were torn down, including the house where General Burnside had his headquarters, with the cannon in the yard, as well as the old Seven Gables Hotel and the little Presbyterian Church. Their sites are now buried at the bottom of Lake Cumberland. The island was created by the dam construction and is ideally suited for recreational use; it was named the General Burnside Island State Park. Between 1958 and 1959, a causeway was built from the mainland to the island. The park was opened in 1958. It offers vacationers a home base from which to explore the many cool, secluded coves along Lake Cumberland's 1,255 miles of shoreline. There is an 18-hole golf course and good year-round fishing.

General Burnside Island

POINTS OF INTEREST   The landscape of the island is gently rolling, covered with bluegrass. Off Hwy. 27,
further south near Stearns, is the Big South
Fork Scenic Railway (376–5330); this runs from Stearns down into the
gorge of the Big South Fork River and Recreation Area.

SIGHTSEEING TOURS   None on the island.

PARKS, BEACHES AND   ***Parks:*** The entire island is a park.
CAMPING   ***Beaches:*** There is a beach and a swimming
pool (open Memorial Day to Labor Day,
noon to 7:00 P.M.) ***Camping:*** The campground is open April 1 through
October 31; there is a 14-day limit, with no reservations. There are
110 sites.

MARINAS   There is a boat launching ramp on the island, but there is nowhere to tie up a private boat. The Burnside Marina, however,
is just off Hwy. 27 (Box 577, Burnside, KY 42519; 561–4223 or 561–
6400). The marina rents deluxe houseboats in 2 sizes, one for 10
persons and one for 8 persons. Pontoons, fishing boats, and ski boats
may also be rented at the marina.

RESTAURANTS   There are no restaurants on the island. At
the golf course you can buy sandwiches
and drinks.

LODGING   There are no accommodations on the island. At Burnside, there are Cumberland
Cove Cottages, 1762 Coomer Rd., Burn-
side, KY 42519; 561–4215;$), they have 1-, 2-, and 3-bedroom units
with decks overlooking Lake Cumberland and the park. Also in Burn-

side are the Sanders Motel (Box 127, Burnside, KY 42519; 561–
4327;$), and the 7 Gables Motel, Box 849, Burnside, KY 42519;
561–4133;$).

RENTALS   There are no cottage rentals.

CONTACT   Superintendent, General Burnside Island
State Park, Box 488, Burnside, KY 42519
(561-4104) or the Regional Information
Center (800/OH BOATS), which will send free maps and brochures.

LOUISIANA

It has been said that when a Louisianian dies and goes to Heaven and finds there is no gumbo, he comes right back. Scholars of folkways and their survival need look no further than this state. In Louisiana, the European heritage permeates the cuisine, culture, and architecture and marks the close and intricate family kinship networks. Here counties are called "parishes," and fiestas and feasts, ghosts and legends, often seem more real than current events.

In shape, the state has been compared to a boot with a "frayed toe" dipping into the Gulf of Mexico. The portion south of New Orleans is a vast terrain full of marsh and islands. It has been greatly influenced by the Cajun culture, and many of the French-speaking people who settled here as shrimpers and fishermen are direct descendants of Jean Lafitte's smugglers and pirates. Most of the archipelago of tropical islands is deserted, but Grand Isle is an exception. The population here is a mixture of French, Portuguese, Spanish, and Filipino. In spring and fall, the island is a major resting place for birds returning from and going toward the tropics; many migratory flyways converge here. The beach is one of the few places in Louisiana where surf swimming and casting can be enjoyed. The offshore oil rigs form a reef environment which attracts an abundance of fish.

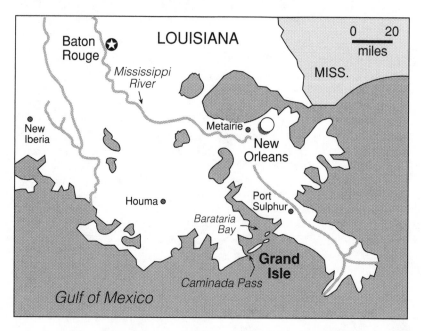

LOUISIANA

GRAND ISLE

Area Code 504

LOCATION   Off the Louisiana coast below Lafourche Parish, at the mouth of Barataria Bay.

SIZE   8 miles long by 1½ miles wide.

ACCESS   *Car:* Follow Louisiana Hwy. 1 south from Thibodaux. *Air:* There is commercial service to New Orleans. *Private boat.*

HISTORY AND DESCRIPTION   Grand Isle is the only state-owned and operated beach on the Louisiana Gulf coast and is particularly well known for its fishing. A 400-foot fishing pier, extending out into the water, is one of the focal points in the park, offering both daytime and nighttime fishing. There are 8 annual fishing rodeos and festivals, including the Caminada Redfish Rodeo in late September and the Lures and Liars Fishing Rodeo in early July.

Grand Isle has figured prominently in state history. As early as the 1730s, the barrier islands near the entrance to Barataria Bay appeared on French exploration maps. The notorious Jean and Pierre Lafitte at one time indulged in piracy activities on the island; many current residents can trace their ancestry to the men who worked with Jean Lafitte. The island serves as a breakwater between the Gulf and the inland maze of waterways of bays and channels leading up to the Mississippi River distributaries (also called "bayous"). The Chênière Caminada community, just beyond the Caminada Pass, at the western end of the island, was devastated by the deadly hurricane and tidal wave of October 1, 1893. Many descendants of the original community still live here. In *The Hard Blue Sky*, Shirley Ann Grau wrote of Cajun life on the island (disguised as the Isle aux Chiens); she knew it from childhood summers spent here. Today the area is sometimes spoken of as the "Cajun Riviera." Bird life is abundant. Common nighthawks are frequently seen, along with other species of birds, such as the common loon, the magnificent frigatebird (late spring and summer), and the semipalmated plover. Shrimp boats pass just offshore, traversing Barataria Pass; dolphins are often visible near the boats.

POINTS OF INTEREST   At Leeville, the Highway 1 overpass spans
Bayou Lafourche; from it you can see a
panoramic view of open marsh land "trem-
bling" on the bank of the gulf of Mexico.

Thibodaux, the parish seat, is an attractive town with New Orleans-
style wrought iron and Gothic church architecture. Fort Livingston is
located on the western edge of Grand Terre Island, across Barataria
Pass from Grand Isle in Jefferson Parish. It is accessible only by boat,
but has a self-guided tour for visitors. It was built in 1835, to protect
New Orleans from an invasion. At present it is not open to the public,
pending repairs.

Port Fourchon, south of Leeville, is a harbor for deep-sea fishing
charter boats and an industrial base for offshore oil drilling. It has
America's only Superport for the gigantic super tankers.

SIGHTSEEING TOURS   The *LA Cruise* (475–6322) is a gambling
cruise ship leaving from Port Fourchon.
Near Houma there are the well-known An-
nie Miller's Terrebonne Swamp and Marsh Tours, at Miller's Landing
on Big Bayou Black, U.S. 90, west of town (879–3934).

PARKS, BEACHES AND   **Parks:** Grand Isle State Park is located at
CAMPING   the eastern tip of Grand Isle. **Beaches:** The
beach is wide with gentle waves; it was af-
fected by Hurricane Gilbert, but the town is putting in jetties and
pumping in sand. There is a swimming area with lifeguards from May
1 through Labor Day, as well as a day-use area with more than 100
picnic tables (not accessible to vehicles). **Camping:** There are trailer
and tent sites, and other amenities, including a barbecue pit at the
state park. Cigar's Marina (787–3220) and Kirkland's Cove (787–
3412) are camper parks on the island; Cigar's has a fishing pier.

Louisiana Heron, Grand Isle

MARINAS   Pirate's Cove Marina (787–3880); 15 transient slips; maximum length 60 feet; approach depth 10 feet; dockside depth 8
feet; electric power—yes; restaurant within walking distance yes.

Cigar's Marina (787–3220); 21 transient slips; maximum length 46
feet; approach depth 25 feet; dockside depth 9 feet; electric power—
yes; restaurant within walking distance—yes.

Bon Voyage Marina (787–3179); 80 transient slips; maximum
length 32 feet; approach depth 5–6 feet; dockside depth 4 feet; electric power—yes; restaurant (oyster bar) within walking distance—yes.

RESTAURANTS   Cigar's Cajun Cuisine, Hwy. 1 (787–2188),
                                     is beside the Grand Isle Bridge. Bobby and
                                     Levita Cheramie added the restaurant to
the marina and and store founded by her father, Landry "Cigar" Cheramie. The restaurant has been widely praised and is said to have the
best crab au gratin in the state.**$$**

Jo-Bob's Restaurant (787–2240) serves good seafood and the
owner has developed a special Jo-Bob burger.**$**

LODGING   There are a number of motels; the Chamber
                                     of Commerce will send a list. The island is
                                     so well known for its fishing that many motels have outdoor seafood cooking facilities. Two are the Barefoot Inn,
Box 92, Grand Isle 70358 (787–2294),**$**; and the Tropical Motel,
Hwy. 1, Grand Isle 70358 (787–3321), which has a swimming pool,
$. Both have apartments as well as rooms, and outdoor seafood-
cooking facilities.

RENTALS   There are a number of cabins, cottages,
                                     and apartments for rent; the Chamber of
                                     Commerce will send a list. Three cottage
facilities are Shady Rest Cottages (787–3367), Sun & Sand Cabins
(787–2456), and Seabreeze Cottages (787–3180).

CONTACT   Grand Isle Tourist Commission, Box 776,
                                     Grand Isle, LA 70358 (787–3700).

MARYLAND

The Chesapeake Bay is the most prominent topographic feature of Maryland, and has, since its earliest colonization, been inextricably linked with Maryland history. In 1608, the Bay was explored and lauded by Captain John Smith as the finest place he had ever seen for "man's commodious and delightful habitation." In 1631, William Claiborne set up a trading post on Kent Island, across the Bay from what is now Annapolis. In 1634, on tiny St. Clements Island near the mouth of the Potomac, Leonard Calvert, brother of Lord Baltimore, knelt and named the province in honor of Henrietta Maria, wife of King Charles I of England. Aboard little ships, the *Ark* and the *Dove*, the band of settlers then moved to an Indian village a few miles away, which they purchased and renamed Saint Maries Citty (now St. Mary's City), south of Solomons Island.

The state has more than 3,000 miles of tidal shoreline. The Chesapeake Bay is a major commercial waterway; it also provides aquatic diversion for 9 million people; on the East Coast only Long Island has more pleasure craft. The area is a paradise for ornithologists, as it is a prime habitat for rare bird species and for waterfowl. Marsh grass and harvested cornfields draw thousands of swans and ducks, along with half a million Canada geese each fall. The Bay has been described as a "demi-Eden"; its position as a geographic buffer between the Eastern Shore and the rest of the state has encouraged the adherence to tradition and independence of thought which mark Smith and Tilghman Islands, particularly. Geologically, the Chesapeake Bay and its islands have been described as "ephemeral"; erosion has caused the disappearance of some islands and has made severe inroads on Smith Island. There have also been problems with pollution which have affected the Bay's bountiful fish, crabs, oysters, and shrimp (H. L. Mencken once called the Bay a "protein factory"), though these conditions have improved of late. To the visitor touring Tilghman or Solomons, or riding out to Smith Island aboard the mail boat or one of the cruise ships, past the tidal creeks and inlets of the Eastern Shore, Captain John Smith's description of the region as a "fruitful and delightsome land" seems very apt.

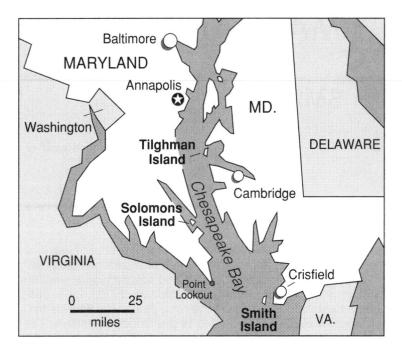

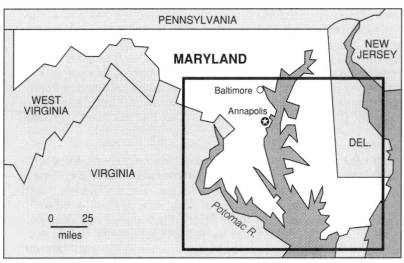

MARYLAND

SMITH ISLAND

Area Code 301

LOCATION In the Chesapeake Bay, 12 miles west of Crisfield.

SIZE Smith Island is actually a group of 3 islands forming an area about 8 miles by 4 miles.

ACCESS *Ferry:* From Crisfield: The *Capt. Tyler II*, a 75-foot sternwheeler with a carpeted, enclosed lounge and top deck with wooden benches (from Somers Cove Marina, Crisfield; 425–2771), takes passengers from to Rhodes Point, where they may dine at the Bayside Inn. The *Capt. Jason II* (425–4471) cruises to the Skipjack Restaurant at Ewell, and the *Capt. Jason* serves Tylerton (both from the Municipal Dock). The *Island Belle II* (425–4271), a smaller vessel, takes passengers to Ewell from the Municipal Dock; passengers may dine at the Harbor Side Restaurant. This is also the U.S. mail boat. The *Teresa Anne* is a freight boat serving Ewell, but passengers may also go along. The cruise ship only runs from Memorial Day through October; the smaller boats run year-round. From Point Lookout, Maryland: The *Capt. Tyler* (425–2771) cruises to the Bayside Inn at Rhodes Point. From Reedville, VA: The *Captain Evans* cruises to Ewell (804/453–3430). *Air:* There is commercial service to Salisbury, MD. **Private boat.**

HISTORY AND DESCRIPTION Smith Island is the largest inhabited offshore island in the Chesapeake Bay. There are three villages, Ewell, Tylerton, and Rhodes Point; the population is about 700. Rhodes Point and Ewell, the capital, are connected by road; Tylerton is separate and does not have road access. The island was named for Captain John Smith, who explored the Chesapeake Bay in 1608. He wrote in his log, "Heaven and earth seemed never to have agreed better for man's commodious and delightful habitation." It was settled in 1657 by English dissenters from Lord Baltimore's colony. The lifestyle here has changed slowly with the passing of time. Descendants of original English and Cornish settlers populate the island, depending on seafood gathering as a livelihood. Some of the ancient modes of speech have survived here; the vowels clang as the watermen discuss their labors in the patois of their English forebears. The principal names here are Evans and Tyler, along with Bradshaw and Marshall; in fact, it is often said that half the people on the island are named Evans. One visitor asked Mrs. Frances Kitching, the famous island cook, why her name was not Evans. "I got married!" she laughed. (She is now retired, but sits on her porch and waves at the passing school bus taking visitors around the island.) There are figs and pomegranates in the yards; the neat Victorian-style white homes are set back from narrow winding lanes paved with crumbled oyster shells. Older residents sit around the Post Office and discuss island matters.

The overpowering feeling in each village is of intimate connection with the Chesapeake Bay, with the gathering and cooking of the shrimp, crabs, and fish which have sustained the economy here for several centuries. You can see the outside floats where crabs are forced to shed their hard shells (producing the delicacy of soft shell crabs); this process goes on all summer on the island. Smith Island soft shell crabs are considered among the finest; New York restaurants clamor for them. The watermen work very hard at oystering, fishing, and crabbing.

It is said that daily life on the island is governed by tide, wind, season, isolation, and the Methodist Church. There has never been a formal local governing body, but that may be about to change. The rustle of developers has been heard on Smith Island, amid the whisper of salt breezes. There is talk of building 100 vacation and retirement homes on the island, and even though the project is couched in terms of "gradual," with homes in the traditional island style, so that they can be "assimilated," many islanders are alarmed. Harry Evans, 72, who has lived on Smith island all his life, does not wish to stop progress, but, on the other hand, he is horrified that the tranquility of Smith Island may be violated. "A hundred condominiums and 200 new people!" he exclaims. Many islanders worry about the effect on the

Rhodes Point, Smith Island

ecology and on island services; others feel they would inject new life on the island and perhaps retain more young people. At the present time, the island is controlled by Somerset County on the mainland; islanders have resisted incorporating themselves, as they are basically against government interference. The development proposed by Sanford Justice of Ocean View, Delaware, however, has prompted residents to reconsider their form of government and to consider taking control of development.

Even the building of the mile-long road between Ewell and Rhodes Point caused controversy; the older residents of Ewell considered it too modern, and asked "Why do we need a road, just so the Tylers can come into town? They got boats." With the road came cars, some of which now rust away on the edges of the road. The 3 churches are all Methodist and ministered to by one clergyman, who travels between the three towns by boat. Smith Island has been called a "theocracy," as people turn to the church for collective guidance in civic matters.

POINTS OF INTEREST   The Glenn L. Martin Wildlife Sanctuary is within view of the villages of Tylerton and Rhodes Point.

SIGHTSEEING TOURS   After the passengers of the cruise ship *Capt. Tyler II* have lunch at Rhodes Point, a school bus takes them on a brief 15-minute tour to Ewell. Tom Horton, an environmentalist and author of *Bay Country*, who lives on the island, conducts ecological tours of its marshes and waters for visiting school groups; these must be arranged in advance.

PARKS, BEACHES AND   **Parks:** There are no formal parks on the is-
CAMPING   land. **Beaches:** There are no recreational beaches on the island; there is a beach, but you need to go by boat to reach it. **Camping:** Tent camping is allowed, but there are no campgrounds.

MARINAS   Mariners may tie up overnight at the Ewell Town Dock, where there are nearby restaurants, but working boats take priority. It is advisable to ask about channel depth before approaching the island; it has been known to be as little as 4½ feet. It may be best to stay in Crisfield, at a marina such as Somers Cove, and make a run to the island for a delicious mid-day meal.

RESTAURANTS   The Bayside Inn, Rhodes Point (425–2771), is reached by the sternwheeler *Captain Tyler II*. The inn overlooks Rhodes Point Harbor and has round tables for ten built around rustic posts; with amazing facility, the inn can serve 150 people simultaneously in about 45 minutes (family style). The inn has delicious crab cakes, ham, corn pudding, homemade rolls, and fresh vegetables. Private boats may dock nearby. Only lunch and dinner are served; call for reservations (if you come by private boat, it may be best to arrive earlier or later than the cruise ship).**$**

The Harbor Side Restaurant, Ewell (425–2201), is served by the tour boat *Island Belle*. This crossing is a family enterprise, as Capt. Tyler's mother, Eloise Tyler, owns the restaurant, which specializes in excellent local seafood (nothing is frozen), along with homemade pies, rolls, and other dishes.**$**

Ruke's Seafood Deck, Ewell (425–2311), has soft shell crabs, cream of crab soup, and crab plates. Open on Sun.**$**

The Skipjack Restaurant, Ewell (425–5571 or 425-3221), is served by the tour boat *Teresa Anne*; it is located near the waterfront in Ewell.**$**

LODGING   The Smith Island Motel, Ewell 21842 (425–4441), run by Doris and Harry Kitching, has 8 rooms. There is also accommodation in the home of Bernice Guy, Ewell 31842 (425–2751). Not all the restaurants serve dinner; ask when you make reservations where you can obtain an evening meal.**$**

RENTALS   Only if arranged privately.

CONTACT   Crisfield Area Chamber of Commerce, Box 292, Crisfield, MD 21817 (968–2500).

SOLOMONS ISLAND

Area Code 301
LOCATION   On the Chesapeake Bay, near the point where the Patuxent River empties into the Bay.

SIZE   About ¼ mile long and a few blocks wide.

ACCESS   **Car:** Via Hwy. 4 from Washington. **Air:** There is commercial service to Washington, DC. **Private boat.**

HISTORY AND   Solomons Island is a retreat long known to
DESCRIPTION   boating people—a quiet community which is becoming something of a tourist center, with 2-story cathedral-style seafood restaurants and interesting little shops. It was originally called Bourne's Island (1680), then Somer-

vell's Island (1740). It became known as Solomons Island in 1870 because of Isaac Solomons oyster-packing facilities. His home still stands on the front of the island. With its superb ice-free harbor and respected shipwrights, Solomons was a major boat-building center on the Chesapeake from the 1870s to the 1920s. The shipyards constructed the schooners, sloops, and bugeyes (the forerunner of the skipjack, the special type of fishing boat indigenous to the Chesapeake) which made up the island's fishing fleet. During the War of 1812, Commodore Joshua Barney's flotilla embarked from here to attack British vessels on the Chesapeake Bay. Ever since then, the deep and protected harbor has been a marine center. Today, across from the hulks of old PT boats, yachts and sailboats crowd the new marinas; weekenders flock to the new waterfront bars and restaurants. The island is low and flat with numerous fishing boats, houses, and docks; it is connected to the mainland by a causeway. There are interesting small boutiques, one specializing in gifts with a flamingo motif.

POINTS OF INTEREST   The Calvert Marine Museum, focusing on maritime history, is well worth visiting. Exhibits include the Drum Point Lighthouse, commissioned in 1883, moved to the museum in 1975, and painstakingly restored, and a notable marine art collection. There is also a small craft collection, along with boat-building exhibits and fossil exhibits. From May through September the J. C. Lore Oyster House, owned by the museum, is open to the public and shows the seafood harvesting and processing business which once flourished on Solomons.

SIGHTSEEING TOURS   The *Wm. B. Tennison*, an historic Chesapeake Bay bugeye, belongs to the Calvert Marine Museum. Cruises are offered to individuals and groups. The ship is operated by Captain Rudy Bennett. It is the oldest Coast Guard-licensed passenger-carrying vessel on the Chesapeake Bay.

On weekends, a 49-passenger paddlewheeler, *Big Wheel*, makes scenic, dinner, brunch, and moonlight cruises; reservations for dinner and brunch cruises need to be made in advance. (Contact Alan G. Bingman, Box 420, Solomons Island, MD 20688; 326/6666).

PARKS, BEACHES AND   **Parks:** The Calvert Cliffs State Park is just
CAMPING   outside Solomons; it has significant fossil
                            deposits dating back to the Miocene Epoch. There are scenic hiking trails. **Beaches:** There are no recreational beaches on Solomons island. **Camping:** There are no campgrounds on the island.

MARINAS   Solomons is rich in marinas of every description; most welcome transients. One is the Harbor Island Marina (326–3441); 15

transient slips; maximum length 100 feet; approach depth 16 feet; dockside depth 12 feet; electric power—yes; restaurant within walking distance—yes.

Another is Bowens' Inn (326–2214), known for its hospitality; this is one of the older establishments on the island; 3 transient slips; maximum length 100 feet; approach depth 10 feet; dockside depth 8 feet; electric power—yes; restaurant within walking distance—yes.

RESTAURANTS   Bowens' Inn (see Lodging; 326–2214); it has been serving watermen since 1918 and is well known for its seafood specials.**$$**

The Harbour Lights Restaurant at the Harbor Island Marina (326–3202) has good views and a very pleasant atmosphere.**$$**

The Lighthouse Inn (326–2444) features seafood and has tall windows overlooking the harbor.**$$**

Solomons Pier (326–2424) is a pleasant restaurant overlooking the Patuxent River. It was built in 1919, as a small 1-room building, but has been expanded 3 times since that time.**$$**

LODGING   Bowens' Inn, Box 35, Solomons, MD 20688 (326-2214); this is an older, smaller inn with 9 rooms.**$**

The Comfort Inn, Lore Rd., Solomons, MD 20688 (326–6303), has a complimentary breakfast.**$$**

The Holiday Inn, Box 1099, Solomons, MD 20688 (326–6311), is a pleasant inn, but has only oblique water views.**$$**

RENTALS   RE/MAX Country Properties (326–2013); O'Brien Realty, Inc., Patuxent Plaza (326–3133).

CONTACT   Charles County/Calvert & St. Mary's, Tri-County Council for Southern Maryland, Box 1634, Charlotte Hall, MD 20622 (884–2144).

TILGHMAN ISLAND

Area Code 301
LOCATION   At the tip of a peninsula southwest of St. Michaels, on Maryland's Eastern shore.

SIZE   3½ miles by approximately 1 mile at the widest point (from many places you can see both the Chesapeake and the Miles River).

ACCESS   *Car:* Via Rt. 33 from St. Michaels. **Air:**
                              There is commercial service to Salisbury.
                              Private boat.

HISTORY AND   "Tilghman—now *that's* the real Eastern
DESCRIPTION   Shore," say the residents of inland places
                              in Maryland. The island is the home port of
many vessels of the Chesapeake Bay skipjack fleet; they bob at anchor
near the small drawbridge at Knapps Narrows, which separates the
island from the main peninsula. A number of fishermen, crabbers, and
oystermen live here, and the island produces more seafood than any-
where else in Talbot County. In hunting and fishing seasons, scores of
sportsmen use Tilghman as their base. Indian relics indicate that
there was a Choptank village on the island in Indian times. In the War
of 1812, the British captured and held the island as a supply base.
When radar was discovered, it was tested on Blackwalnut Point at the
bottom of the island.

POINTS OF INTEREST   On Tilghman, the small boat basins and
                              quiet country roads make up the land-
                              scape. For diversion, visitors may want to
go in to St. Michaels, and visit the Chesapeake Bay Maritime Museum
(745–2916). This is a major nautical museum, with 12 buildings,
floating exhibits, a boat-building shop, models, paintings, and other
marine artifacts; there is also the rare cottage-type Hooper Strait
Lighthouse, first lit in 1879 and moved to the museum in 1966.
    St. Mary's Square Museum (745–9535) in St. Michaels is an early
half-timbered building which has historical artifacts.
    The Oxford-Bellevue ferry, established in 1683 and thought to be
the oldest privately-owned one in the country, is south of St. Michaels,
not far from Tilghman. It is well worth the drive around to Bellevue for
a brief trip on the ferry to Oxford, a delightful town which flourished as
a port in the 17th century.

SIGHTSEEING TOURS   None on the island, but the *Patriot* (745–
                              3100) offers cruises from St. Michaels
                              along the Miles River, past the summer
homes of famous people such as the opera star John Charles Thomas.

PARKS, BEACHES AND   **Parks:** Tilghman Park, with wetlands and a
CAMPING   bridge, has pleasant walks and many birds.
                              Beaches: There are no recreational
beaches on Tilghman. **Camping:** There is no camping.

MARINAS   Bay Hundred Restaurant and Marina (886–
                              2622); 87 transient slips; maximum length
                              50 feet; approach depth 9 feet; dockside

depth 6 feet; electric power—yes; restaurant within walking distance—yes.

Chesapeake House (886–2123); 10 transient slips; maximum length 100 feet; approach depth 5 feet; dockside depth 5 feet; electric power—yes; restaurant within walking distance—yes.

Severn Marine Services (886–2159); 20 transient slips; maximum length 60 feet; approach depth 7 feet; dockside depth 7 feet; electric power—yes; restaurant within walking distance—no.

RESTAURANTS   Bay Hundred Restaurant Co., at the Knapp Narrows Bridge (886–2622), has delicious seafood, along with a cozy library in the lobby. In case you are dining alone, you can choose *Week-end Marriage* by Faith Baldwin or Grace Miller White's *The Secret of the Storm Country* for company. The seafood is fresh and deliciously prepared.**$$**

The Bridge Restaurant (886–2500) is at the Knapp Narrows drawbridge, and has good water views and seafood specialties.**$$**

LODGING   Harrison's Chesapeake House Country Inn and Sport Fishing Center (886–2123) is a sprawling large white complex; part of the inn was a large country house with porches. Before the turn of the century, people arrived here by steamboat and horse and buggy to enjoy Captain Levin Harrison's hospitality. Today, there are excellent home-cooked Eastern Shore meals, with seafood specialties; there are also "Buddy Plan" fishing packages which include meals, boat, and tackle.**$$**

Tilghman Inn and Lodging (886–2141) has 20 rooms and is situated by the water; you can have steamed crabs on the Narrows Deck, watching the boats docked, or dine more formally at the Captain's Table. Many of the rooms have water views.**$**

RENTALS   The closest realtors are in St. Michaels.

CONTACT   Talbot County Chamber of Commerce, Box 1366, Easton, MD 21601 (822–4606).

MISSISSIPPI

The lyrical name of the river and the state is thought to have derived either from the Choctaw word for "beyond age" or the Illinoian one for "great water." The state was first explored by Hernando de Soto; he looked for gold here in 1540–41. In the late 1680s, it was claimed for France by Sieur de la Salle. The French were succeeded by the British and the Spanish before Americans staked their claim and Mississippi became a U.S. Territory.

The coastal section has been said to have a "lazy halcyon atmosphere . . . where . . . worry and tautness are vanquished by a conspiracy of summer breezes, winter greenery, blue waters, and foreign gayety . . . the Coast is recognized first and last as a pleasure resort." The March Gulf Coast Pilgrimage which takes place in Biloxi draws hundreds of tourists, who visit ante-bellum homes, as well as more modern structures, and gardens ablaze with abundant azaleas, crape myrtle, magnolias, and camellias.

The islands in the Gulf, unfortunately, have not always fared well. In 1969, Ship Island was divided by Hurricane Camille into two islands, West Ship and East Ship. Long before Camille, Ship island had had a chaotic history, with marauding pirates, then control by French, British, Spanish, and finally United States forces. Another Gulf island, Caprice, which had a resort and gambling casino in the early 1920's, was also rich in sea oats. At that time, all the sea oats were harvested and sold to a Chicago florist, and, in 1926, a hurricane destroyed the unanchored dunes; now a submerged sand bar is all that is left of Caprice.

"I wonder how long it will be before nature and man will accept each other again," wrote artist Walter Inglis Anderson, who camped on many of Mississippi's Gulf islands and sketched the wildlife he found. Today, Ship Island is a Wildlife Sanctuary and, along with several other nearby islands, is under the protection of the Gulf Islands National Seashore. Ship Island is accessible by excursion boat, and still, despite the devastation of Camille, retains the sea oats, sandy beaches, sandpipers, and swallows which marked the island during the chaotic centuries of privateers and early colonists.

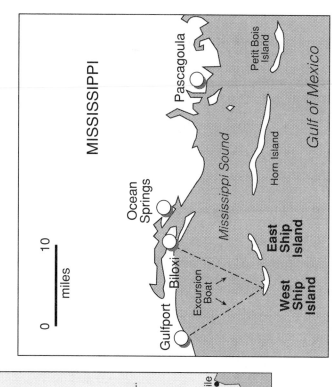

MISSISSIPPI

Pascagoula

Ocean
Springs

Gulfport

Biloxi

Excursion
Boat

West
Ship
Island

East
Ship
Island

Mississippi Sound

Horn Island

Petit Bois
Island

Gulf of Mexico

0   10

miles

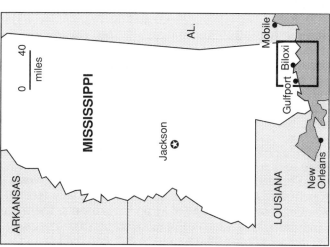

ARKANSAS

MISSISSIPPI

Jackson

LOUSIANA

New
Orleans

AL.

Mobile

Gulfport Biloxi

0   40

miles

MISSISSIPPI

SHIP ISLAND
(West Ship Island and East Ship Island)

Area Code 601

LOCATION — In the Gulf of Mexico 12 miles south of Biloxi.

SIZE — The island was divided by Hurricane Camille in 1969, and almost a mile of open water now separates the 2 parts of the island. West Ship is 3 miles by ¼ mile; East Ship is 4 miles by ¼ mile.

ACCESS — *Ferry:* Tour boats fom Biloxi and Gulfport now visit the island from March through October; they run twice daily from Memorial Day through Labor Day and less frequently in the spring and fall. From Biloxi: The *Pan American* (2808 Lewis St., Biloxi 39531; 432–2197). The pier is behind the Buena Vista Motel, 5 blocks east of the lighthouse. From Gulfport: The *Island Clipper* and the *Pan American Clipper* (514 Iroquois, Biloxi 39530; 864–1014). They depart from Bert Jones Yacht Harbor near the Port of Gulfport. *Air:* There is commercial service to the Gulfport-Biloxi Airport. *Private boat.* Private boats may dock near Fort Massachusetts on West Ship island all year.

HISTORY AND DESCRIPTION — Owing largely to Hurricane Camille, Ship Island is not a tropical paradise. The western half has been swept clean of all evidence of its previous inhabitants; it is now a barren stretch of sand sparsely covered by sea oats and saltgrass. A very well constructed Civil War fort on the west tip and a stand of pines, palmettos, and live oaks on the eastern half survived the hurricane. The island's very feeling of complete isolation, however, is one of its principal assets. There is an atmosphere of serenity on its deserted beaches; the only sounds breaking the silence are the murmur of the surf and the cries of wild birds.

Ship Island is a wildlife sanctuary under the jurisdiction of the Gulf Islands National Seashore; it is a haven for seagulls, sandpipers, red wing blackbirds, and flocks of small swallows which nest in the many arches of the fort. A Park ranger and, in summer, a maintenance man, are the only human inhabitants allowed on the island at night. It is a carefully supervised tourist attraction where visitors come by excursion boat or private boat.

The island was not always so serene. Pierre le Moyne, Sieur d'Iberville, the French explorer, first set foot on it in 1699. It was to Ship Island that 80 marriageable girls destined to be wives for the early colonists came in 1704. They were carefully selected by a French bishop and brought their chests, or *casquettes*, with them; they were called "casket girls." Long before the Gulf Coast was colonized in the late 17th century, Ship Island was frequented by privateers and pirates who raided the gold-laden Spanish galleons as they sailed in the Gulf. The French lost the area to the British, who in turn lost it to the Spanish after the American Revolution. It officially became part of the United States when it was annexed in 1810.

In 1856, Jefferson Davis authorized construction of a fort at its west end to defend Ship Island Pass (a major waterway to New Orleans); the walls, however, were only 6 feet high and it was never completed, though the brick and stonework were of the highest caliber. It was lost to Union forces in 1861. From 1864 until the war's end, the island was a federal prison site where Confederate and political prisoners were held under abject conditions. Here General Benjamin Butler, who headed Union forces in New Orleans, arrested and imprisoned an outspoken Senator's wife with her maid; the 2 women lived in a boxcar for several months, causing Jefferson Davis to declare Butler "an outlaw who deserves to be shot." The hurricane destroyed the graves of more than 150 Confederate soldiers who were buried on the island. Yellow fever victims were also buried here when the east end of the island was a quarantine station and hospital; vandals stole markers from their graves.

Today, from April through October, excursion boats ply the channel daily from Biloxi and Gulfport. Family groups spread picnic lunches, children wade and swim, and visitors tour the fort. At twilight, however, the last boat leaves, and with it all the visitors. The beach is deserted and the sun dips behind the fort, which is left once more with the ghosts of past scenes of piracy and wars.

Horn Island, 12 miles long and ¼ mile wide, and Petit Bois Island,

West Ship Island

6 miles long and ¼ mile wide, are National Wilderness islands which are also part of this section of the Gulf Islands National Seashore, though there is no scheduled boat service to these islands from the mainland. Private boats are authorized by the Park Service to go to these islands from Pascagoula and Ocean Springs; contact Park Service for details.

POINTS OF INTEREST   Fort Massachusetts (see History and Description section). The William M. Conyer Visitor Center on the mainland at Davis Bayou has an audiovisual program and exhibit on park resources.

SIGHTSEEING TOURS   Park rangers offer tours of the Fort on West Ship Island. There are boat marsh tours from here in summer.

PARKS, BEACHES AND   **Parks:** The islands are part of the Gulf Is-
CAMPING   lands National Seashore. **Beaches:** The swimming beach on West Ship Island has a bathhouse and lifeguards; there are no lifeguards at East Ship, Horn, or Petit Bois Islands and the surf is very treacherous. **Camping:** Primitive camping is permitted in all locations on East Ship, Horn, and Petit Bois Islands. Food and drinking water must be packed in. There is limited food service on tour boats and water is offered on West Ship Island, which, in summer, also has a snack bar. A boat shuttle service to Horn Island is available for backpackers; check at the William M. Colmer Visitor Center. Davis Bayou, on the mainland, has a number of year-round facilities, including a campground.

MARINAS   There are no marinas, but private boats may dock near Fort Massachusetts on West Ship Island.

RESTAURANTS   None; there is a snack bar on West Ship Island during the summer which sells a limited range of foods, suntan oil, and a few other necessities.

LODGING   None.

RENTALS   None.

CONTACT   Gulf Islands National Seashore, 3500 Park Rd., Ocean Springs, MS 39564 (875–9057).

NORTH CAROLINA

It has for years been said of North Carolina that the state is a "vale of humility between two mountains of conceit." Her islands, though modest in number and in population, are at the apex of desirability, both to live on and to visit. For one thing, they are attractively remote, especially the Outer Banks. State ferry service between Cedar Island and Ocracoke was not established until 1960; service between Hatteras and Ocracoke was started in 1953. Until 1977, when the Ocracoke-Swan Quarter state service began, Ocracoke islanders had to drive round trips of 400 miles to serve on juries in Hyde County. Hatteras, Bogue Banks Island, and Wrightsville Beach, are all, fortunately, evaded by Rt. 95. Portsmouth, Bald Head, and Ocracoke are not accessible by car. Large portions of all the island except Wrightsville Beach and Bogue Banks are now protected by environmental restrictions, and, on those 2, growth is restrained. During the past half-century, the Cape Hatteras and Cape Lookout National Seashores were created on a 130-mile strip of islands along the Outer Banks.

The state has about 320 miles of sea front; the long chain of islands or "banks" are constantly shifting. Three famous capes extend into the ocean from the islands; Hatteras, which has been called the "graveyard of the Atlantic," Cape Lookout, and Cape Fear. Sand dunes, the red beach daisies or gaillardia, low sea elder shrubs, and sea oats characterize all the beaches; it sometimes seems there are more sea oats than people, so successful have been conservation measures to avoid their depletion. The Ocracoke telephone book has 3 residential pages; Portsmouth is a ghost island, and Bald Head has a small colony of permanent residents. The climate reaches the subtropical zone on Bald Head; on the others there is a pleasant change of seasons. Fall, in fact, is considered by some connoisseurs to be the best time to visit the Outer Banks, when the summer crowds have vanished yet the weather is still balmy. Winter, with its absence of tourists, will suggest the way these barrier islands were when settled by the English over 3 centuries ago (Elizabethan accents are still detectable on the Outer Banks).

The ocean off the North Carolina coast is like no other, sapphire and tranquil at dawn in summer, whipped to a billowy aquamarine froth by late afternoon winds and northeasters, foaming and white at night, grey and turbulent in winter, frenzied during hurricanes. The Hatteras currents can be treacherous, as can those near all inlets. Don't come to the North Carolina islands in search of a slick big-city resort atmosphere. But a calm sunny day on the wide bright strand, punctuated by ocean dips and beach walks (past shingled cottages, perhaps, and out to the end of a fishing pier) can be incomparably refreshing.

Equally restorative, in a different way, is a moonlight walk over the
dunes and out on the beach, toes wriggling through phosphorescent
eddies, or through a small beach settlement, with the day's sand just
settling on the floors of the shingled cottages, floor lamps illuminating
a family game table, shell treasures lined up on slender banisters,
porch conversation muted against the dim background of crashing
waves.

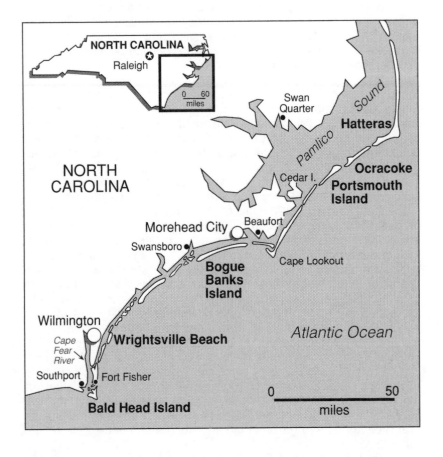

NORTH CAROLINA

BALD HEAD

Area Code 919

LOCATION   Southeast of Southport, south of Wilming-
                      ton, almost at the South Carolina border.

SIZE   13,000 acres.

ACCESS   **Ferry:** From 704 E. Moore St., Southport
                      (Bald Head Island Management, Inc., P.O.
                      Drawer 10999, Southport, NC 28461; 457
6763 or NC only 800/722–6450). **Air:** The Brunswick County Airport
can accommodate private planes; it is 6 miles from the boat dock.
There is commercial service to Wilmington and Myrtle Beach. **Private
boat.**

HISTORY AND   Sentinel of the "Cape of Feare," which for
DESCRIPTION   centuries has been the scourge of mari-
                      ners, Bald Head Island is at the mouth of
the Cape Fear River. As early as 300 A.D., it was an Indian campsite.
In 1524 Giovanni da Verrazano sailed past it, exploring the coast, and
in 1663 Capt. William Hilton surveyed the land along the river. The
next year, settlers from Barbados arrived and began building frame
houses. Shipping between England and these settlements flourished,
and piracy became a lucrative operation. Bald Head served as a base
from which infamous pirates such as Major Stede Bonnet and Edward
"Blackbeard" Teach set forth to prey on vessels; Bonnet set false
lights on the Bald Head beaches and lured ships to their destruction.
In July and August of 1718 alone, he captured 13 ships; he was captured in September and hanged in Charleston. Blackbeard was also
captured and died that year. During the Revolution, General Cornwallis
quartered some of his troops here.
   During the later years of the Civil War, when the other Confederate
ports were virtually closed by the Union blockade, the mouth of the
Cape Fear River servicing the port of Wilmington was kept open, in
large part due to the awesome Whitworth rifled cannons at Fort Fisher,
across New Inlet from Bald Head. Blockade runners, built low to the
water and painted the color of fog, would slip in close to the surf north
of the fort at night. At first light, they would run down the beach just
outside the surf. If they made it under the guns of Fort Fisher, they
needed to fear nothing afloat. The unfortunate ones are the subject

today of underwater archaeology by the North Carolina Department of Archives and History, and artifacts may be viewed at the museum the Department maintains at Fort Fisher. The Fort finally fell in January, 1865. After the war, a lifesaving station was established on the island and accomplished many rescues.

At one time, the island was home to about 150 people. In 1916, Thomas Frank Boyd bought Bald Head and renamed it "Palmetto Island"; he built a pier, a pavilion, and a hotel, and sold lots, but the Depression eradicated his dreams. Frank O. Sherrill, owner of the S & W Cafeteria chain, purchased the island in 1938 and attempted to fill in marshlands, build a bridge and homes for 60,000 people, and create a city he said would be better than Miami, but early environmentalists stepped in, questioning the desirability of such "progress." Other plans for development were made and collapsed. Fortunately for the future of Bald Head, Texas oilman George P. Mitchell purchased the island in 1983. A philanthropist and visionary, he realized how easily its natural beauty might be destroyed, and proceeded with a unique conservation-minded philosophy to develop the island. There was one principal mandate: "Bald Head Island will be a private seaside community, sensitive to the fragile nature of the island's ecosystem and to the simple philosophies and scale of island lifestyle around the turn of the century." As his sons Kent and Mark Mitchell express it, the family aimed to fulfill a lifelong quest for an "idyllic seaside retreat . . . not as intruders, but as partners with nature." Mitchell believed in acting in concert with nature and in enhancing the environs; he deeded almost 10,000 acres of marsh and estuarine areas to North Carolina as a permanent wilderness. Only one-fifth of the landscape can be developed, and even that area is subject to cov-

"Old Baldy," Bald Head Island

enants intended to preserve natural vistas and leave the terrain as little disturbed as possible. Future structures will resemble those in celebrated seaport towns such as Edgartown and Nantucket, Massachusetts.

The Bald Head Conservancy was founded in 1983 with the special aim of conserving the natural resources of Bald Head Island, particularly the loggerhead sea turtle nests. Every summer, giant loggerhead sea turtles return to Bald Head Island to lay their eggs; the nests are marked and monitored. There is a maritime forest with palm trees, loblolly pines, and dogwoods, all beneath a canopy of live oaks. Tidal creeks teem with ibis, mosquitoes, egrets, herons, ospreys, and other flocks of migratory birds.

Bald Head is now a unique and exclusive haven, a residential resort community, with amenities possessed by other resorts, plus many added dimensions. Unlike some resorts, all homes and condominiums are designed to blend in with the natural growth on the Island and reflect its history. The island has a 14-mile stretch of virtually deserted wide sand beach, bordered by sand dunes and waving sea oats. Automobiles are prohibited, but you may rent an electric golf cart. Day visitors may bring a picnic cooler over on the ferry and travel along the winding, shady Federal Road to East Beach in a rented electric golf cart. There is a gourmet grocery store in the administration building near the ferry landing which stocks sandwich supplies, wine, and myriad other necessities. Electric vehicles for touring the island, bicycles, canoes, beach equipment, and charter fishing boats are available for rental. Among the property owners is artist Bob Timberlake, who has depicted Bald Head and whose work has been exhibited in the Corcoran Gallery in Washington and the Isetan Art Gallery in Tokyo. Many of those who own homes on the island today had childhoods on other Southern islands that are now sadly developed; no one mourns the absence of automobiles.

Ferry service to Bald Head Island began in 1976, with the *Bald Head I*, designed and built by Capt. Herman Sellers (a long-time ship pilot) from the hull of an old LCM–6. The *Adventure* began operation in 1983; she was constructed as a transportation boat to offshore oil wells. The *Revenge*, currently used, is named for the pirate Stede Bonnet's boat.

POINTS OF INTEREST   The island is the home of "Old Baldy," built in 1817 and standing 109 feet high; this is the oldest lighthouse on the North Carolina coast. (Funds to complete a lighthouse already under construction were appropriated by Congress in 1792; the letter was signed by Thomas Jefferson.) From 1817 to 1903, the lighthouse was in continuous use; it was decommissioned in 1935. The Old Baldy Foundation is hoping to raise enough money (about $250,000) to restore the lighthouse completely, so that visitors may climb the dark, narrow steps to the top for a panoramic view of the Atlantic Ocean, the Cape Fear River, and nearby islands.

The Bald Head Island Chapel, recently completed, was designed to take full advantage of the live oaks and distant water view; its curved rafters are identical in design to a 200-year-old prototype.

Southport itself is a charming seaport city; the film *Crimes of the Heart* was shot on location in one of the old houses here.

SIGHTSEEING TOURS   None.

PARKS, BEACHES AND   **Parks:** Much of the island has been pre-
CAMPING   served by the Bald Head Conservancy.
                                Beaches: East Beach is wide and isolated,
offering surf fishing and good swimming. Umbrellas are available at the Gazebo, at the entrance to the beach, which also has restrooms and battery chargers for the golf carts. **Camping:** Overnight camping is not allowed on the island.

MARINAS   The Bald Head Island Marina (457–4758)
                                attracts many local sailors as well as tran-
                                sient yachtsmen making their way along
the Inland Waterway; 25 transient slips; maximum length 60 feet; ap-proach depth 6 feet; dockside depth 6 feet; electric power—yes; res-taurant within walking distance—yes.

RESTAURANTS   In the summer of 1989, the restaurant will
                                be located in the administration building
                                by the harbor, seating about 100 people
and serving three meals a day.**$$** The public will be welcome by res-ervation. A new 23,000-sq. feet clubhouse is being constructed and is expected to open in 1990. The former inn is no longer open.

LODGING   Many types of accommodations are avail-
                                able, ranging from shake-shingled ocean-
                                front cottages to bungalows within the mar-
itime forest.**$$$** For all accommodations, contact Bald Head Island Management, Inc.

RENTALS   There are privately owned island homes for
                                rent; they come equipped with electric
                                carts. Contact Bald Head Island Manage-
ment, Inc.

CONTACT   Bald Head Island Management, Inc., P.O.
                                Drawer 10999, Southport, NC 28461
                                (457–6763; US except NC 800/443–
6305; NC 800/722–6450).

BOGUE BANKS ISLAND

Area Code 919

LOCATION   Bogue Banks Island is the southernmost of
                                the Outer Banks; it is a long barrier beach
                                paralleling the coast between Swansboro
and Morehead City and bounded by Bogue Inlet and Beaufort Inlet.

SIZE   Approximately 30 miles long by a few
                                blocks wide.

ACCESS   *Car:* By bridge from the mainland just north
                                of Swansboro or from Morehead City. *Air:*
                                There is commercial service to New Bern.
                                Private boat.

HISTORY AND   As early as 1525, the Banks were men-
DESCRIPTION   tioned as highly desirable because of their
                                supplies of water, fresh meat, fish, and
wood. Three Indian tribes populated the area, the Hatteras, the Core,
and the Neuse tribes. In 1720 the land was granted to Christopher
Gale, Chief Justice of the Province of North Carolina. His descendants
sold it in parcels. In 1713 the town of Beaufort was laid out; by 1722
there was a substantial shipping industry there. Pirates roamed the
coast, however, and several forts were built to defend the town. Fort
Macon still survives (*see* Parks).

Bogue Banks Island has several settlements: Atlantic, at the northern end, and Pine Knolls, Salter Path, Indian Beach, and Emerald Isle
at the southern end. Atlantic Beach has high-rise condos and is more
commercial than the remainder of the island; there is a rather tawdry
section just over the bridge with taverns and pool halls. Further down,
however, the urban section gives way to beautiful dunes, sea oats,
and occasional motels, and, even further south, unspoiled beach reminiscent of Nags Head in the 1950s and earlier (though the ubiquitous
condos are encroaching). The island has 8 fishing piers and 29 miles
of beach; it has been termed the "Crystal Coast" by the Chamber of
Commerce, a name which does not have historical associations but
does summon valid images of the fine sand and smooth dawn surf
(which often changes to rolling, crashing waves later in the day). The
towns are largely cottage communities, and weekly rentals are popular with visitors. At one point the Rockefeller family owned a good bit
of the island and had an estate near Salter Path. They sold the area
from Salter Path down to Emerald Isle to developers, but the island is
still comparatively undeveloped. A bridge was not built at the southern
end until after the Korean War.

Just over the bridge from Atlantic is Morehead City, which in turn is
linked by bridge with the port town of Beaufort.

POINTS OF INTEREST   Fort Macon State Park (*see* Parks).

SIGHTSEEING TOURS   None on the island.

PARKS, BEACHES AND   **Parks:** There are 2 state parks on the is-
CAMPING   land, Theodore Roosevelt at Salter Path
                              and Fort Macon at the northern tip, beyond
Atlantic. Theodore Roosevelt does not have any recreational facilities,
but has an unspoiled setting with rare coastal-zone flora. There is a
nature study trail and Marine Resources Center. Fort Macon State
Park, which commemorates a key Civil War fort, is on 389 acres of
land, and includes a museum and a refreshment stand. It has a beach
area, and surf fishing, hiking, picnicking, and nature study are available. Hammocks Beach State Park, on Bear Island, just south of
Bogue Banks Island, is not far from Emerald Isle. From June through
Labor Day, a ferry runs here from Swansboro; there are showers, picnic tables, showers, restrooms, and a refreshment stand, but other-
wise the island consists of beach, dunes, and general wilderness. Call
326–4881 for ferry reservations. **Beaches:** The strand here is wide
and sandy. It is one of the few "East-West" beaches on the Atlantic
coast, which means that the sun may be seen both rising and setting
over the ocean. **Camping:** Holiday Travel Park, on the ocean, and
Bridgeview Campground, on Bogue Sound.

MARINAS   At Emerald Isle, there is the Island Harbor
                              Marina (354–3106); 5 transient slips;
                              maximum length 60 feet; approach depth
7 feet; dockside depth 7 feet; electric power—yes; restaurant within
walking distance—no.

RESTAURANTS   The Beaufort House Restaurant, 502 Front
                              St., Beaufort (728–7541), in the restored
                              town center, has a Williamsburg decor and
gourmet seafood dishes served by waitresses in colonial costume.**$**
   The Channel Marker Restaurant, on the causeway in Atlantic Beach
(247–2344), has fresh seafood and an atrium lounge with a deck
overlooking Bogue Sound.**$$**
   The Islander Restaurant and Lounge just off Hwy. 58, east of the
Emerald Isle high-rise bridge (354–3111), offers many seafood spe-
cialties; it is known for the seafood buffet Wed.-Sat.**$$**
   The Sanitary Fish Market and Restaurant, Evans St. between 5th
and 6th (247–3111), in Morehead City, established in 1938, is the
largest seafood restaurant on the North Carolina coast and draws
people from all over the state; it serves superb fresh seafood in a
simple setting.**$**
   Smithfield's Chicken 'n' Bar-B-Que, Hwy. 58, Indian Beach, has good
barbecue and is popular with families.**$**
   Mrs. Willis' Restaurant, Bridges St., Morehead City (726–3741),

has barbecue from an old family recipe and other home-cooked southern dishes.**$**

LODGING   The John Yancey, Box 790, Atlantic Beach
                               28512 (726–5188), is one of the older es-
                               tablishments on the beach, but is popular
and friendly. In the Pine Knoll Shores section of the beach, it has an
1,100-foot private beach and many spacious oceanfront rooms.**$$**
   A Place at the Beach: A Fairfield Resort and The Sands: A Fairfield
Resort (247–2636) are two oceanfront resorts, both on Rt. 58, offer-
ing apartments with daily rates.**$$$**
   At Emerald Isle, people usually rent houses.

RENTALS   There are a large number of realtors; the
                               Chamber of Commerce will send a list. Two
                               are Emerald Isle Realty, 201 Emerald Dr.,
Emerald Isle 28594 (354–3315), and Resort Realty, Atlantic Station
Shopping Center, Atlantic Beach, NC 28512 (247–2483).

CONTACT   Carteret County Chamber of Commerce,
                               3401 Arendell St., Box 1198, Morehead
                               City, NC 28557 (726–6831).

HATTERAS

Area Code 919
LOCATION   Hatteras Island is one of the more southern
                               islands in the Outer Banks; it lies between
                               Nags Head and Ocracoke Island.

SIZE   The island is approximately 50 miles long.

ACCESS   *Car:* Rt. 12 down the Outer Banks from
                               Nags Head. *Ferry:* From Ocracoke Island
                               (40 minutes); this is a free ferry and you do
not need reservations (for information, contact the Hatteras Ferry Terminal, Hatteras, NC 27943; 986–2136). *Air:* There is a private airstrip
at Frisco. *Private boat.*

HISTORY AND   Hatteras is a small resort town and fishing
DESCRIPTION   village. The ferry route here from Ocracoke
                               is one of the oldest on the Outer Banks. As
early as April 1953, Frazier Peele instituted service between Hatteras
and the northern end of Ocracoke Island. It lies on the south end of
Hatteras Island beside the Hatteras Inlet. The Hatteras shoreline is at
the heart of the "graveyard of the Atlantic," where more than 600 ships

have been lost. Many Outer Banks cottages are decorated with ships' nameplates, such as *Peconic*, *Emma C. Cotton*, *Mary Lee*, and *William H. Macy*—grim reminders of the dangers of the turbulent, shifting shoals. As early as 1870, villagers served as members of the U.S. Life Saving Service, participating in rescue efforts; others manned the lighthouses built to guide mariners.

The Outer Banks, despite their isolation, have long been known to attract tourists. In 1970, the centennial of the illumination of the present lighthouse was celebrated. The souvenir booklet commemorating the event was dedicated "to the highly adaptable citizens of Dare who have been stockmen, lifesavers, fishermen and now entrepreneurs. The dramatic surge of tourism is merely a new blessing from the sea." If it were not for the Park Service, however, the "surge of tourism" might threaten to topple the lighthouse itself. Hatteras has been protected from overdevelopment because the island is part of the Cape Hatteras National Seashore Recreational Area and under the strict control of the National Park Service. The Seashore area covers about 45 square miles on the Outer Banks, including part of Ocracoke island and the southern portion of Bodie island. Along Rt. 12 there are a number of other small settlements: Avon, Buxton, Frisco, Rodanthe, Waves, and Salvo. The island has 3 fishing piers, at Rodanthe, Avon, and Frisco. The oceanside is largely protected, though developers are now attempting to pounce on inland terrain, especially in Buxton. There are still many small shops, including the workshops of decoy carvers.

Oregon Inlet is a major center of sport fishing activity, and about 35

Cape Hatteras
Lighthouse

charter boats operate at the Oregon Inlet Fishing Center (as Park Service concessionaires, they all charge the same, but reserve well in
advance). The Hatteras Marlin Tournament is held at the village of
Hatteras in June.

POINTS OF INTEREST   The candy-striped Cape Hatteras Lighthouse, built between 1869 and 1870, is
208 feet high, the tallest brick lighthouse
in the U.S., and one of the area's best-known landmarks. Exhibits and
a book store occupy the former lighthouse keeper's quarters (the Hatteras Island Visitor Center), built in 1854.

Just north of the lighthouse, at Rodanthe, there is a living history
re-enactment, demonstrating lifesaving equipment, at the Lifesaving
Station (summers only). At Frisco, there is the Native American Museum, featuring authentic Indian artifacts.

The Pea Island Wildlife Refuge, at the northern end of the island, is
reached from Bodie Island via a 3-mile long bridge spanning Oregon
Inlet.

SIGHTSEEING TOURS   The *Miss Oregon Inlet*, at the Oregon Inlet
Fishing Center (441–6301) offers twilight
cruises as well as fishing trips.

PARKS, BEACHES AND   **Parks:** Most of the island is part of the
CAMPING   Cape   Hatteras   National   Seashore.
                          Beaches: Hatteras Island, with its dunes,
sea oats, wide strand, and easy access points, seems to be almost
everybody's idea of a wilderness beach. **Camping:** There are a number
of private campgrounds on the island, including the Hatteras Sands
Camping Resort, Box 295, Hatteras Village NC 27943 (986–2422),
near the ferry dock; it has an Olympic-sized pool. There are National
Park Service Campgrounds at Oregon Inlet, Cape Point (the largest of
the NPS campgrounds on the Outer Banks), Frisco (isolated without
utilities), and Salvo; for reservations write Box 2715, San Francisco,
CA 94126 (no telephone reservations). They are operated on a first-
come, first-served basis. Bring mosquito netting and long tent stakes
for sand.

MARINAS   Hatteras Harbor Marina, Hatteras Harbor
               (986-2166); 44 transient slips; maximum
               length 65 feet; approach depth 6 feet;
dockside depth 8 feet; electric power—yes; restaurant within walking
distance—yes. At the northern tip of the island, the Oregon Inlet Fishing Center (441–6301) is a major center of sport fishing activity but
also welcomes transients; 7 transient slips; maximum length 55 feet;
approach depth 5 feet; dockside depth 7 feet; electric power—yes;
restaurant within walking distance—no (but delicious breakfasts are
served at the marina restaurant from 5 A.M. to 9 A.M.). Village Marina,

Hatteras Village (986–2522); 40 transient slips; maximum length 26 feet; approach depth 7 feet; dockside depth 7 feet; electric power—no; restaurant within walking distance—yes.

RESTAURANTS   The Channel Bass Restaurant, Hwy. 12, in Hatteras (986–2250), run for many years by the Harrison family, is known for its excellent seafood and does its own baking. Open Apr.-Nov.**$$**

Emily's Soundside Restaurant, Waves Village (987–2383), operated by Emily and Jim Landrum, is not far from the Chicamacomico Lifesaving Station. It has an upstairs room with an exceptional view, famous biscuits, and good seafood.**$$**

The Gingerbread House, Frisco (995–5204), is a Bavarian coffee shop/bakery run by Carlos Caruso. If you arrive from an early Ocracoke ferry, it makes an excellent place for a coffee break; going the other way, you might take along some goodies for lunch or tea on the ferry (which does not have food).**$**

The Pilot House, Buxton (995–5664), rebuilt following a 1987 fire, is on the sound with an excellent view, especially at sunset. They serve fresh fish and good homemade desserts.**$$**

LODGING   There are many motels scattered along the island; the following is a sampling. A full accommodations directory is available from the Chamber of Commerce.

The Cape Hatteras Motel, Rt. 12, Buxton (995–5611), has a whirlpool, tennis courts, a sauna, and kitchen units and cottages as well as motel rooms. It was recently renovated by owners Carol and Dave Dawson. Book well ahead.**$**

The Hatteras Island Resort, Box 8, Rodanthe, NC 27968 (US except NC 800/331–6541; NC 800/682–2289), is at the head of the Hatteras Island Fishing Pier; guests have sightseeing privileges.**$$**

The Kona Kai, Box 429, Avon, NC 27915 (995–4444; US except NC 800/845–6070), is the most deluxe establishment on Hatteras, providing an unexpected South Seas presence. It is on the ocean, but the lowest levels of rooms are hidden by sand dunes and they do not have an ocean view.**$$–$$$**

The Lighthouse View Motel, Hwy. 12, Buxton (995–5680), is one of the vintage motels on the island, with efficiencies and apartments as well as rooms. It has been operated for many years by the Hooper family.**$**

The Sea Gull Motel, Hatteras, NC 27943 (986–2550), has oceanside units and pleasant landscaping.**$**

RENTALS   Midgett Realty, Hatteras Village, NC 27943 (800/527–2903), run by one of the oldest families on the Outer Banks, handles vacation rentals.

Hatteras Realty, Hwy. 12, Box 249, Avon, NC 27915 (995–5466), also has cottages for rent.

CONTACT	The Outer Banks Chamber of Commerce, Box 1757, Kill Devil Hills, NC 27948 (for Hatteras Island, call 995–4213).

OCRACOKE ISLAND

Area Code 919

LOCATION   Below Hatteras Island, on North Carolina's Outer Banks; this is the last of the Outer Banks with a road.

SIZE   17 miles long.

ACCESS   ***Ferry:*** There are toll ferries from Cedar Island and Swan Quarter, each taking about 2½ hours; reservations are necessary (for departures from Ocracoke call 928–3481; departures from Cedar Island call 225–3551; departures from Swan Quarter call 926–1111; office hours 6:00 A.M.–6:00 P.M.). From Hatteras Island there is a free ferry and you do not need reservations; (for information, contact the Hatteras Ferry Terminal, Hatteras, NC 27943; 986–2136). ***Air:*** There is a private airstrip on the island. ***Private boat.***

HISTORY AND   Ocracoke Island is one of the barrier is-
DESCRIPTION   lands forming the Outer Banks; it is part of the Cape Hatteras National Seashore, established in 1953. It was explored, though not settled, in 1585 by an expedition led by Sir Walter Raleigh. A settlement by pilots was officially recognized in 1715, and in 1753 the Colonial Assembly designated Ocracoke a town. It is a rare visitor to Nags Head or Hatteras who does not schedule a trip to Ocracoke Island from Hatteras Island, perhaps ostensibly to see Blackbeard's Hideaway or the British Cemetery, but secretly to ride the ferry across Hatteras Inlet. The town of Ocracoke is a small resort which retains most of its old charm, thanks to its remoteness. Built around circular Silver Lake, it is a fishing village with roots dating back to before the days when Blackbeard made the island one of his favorite retreats; he was killed in Ocracoke Inlet in 1718, by Royal Navy Lt. Robert Maynard and his crew (legend holds that his body swam 7 times around the ship before sinking). Pleasant shingled houses, hedges, and sandy streets, which wind below mossy live oaks, give the town a tranquil flavor.

The island has about 25 semi-wild russet ponies, cared for by the National Park Service. There is speculation about their origin; the most popular legends say they were from the West Indies and swam from Sir Richard Grenville's ship *Tiger*, when it was grounded in Ocracoke Inlet, or that they survived Spanish shipwrecks. The Pony Pen is about 6 miles southwest of the Hatteras-Ocracoke ferry landing on the sound side; if you don't see the ponies, they may be in their shelter, but it is not advisable to enter the pen.

The danger of commercial growth worries many islanders. One is Col. Wesley Egan, a retired Air Force officer who owns the Berkeley Center Country Inn. He fears the island is developing too rapidly and hopes motel and house building will "slow down voluntarily, rather than by zoning legislation." Rudy Austin, whose family is one of the oldest on Ocracoke, agrees that developers often obey the letter rather than the spirit of the law. For instance, a 35-foot height limitation was deviously interpreted as the average height of the roofline, allowing ugly structures with intrusive dormer windows to be built on Silver Lake, dominating the more modestly scaled village. Ricky Tillett, a native islander whose accent reflects traces of his 17th-century Dover ancestors, says, "we're growing too fast for our own good, and the big motels are overtaxing our water and sewer facilities; it could pollute Silver Lake." All islanders have a horror of the "Nantucketization" of Ocracoke, with outsiders buying up property, inflating prices, and making it economically unfeasible for natives to remain in their ancestral houses.

POINTS OF INTEREST   The Ocracoke Lighthouse, built in 1823, is second oldest in use on the Atlantic coast and the oldest operating lighthouse still in use on the North Carolina coast (Old Baldy, on Bald Head Island, was built in 1817 but is not in use). It is 75 feet tall.

The Ocracoke Visitor Center, next to the ferry slip (928–4531), is run by the National Park Service and has exhibits and an information booth.

The British Cemetery is the burial ground for four World War II British sailors washed ashore from the *HMC Bedfordshire* in May 1942.

Ocracoke Lighthouse

SIGHTSEEING TOURS   The Ocracoke Trolley (928–4041) tours the area, stopping at Blackbeard's Hideaway and other points of interest; it runs 3 times a day Mon.–Sat. and twice on Sun.

Squire Eley's Carriage (928–1101) offers carriage tours of the island.

Bus tours are given by Irvin Garrish (928–4571).

PARKS, BEACHES AND   ***Parks:*** Most of the island is part of the
CAMPING   Cape Hatteras National Seashore.
Beaches: The beaches north of the town of Ocracoke are uncrowded, wide, and appealing, with dunes and sea oats. There are parking lots and boardwalks leading to the beach at several points. There are lifeguards at the beach near the airstrip. ***Camping:*** Reservations are required at the Ocracoke Campground, run by the National Park Service; write Box 2715, San Francisco, CA 94126 or visit or write Ticketron (Dept. R, 401 Hackensack Ave., Hackensack, NJ 07601; no telephone reservations). Two private campgrounds are Teeter's (928–3511), one of the older ones on Ocracoke with grass and trees, and the Beachcomber (928–4031), the newest one, which is almost a mile from the beach.

MARINAS   Ocracoke Public Dock (928–5111); 22 transient slips; maximum length 100 feet; approach depth 7 feet; dockside depth 6 feet; electric power—yes; restaurant within walking distance—yes. There is a 14-day limit in summer. O'Neal's Dockside (928–1111) is very central, with a grocery store and other amenities; 9 transient slips; maximum length 80 feet; approach depth 10 feet; dockside depth 10 feet; electric power—yes; restaurant within walking distance—yes. The Silver Lake Marina, run by the Park Service, has 400 feet of frontage on Silver Lake on a space-available basis (14-day limit in summer).

RESTAURANTS   The Back Porch (928–6401), owned by John and Debbie Wells, is very popular, with a screened porch and fresh fish; there are imaginative entrees such as shrimp in caper butter.**$$**

Capt. Ben's (928–4741) has been at the same location for more than a decade. The restaurant has a life-size mannequin of Blackbeard and a nautical decor. Specialties are prime rib and fresh fish.**$$**

The Island Inn (*see* Lodging) has very good seafood in a low-ceilinged dining room, which evokes the flavor of a country inn. The restaurant is managed by Chester Lynn, who has returned to some of the original recipes which made the inn famous (such as hushpuppies and crab cakes).**$$**

The Pony Island Restaurant serves Pony Island Clam Chowder and has good seafood dishes.**$$**

LODGING The Anchorage Inn, Box 130, Ocracoke Island 27960 (928–1581), is a large new structure, quasi-Victorian in style, with porches and harbor views overlooking Silver Lake. It is well located for exploring Ocracoke on foot. It has its own dock where, if you wish to go to Portsmouth Island, you can arrange to be picked up.**$$**

The Berkeley Center Country Inn, a renovated older home that is now a guest house, is a few steps from the harbor; breakfast is offered in the main house. It is owned by Col. Wesley Egan, who is an expert on island history and willingly shares insights about the island with guests.**$$**

The Boyette House, Box 39, Ocracoke NC (928–4261), is a new motel but retains the flavor of a gracious old inn, with rocking chairs on porches, a spacious lobby, and a library. The Boyette family began innkeeping on the island in 1941; the present innkeeper is Lanie Boyette-Wynn.**$$**

The Island Inn, Box 9, Ocracoke NC (928–4351), is the vintage Ocracoke hotel, published in *Historic Hotels of the South* and other guidebooks; it has a heated outdoor pool.**$$**

RENTALS Ocracoke Island Realty, Box 238, Ocracoke (928–6261), has over 125 cottages available.

CONTACT Ocracoke Visitors' Center, Ocracoke, NC 27960 (928–4531); the Outer Banks Chamber of Commerce, Box 1757, Kill Devil Hills, NC 27948 (Hatteras Island 995–4213).

PORTSMOUTH ISLAND

Area Code 919

LOCATION East of Pamlico Sound, below Ocracoke Inlet.

SIZE 18 miles by approximately 2 miles at its widest.

ACCESS *Ferry:* Don Morris runs the *Green Grass* several times daily from Atlantic to an area north of Drum Inlet on the southern end of Portsmouth Island (Don Morris, Morris Marine, Star Route 763, Atlantic, NC 28511 (225–4261). Rudy Austin and his father, Junius Austin, offer charter service from Ocracoke to the northern end of Portsmouth Island; call Rudy Austin (928–4361 or 928–4281). *Air:* There is a private airstrip on Ocracoke Island. *Private boat.*

HISTORY AND   Portsmouth Island is part of the Cape Look-
DESCRIPTION   out National Seashore—a low, narrow,
                          chain of islands running from Ocracoke In-
let on the northeast to Beaufort inlet on the southwest. The Cape
Lookout Bight area, on the lower island, is served by ferry from Harkers
Island, and there is service from Davis to near Great Island.

Portsmouth Island, closest to Ocracoke, was once well-populated;
today, the only resident is a National Park Service caretaker for Portsmouth Village. The village is essentially a ghost town, but it had an
illustrious past. It was established in 1753, and by 1770 was the largest settlement on the Outer Banks. Ocracoke Inlet was the major trade
route through the Outer Banks to such ports as Wilmington (in 1842,
over 1,400 vessels and two-thirds of the exports of the state passed
through Ocracoke Inlet), but heavily laden ships could not sail through
the shallow inlet and transferred their cargo to shallow draft boats at
Portsmouth. In 1846, a deeper inlet was opened at Hatteras by a
storm, and shipping shifted north. After the Civil War, many people
left Portsmouth, never to return. The population steadily declined, to
320 in 1870, 222 in 1880, 104 in 1930, and 17 in 1956. With the
death of Henry Pigott, the last male resident, in January, 1971, the
last two residents, Elma Dixon and Marian Babb, reluctantly moved to
the mainland. During the early part of the century, there were many
wrecks, recalled by Ben Salter in his book *Portsmouth Island*. A long-
time resident of the island, he describes the May 1903 demise of the
Vera Cruz in May 1903, with sheep and 421 people, and the 1907
wreck of the *John L. Snow*, which was carrying a complete hotel to
New York. In 1976, new life came to Portsmouth with the establishment of the Cape Lookout National Seashore. The 250-acre historic
district of Portsmouth Village is listed on the National Register of Historic Places, and buildings are slowly being restored.

POINTS OF INTEREST   Portsmouth Village is of substantial inter-
                          est as a ghost town. It must be reached by
                          private boat or by charter boat from Ocra-
coke (see Access); it is also accessible along the beach from the lower
part of the island, but only with a 4-wheel drive vehicle. There are no
roads on the island, so only 4-wheel drive vehicles are transported
(from Atlantic, not Ocracoke; a free permit from the National Park Service is necessary). The fishing on the island is very good, but there is
virtually no shade or shelter. If you want to come from Ocracoke, call
Junius Austin or his son Rudy (see Access). They will pick you up at
one of the Silver Lake docks and speed you over to the Haulover Pt.
Dock on the island, making a return run whenever you wish. Some
people only want time to see Portsmouth Village and others plan to
visit the beach as well. The Austins also run shelling charters to Drum
Shoal, which is rising and may join Portsmouth Island.

Despite the limited access, a surprising number of people have
found their way to the island; a look at the guest register on a single

August day in 1988 revealed visitors from North Carolina (Murray D. Adams had made his sixth visit of the year), Michigan, Pennsylvania, California, New York, Philadelphia, and West Virginia. "Our ancestors were Dixons," wrote Regina Burdette of West Virginia. "Lovely and natural," wrote Michael Woollen of Philadelphia. Two buildings are open, the Dixon/Salter House, which has a visitor center and small museum, and the Church. The museum has photographs of island gatherings; the Babbs and Dixons were sitting on their porches hearing instrumental music in 1944. Other buildings include houses, the school house, the post office and general store, and the Life Saving Service Complex. You must wear sturdy walking shoes, as the walkway from Haulover Pt. Dock may be covered in water. Take mosquito repellent, suntan lotion, a hat, and food and drinking water.

"For Portsmouth Village to work, people have to take a personal interest and have their hearts in it," says Rudy Austin of Ocracoke, whose father, Junius, worked on the island before it was taken over by the Park Service. Portsmouth Village is a rarity among Park Service properties, more isolated than most yet depicting an entire era. Its location, on the beautiful Cape Lookout National Seashore, insures its continuing appeal.

SIGHTSEEING TOURS   None.

PARKS, BEACHES, AND   **Parks:** The entire island is part of the Cape
CAMPING   Lookout National Seashore, run by the National Park Service. **Beaches:** The beaches
are superb here, wide, with excellent shelling. There are strong riptides, however, so do not swim alone. **Camping:** Permitted on the beach, but not in Portsmouth Village because of the fire hazard. Insect repellent and mosquito netting are an absolute necessity; the mosquitoes are very aggressive. Visitors need also to bring all food and drink and take away all trash.

Portsmouth Island

MARINAS	None, but private boats may tie up at Haulover Pt. Dock.
RESTAURANTS	None
LODGING	Kabin Kamps, 17 rustic older cabins, along with 8 new ones sleeping from 4 to 12 people, are available for rent on the lower

part of the island (not near Portsmouth Village). Contact the Morrises (see Access); they are concessionaires for the National Park Service.

RENTALS	None
CONTACT	Cape Lookout National Seashore, National Park Service, Box 690, Beaufort, NC 28516 (728–2121).

WRIGHTSVILLE BEACH

Area Code 919

LOCATION	Approx. 2 miles from the Intracoastal Waterway and 10 miles from Wilmington.
SIZE	2 miles by 1–2 blocks.
ACCESS	***Car:*** Rts. 74 and 76 from Wilmington. ***Air:*** Commercial service to Wilmington. ***Private boat.***
HISTORY AND DESCRIPTION	Wrightsville Beach was developed at the end of the 19th century, principally as a summer resort for Wilmingtonians. Accord-

ing to historian Lewis Philip Hall, a shell road as far as Wrightsville Sound had been built about 1876, and a Wagonette, drawn by horses, conveyed passengers to a resort village there. The Wilmington & Sea Coast Railroad was constructed in 1888 to Wrightsville Sound, and on to Hammocks (now Harbor Island), via a trestle built the same year. The maiden run of the steam railroad was June 17, 1888. A footbridge across Banks Channel to Wrightsville Beach (then called Ocean View Beach) was opened on July 1, 1888. In 1889, the railway was extended to Wrightsville. A restaurant (Brown's), 2 bath houses, and the Carolina Yacht Club (built in 1853 and the second oldest in America, after the New York Yacht Club) were the only buildings there. In 1899, a severe storm damaged the trestles and many cottages. In 1902, electric trolley service to Wrightsville began. For many decades, the trolley provided the only access, stopping at various stations on the southern end of the island.

Lumina, at Station Seven, was a pleasure palace built in 1905 by Consolidated Railways, Light and Power Company (later Tidewater Power Company) to attract people to the beach. It was lit by 600 incandescent light bulbs and had an orchestra shell, a screen mounted in the surf for silent movies, and children's events. For 68 years, until its demolition in 1973, Lumina attracted thousands of people, and all across the South there are those with memories of the nightly dances, with the sounds of Cab Calloway, Kay Kyser, Lionel Hampton, Louis Armstrong, Tommy Tucker, and Charlie Spivak. Dowager chaperones supervised courtships between eligible young gentlemen in full evening dress and elegantly dressed girls; behavior was circumspect and the dances formal. During the day, the pace was slow but always festive; Wilmington grocery stores would send down ice cream and cake on the trolley for children's birthday parties. There were moonlight beach walks, lunches on cool porches with tall glasses of frosty iced tea with a sprig of mint, and shrimp salad with the tiny tender shrimp which are caught amid the muddy marshes and eaten as fresh as possible. Always there was good swimming, shell-collecting, and boat-riding. More cottages were built—grand ones fronting on both the ocean and the sound, as well as more modest structures. A raised boardwalk made its shaky way down portions of the beach, branching into the porches of shingled cottages, all on stilts in case of high water. The whole network was a triumph of anti-hurricane optimism. Amusement arcades were outlawed, early and emphatically, by the Board of Aldermen (one member who was influential in opposing such decadence was the writer's father, Richard Oscar "Rock" Grant). At first people came only for the summer season, but gradually some houses were winterized; many people now live on the island year-round. Today there are still holiday sailboat races in Banks Channel (a new form of entertainment is "rafting up," tying large ketches and sloops together and anchoring out for race-watching parties). On the Saturday after Thanksgiving, the Holiday Flotilla and Christmas Parade is held, with dozens of elaborately decorated boats carrying out various themes and competing for prizes.

For many generations, Wrightsville Beach has been a family resort area; the extent of evening entertainment is an occasional beer or, the current rage, French vanilla or honey almond yoghurt at Ms. Muffet's Yoghurt Shop just over the causeway. Families who sold their beach houses in the 1960s for a few thousand dollars can't retrieve them now for 30 times that, regardless of hurricanes. The beach is still welcoming and restful. The small piers silhouetted against the sunset over the sound, the chilly but happily deserted winter beaches, the large stalwart fishing piers, graceful sea oats, and rust beach flowers haven't changed since the trolleys first rumbled and creaked down the causeway and over the narrow bridge. But if the clock could be turned back, just a little, if Lumina could be reassembled and a mile or so of high beach boardwalk restored, with the incoming tide foaming up on the beach underneath and sand fiddlers scurrying—would it not be a more amiable place, after all?

Wilmington, 10 miles west, is one of North Carolina's most historic port cities (settled in 1732); it is the largest town on the North Carolina coast and is the commercial center for Wrightsville Beach as well as a large adjacent rural area. Wilmington College (U.N.C.W.), once a small community college, has greatly expanded and is now one of the major institutions within the University of North Carolina system.

POINTS OF INTEREST   Just over the drawbridge from Wrightsville Beach, on Airlie Road, is Airlie Gardens, which contains unique formal gardens and is open in the spring.

In Wilmington, points of interest include the *U.S.S. North Carolina* Battleship Memorial (the *Captain Maffit* passenger ferry goes across to the battleship and stops at the newly completed Riverfront Park).

Wilmington has a number of historic buildings, including the Governor Dudley Mansion, Thalian Hall (1858, a restored theater where Lillian Russell and Tyrone Power once performed); the Burgwin-Wright House (c. 1770), used by General Cornwallis as his headquarters during the Revolution; and the Zebulon Latimer House (1852). Combination tickets are available for the Historic Wilmington Tour, covering about 7 blocks (by foot or car, but parking is limited). The renovated downtown area includes the Cotton Exchange and Chandler's Wharf, which have boutiques and restaurants as well as historical displays. The Wilmington Railroad Museum has exhibits about railroads which have operated here since 1840.

New Hanover County Museum of the Lower Cape Fear, 814 Market St., preserves historic treasures of the region.

Not far from Wrightsville and Wilmington are Orton Plantation (an historic rice plantation with beautiful gardens, house not open) and Poplar Grove Historic Plantation, where hostesses in period dress conduct scheduled tours.

SIGHTSEEING TOURS   None at Wrightsville, but, on the Cape Fear River in Wilmington, 10 miles away, there are sightseeing cruises aboard the *Henrietta II* (392–1140) or the *Captain J. N. Maffitt* (343–1776). There is a town-sponsored walking tour of some of Wilmington's historic buildings.

PARKS, BEACHES AND   **Parks:** There is a large park at Wrightsville,
CAMPING   just across from the Seapath Yacht Club Transient Dock. There are 2 regional beach access points, one at either end of the beach. In Wilmington, Green-

field Gardens is a 185-acre municipal park with a 5-mile scenic drive around a lake containing ancient cypress trees; it is particularly beautiful in spring when the azaleas are in bloom. **Beaches:** The beach is excellent for swimming and sunbathing; there are beach access points on the southernmost end and at Johnny Mercer's Pier. **Camping:** No camping is allowed on the beach; the nearest campground is Camelot Campground, 7415 Market St. (on Hwy. 17 N).

MARINAS   Wrightsville is one of the most popular stops on the Intracoastal Waterway, owing to its many marinas and restaurants. It is not unusual to see noteworthy craft such as the *Monkey Business* (of Gary Hart notoriety) moored here.

Seapath Yacht Club Transient Dock (256–3747); 36 transient slips; maximum length 150 feet; approach depth 10 feet; dockside depth 10 feet; electric power—yes; restaurant within walking distance—yes.

Wrightsville Marina (256–5770); 25 transient slips; maximum length 100 feet; approach depth 10 feet; dockside depth 10 feet; electric power—yes; restaurant within walking distance—yes.

Bradley Creek Marina (256–2282); 6 transient slips; maximum length 100 feet; approach depth 6 feet; dockside depth 6 feet; electric power—yes; restaurant within walking distance—no.

RESTAURANTS   The Bridge Tender, Airlie Road (256–4519), overlooks the Intracoastal Waterway and specializes in seafood; it is just south of the drawbridge over the waterway.**$$**

The Causeway Cafe (256–3730), just over the bridge, next to Redix, serves Belgian waffles for breakfast and fresh local seafood; it has good home cooking.**$**

The Crystal Restaurant, 703 S. Lumina (256–9083), at the Crystal Pier, serves seafood in the atmosphere of an oceanfront pier.**$$**

The Dockside, 1308 Airlie Road (256–2752), is an informal restaurant with a shaded deck overlooking the Intracoastal Waterway.**$**

The King Neptune, 11 N. Lumina (256–2525), serves good classic seafood and has nautical murals.**$$**

The Middle of the Island (256–4277), on the causeway to the beach, is very good for breakfast and light meals.**$** Another popular place is Robert's Deli (256–9708), on the beach, for light sandwiches and lunches; it has an informal decor.**$**

The Pepper Mill, in the Landing at Wrightsville Beach (256–4579), is a Mediterranean restaurant with good Italian veal and pasta, along with seafood.**$$**

Skinner and Daniels Barbecue, 5214 Market St. (799–1790), on the road to Wilmington, has long been a local favorite for eastern North Carolina barbecue (uncontaminated by tomato sauce) and Brunswick stew.**$**

LODGING The Blockade Runner, 275 Waynick Blvd., Wrightsville Beach, NC 27480 (256–2251), is the major hotel; it replaced the old wooden Ocean Terrace and has rooms with good ocean views.**$$$**

The Holiday Inn, 1706 N. Lumina Ave., Wrightsville Beach 28480 (256–2231), is on the ocean and has balconies or patios.**$$–$$$**

The Surf Motelminium, Box 489, Wrightsville Beach 28480 (256-2275), has good access to the dunes and wide beach; it is near one of the fishing piers.**$$$**

RENTALS There are many cottages and apartments for rent at Wrightsville. Among the realtors handling rentals are Bryant Real Estate, 1001 N. Lumina Ave., Wrightsville Beach 28480 (256–3764); Intracoastal Realty, 534 Causeway Dr., Wrightsville Beach 28480 (256–3780); Bland and Associates, Realtors, 204 Causeway Dr., Wrightsville Beach 28480 (800/432–4595); and Wrightsville Beach Realty, 1 Lumina Ave., Wrightsville Beach 28480 (256–4561).

CONTACT Greater Wilmington Chamber of Commerce, Box 330, Wilmington, NC 28402 (762–2611).

Wrightsville Beach

SOUTH CAROLINA

For more than 300 years, the Lowcountry of South Carolina has offered a wealth of historic attractions, along with sandy shores and winding rivers. Spanish explorers were sailing along the present-day South Carolina coast less than 30 years after Europeans discovered America. In 1526, the Spanish made the first attempt at establishing a settlement in the state on Winyah Bay (near what is now Georgetown). In 1562, a group of French Huguenots, led by Jean Ribaut, landed near what is now Parris Island. The first permanent settlement was made in 1670, across from Charleston at Albemarle Point; in 1680, the settlers moved across the Ashley River to the present site of Charleston.

South Carolina's 280 miles of coastline is graced with a variety of appealing islands. Some have ramshackle beach cottages with a cachet all their own; some have posh yet deliberately rustic and understated resorts; some have wilderness. However, even the new developments have been marked by attention to conservation and wildlife management, resulting in a remarkable symbiosis between man and nature. The character of the South Carolina coast changes as the traveler goes south past the commercial Grand Strand, of which Myrtle Beach is the center. The islands, beginning with Pawleys Island and ending with Daufuskie Island, near the Georgia border, offer vacationers the best of past and present, combining miles of the solitary beaches which greeted the early explorers with modern accommodations.

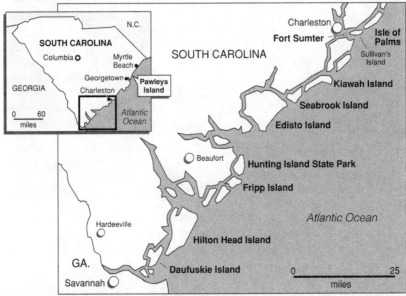

SOUTH CAROLINA

DAUFUSKIE ISLAND

Area Code 803

LOCATION The island is about 4 miles from Hilton Head, north of Savannah.

SIZE 5 miles by 3 miles.

ACCESS ***Tour boat:*** from Hilton Head Island. Two boats leave from Broad Creek Marina, the *Daufuskie Queen* (681–7918) and the *Safari* (785–5654); the *Adventure* leaves from Shelter Cove (785–4558), and the *Vagabond* (842-4155) leaves from the Harbour Town Yacht Basin (see *Sightseeing*). There is service to the Melrose development leaving from Salty Fair Village. **Air:** There is commercial service to Hilton Head Island. **Private boat.**

HISTORY AND DESCRIPTION Daufuskie is an isolated sea island with a recorded history dating from the 1700s. The name of the island is said to be a corruption of the answer the Hilton Head Gullahs gave early visitors, when asked what the island in the distance was: "Da Fus Key" (the first key). According to the Rev. Dr. Robert E. H. Peeples, President of the Hilton Head Island Historical Society, Daufuskie Island has always been an agriculturally oriented island. Many of the old Gullah traditions are preserved here. Most of the island has been held since *ante bellum* years in 5 substantial plantations: Haig's Point, Melrose, Oak Ridge (also known as Ingleside), Webb, and Bloody Point. The southwest corner, formerly the Bland-Martinangele-Chaplin property, was sold off in small tracts suitable for subsistence-type living (fishing, crabbing, oystering), and had a population of several thousand, but the population declined to fewer than 75 residents when the Savannah River became too polluted for these activities. Since then, a 2-room elementary schoolhouse has been sufficient for the island's needs. Pat Conroy wrote about Daufuskie in his novels *The Water is Wide*, subsequently made into the film *Conrack*, and in *The Prince of Tides*.

Several residential, resort, and recreational projects are now underway which may well change the character of the island to some extent (though such developments will probably remain private).

Approximately 70 percent of the island is now divided into 4 parcels of land: Haig Point, purchased by the International Paper Co. in Oct. 1984 is 1,040 acres; it was uninhabited at that time, just overgrown natural jungle. The Melrose Club has approximately 750 acres, and there are 2 other parcels, the Webb Tract (730 acres) and Oak Ridge (340 acres), on which International Paper holds an option. The remaining 30 percent of the island is owned by small landowners, the original indigenous population, approximately 59 people; they are mostly black, female, and elderly.

Melrose is on the site of a plantation whose history dates back to the early 1800s. Land on Daufuskie Island was acquired by David John "Money" Mongin, one of a long line of Mongins (mostly named David John and John David) who were originally of French Huguenot descent. His son, William Henry Mongin, and his wife, Isabella, built the original huge home, destroyed by fire in 1912. The Melrose development includes a 50-room replica of the original, along with beach cottages, a golf course, and other resort amenities. The principal concept, so far as the Melrose and Haig Point developments are concerned, is privacy and exclusivity; they do not offer regular sightseeing tours of their properties but, if you have a serious interest in buying land or a membership, they will be glad to escort you to the island. At Melrose, there are 1,550 memberships available for $65,000 each; you do not really own your land there, but buy a membership, which entitles you to a 1/1550th interest. Melrose now has 2 restaurants open; there will be 3. There are no permanent residents yet, but members may stay in the Inn.

Haig Point is being developed as private residential community with its own private club. It is not open to the public, though people with a particular interest in buying property may come for an investigatory visit. Transportation to island is by private ferry. A limited number of memberships are available in the Strong dining club. Newton ("Tommy") Houge, a carpentry foreman on the Haig Point project, says that island natives do not mind having the residential community built, but do worry that it will cause their taxes to rise so that they will be unable to live on the island. Houge and his workmen have found a surprising number of whiskey still sites on the island; he says deer and rattlesnakes are both abundant.

POINTS OF INTEREST   The main points of interest are the Silver Dew Winery, the old cemetery, and the old church; all may be seen on the bus tour described under Sightseeing Tours.

SIGHTSEEING TOURS   The Daufuskie Island Adventure tour continues on the island in open-air buses driven by native Daufuskie islanders (see Access). There are also tours on the island given by the 2 development companies to serious prospective buyers.

From Hilton Head, South Beach Marina (842–4155), the *Gypsy* makes narrated sea life and nature cruises. The *Vagabond* also makes ocean cruises in the afternoon (842–4155).

PARKS, BEACHES AND CAMPING

Parks: There are no public parks on the island. **Beaches:** The beach here is wide and sandy. **Camping:** No camping is allowed.

MARINAS

Cooper River Landing (681–7335); 2 transient slips; maximum length 100 feet; approach depth 20 feet; dockside depth 20 feet; electric power—yes; prior arrangements would have to be made with the Haig Point Co. to eat at the restaurant.

The Haig Point Company plans a large marina when they develop the Webb tract.

RESTAURANTS

The Melrose and Haig Point restaurants are not open to the public. As a member of the Strong Club, one can dine in the restaurant at Haig Point Plantation; Melrose has 2 restaurants, but they are only open to those with Melrose memberships.

LODGING

At Haig Point, there are not at present any condos or hotels. There are 2 buildings with guest suites; one is the Haig Point Lighthouse, built in 1872, and the other is the Strong Mansion. This building was originally put up on St. Simons Island, Georgia, in 1910 and moved to Haig Point in 1986 as a welcome center; it has 4 guest suites, a cocktail lounge and a dining room. People may stay here if they are guests of the corporation or guests of property owners.

RENTALS

No, except arranged privately with members.

CONTACT

The Melrose Co., Box 6779, Hilton Head Island, SC 29938 (785–6688), or Haig Point Plantation, International Paper Realty Co., Box 7319, Hilton Head Island, SC 29938 (800/992–3635).

EDISTO ISLAND

Area Code 803

LOCATION

Approx. 40 miles south of Charleston on Highway 174 in Colleton County.

SIZE

3 square miles.

ACCESS

Car: Rt. 174 from Hwy. 17. **Air:** There is commercial service to Charleston. **Private boat.**

HISTORY AND   Edisto Island was named for a tribe of In-
DESCRIPTION   dians (the Edistows). Although it is thought
                     to have been settled by the Spanish origi-
nally, the Earl of Shaftsbury bought the land in 1674 from the Indians,
reportedly for cloth, hatchets, beads, and other goods. In 1686, the
Spanish raided the English settlement, carrying off loot "of great
value," including slaves and silver. During the 18th century, rice cul-
tivation was tried, but it was unsuccessful because of the lack of fresh
water. Indigo was then tried, but the Revolution eliminated that trade;
later in the century, Sea Island cotton became king. From then until
the Civil War, Edisto was a fabulously wealthy kingdom with many
plantations and affluent planters. Settlement of the beach as a resort
began in the 1920s, and has progressed steadily ever since. Most of
the plantation homes have disappeared owing to fire or neglect, and
little evidence remains of the grandeur of the Camelot which once
existed here (though some plantations are preserved along the river
front).

The island is bounded by the sea on the coast and the 2 branches
of the Edisto River on the north and south. It is a family-oriented
beach, and very popular with South Carolinians; it has historically
been the site of beach homes for families in Colleton and Charleston
Counties.

POINTS OF INTEREST   The Indian Shell Mound, on Scott Creek, is
                            of interest. The Wildlife Management Area,
                            on adjacent Bear Island, has good fishing
and hunters will find deer, dove, duck, and quail in season; call the
Game Warden at 844–2952 for further information.

SIGHTSEEING TOURS   None, but the Indian Mound Self-
                          Interpretive Trail is excellent for observing
                          the subtropical fauna and flora, as well as
shorebirds and songbirds.

PARKS, BEACHES AND   **Parks:** Edisto Beach State Park, with 1,255
CAMPING   acres, occupies a prime site on the ocean
                            side of the island, **Beaches:** The beach is
wide, quiet, and peaceful; surf fishing for bass, trout, whiting, drum
and sheepshead is a popular pastime. There are lifeguards during the
summer months. **Camping:** There are 75 oceanside campsites (some
may be reserved in advance) and 5 2-bedroom vacation cabins in a
quiet wooded area overlooking the salt marsh and Scott Creek; these
are very popular and need to be reserved months in advance.

MARINAS   Edisto Marina, 3702 Dock Site Rd. (869–
                 3504); 12 transient slips; maximum length
                 95 feet; approach depth 12 feet; dockside
depth 20 feet; electric power—yes; restaurant within walking distance—yes.

RESTAURANTS Collins Restaurant and Pavilion, Hwy. 174 (869-2235) **$**; and the Dockside, 3729 Dock Site Rd. (869–2695) specialize in seafood.**$** Salty Mike's Restaurant (Bay Creek Villas, 869–3520) is also well known.**$**

At Fairfield Ocean Ridge, the Planters Oak Restaurant and Lounge (869–5170) offers Lowcountry seafood specialties and is open to the public. The complex was built around a mighty oak tree; glass-enclosed, it is often the scene of night forays by masked raccoons.**$$**

LODGING Fairfield Ocean Ridge, 1 King Cotton Rd., Box 27, Edisto Beach, SC 29438 (869–2561; SC 800/922-3330), is a resort with efficiencies and condominiums, away from the ocean, but with many units overlooking the golf course. It has a children's recreation program, rental bicycles, and a playground. In season a covered tram runs non-stop between the resort and the beach cabana.

RENTALS Many private cottages (some beachfront) are for rent. Edisto Sales and Rentals Realty, 1405 Palmetto Blvd., Edisto Beach 29438 (869–2527), and the Atwood Agency, Box 10, Edisto Island 29438 (869–2151), both handle rentals.

CONTACT Edisto Beach State Park, 8377 Cabin Road, Edisto Island, SC 29438 (869–2156; reservations 869–2756).

FORT SUMTER

Area Code 803
LOCATION In Charleston Harbor.

SIZE 1½ acres.

ACCESS **Boat:** Fort Sumter is reached by tour boat from the Charleston City Marina on Lockwood Blvd. in Charleston or Patriots Point in Mount Pleasant (Box 59, Charleston, SC 29402, 722–1691). **Air:** There is commercial service to Charleston. **Private boat.**

HISTORY AND DESCRIPTION Fort Sumter, rising majestically from the depths of the harbor, is built on a manmade island. Construction began in 1829. On December 26, 1860, it had still not been completed when, under cover of darkness, Major Robert Anderson of the Union army moved his troops from Fort Moultrie to Fort Sumter. South Carolina was the first Southern state to secede, passing its Ordinance of Secession December 20, 1860. The surrender of Fort Sumter was demanded on April 11, 1861. On April 12, 1861, Confederate forces at Fort Johnson fired the first shot of the Civil War at the Union-occupied Fort Sumter and after 2 days the garrison surrendered. The South then held the Fort. From Morris Island, Union forces bombarded the Fort from 1863 to 1865—one of the longest sieges in modern warfare. By the time it was evacuated by Confederate forces, on February 17, 1865, it was a heap of rubble, but its cracked, crumbling remains have been restored and Fort Sumter is now a National Monument. National Park Service guides conduct walking tours of the ruins and explain the plan of the original stronghold. Artifacts from the fort are displayed in a museum.

POINTS OF INTEREST   The National Monument also includes Fort Moultrie, located 1½ miles east, on Sullivan's Island (accessible by car). Here there is a Visitor Center with an audiovisual program depicting the evolution of seacoast defenses. It was here in 1776 that Col. William Moultrie and his men drove off a squadron of nine British warships at the Battle of Sullivan's Island, the first significant victory of the Revolution for the United States. Sullivan's Island is also known as the setting for Edgar Allan Poe's short story "The Gold Bug."

SIGHTSEEING TOURS   Fort Sumter Tours (see Access) offers tours of the Fort; these tours take 2½ hours and also include a narrated tour of Charleston Harbor. The same company offers dinner cruises aboard the 102-foot yacht *Spirit of Charleston* (722–2628 for reservations). The cruises include live entertainment, dancing, and cocktails.

The 50-minute carriage tours are one of the most visible tourist features of Charleston. Several companies operate the tours, including Charleston Carriage (577–0042) and the Old South Carriage Co. (723-9712). They leave from numerous points in the historic district.

There are also trolley tours (577–0053).

PARKS, BEACHES AND   **Parks:** Fort Sumter is under the supervision
CAMPING   of the National Park Service. **Beaches:** The island does not have a recreational beach. **Camping:** No camping is allowed.

MARINAS   None, but private boats may tie up at the pier and passengers may tour the Fort.

RESTAURANTS   There are no restaurants and no snack bars on the island, but snacks and drinks are available on the tour boat. Charleston itself has a seemingly never-ending variety of restaurants.

LODGING   None; visitors usually stay in Charleston.

RENTALS   None.

CONTACT   Superintendent, Fort Sumter, 1114 Middle
                               St., Sullivan's Island, SC 29482 (883–
                               3123).

FRIPP ISLAND

Area Code 803

LOCATION   19 miles east of Beaufort, on US 21, adja-
                               cent to Hunting Island State Park.

SIZE   3,000 acres.

ACCESS   *Car:* Highway 21 from Beaufort. *Air:* There
                               is air service to Charleston and there is a
                               3,430-foot airstrip at Beaufort for private
planes. *Private boat.*

HISTORY AND   Fripp Island is one of the Lowcountry is-
DESCRIPTION   lands edged by white beaches and forested
                               with palmettos and moss-covered live
oaks. It was named after Johannes Fripp, the captain who was given
the island in appreciation for guarding the English-held coast from the
Spanish. The whole island, developed largely in the 1970s, falls
within the bounds of a single private community; there is 24-hour security. It has been called an "islander's island," and advertises itself
as "The Uncrowded One," an ocean retreat which has not been developed in a high-density commercial way. There are a variety of accommodations as well as private homes on the island. It has long been
undisturbed by people; in fact, it is the natural habitat of many forms
of wildlife. As you enter, a sign warns, "$1,000 fine for Feeding or
Molesting the Alligators."

POINTS OF INTEREST   Hunting Island State Park (see entry) has
                               an historic lighthouse; there are also
                               sights of interest in Beaufort, including the
Beaufort Museum, which has Civil war relics and plantation handicrafts; the Penn Center on St. Helena Island, the first school for freed
blacks established in the South; the Parris Island Museum, which relates the history of Parris Island and has a collection of vintage Marine
Corps uniforms and weapons; and the George Elliott House Museum,
built in 1840 and used as a Federal hospital during the Civil War.

SIGHTSEEING TOURS   None.

PARKS, BEACHES AND   **Parks:** There are no parks on the island,
CAMPING   but Hunting Island State Park is adjacent.
Beaches: There are 3½ miles of uncrowded
beach. There has been an erosion problem, but renourishment may
preserve the wide beaches which characterize much of the South Carolina coastline. **Camping:** No camping is allowed.

MARINAS   The Fripp Island Marina (838–2832) has
space for transient boats as a rule, except
for holiday weekends, when reservations
are recommended; maximum length 50 feet; approach depth 5 feet;
dockside depth 16 feet; electric power—yes; restaurant within walking distance—yes.

RESTAURANTS   The Beach Club Restaurant, recently remodeled, also has an ocean view and
serves seafood and steaks.**$$** The 19th
Hole, in the golf course clubhouse at Ocean Point, has an ocean view
and serves breakfast, lunch, and snacks.**$** The Speranza Restaurant,
at the marina, serves full meals.**$** (The public may dine in the restau-
rants with advance reservations; 800/845–4100).

LODGING   There is accommodation in villas, efficien-
cies, and rental homes. The villas have
both nightly and weekly rates; in summer,
there is a 2-night minimum. Most homes have weekly rates only in the
summer, but may have nightly rates in the March-May Sports Season
or the December-February Winter Season.**$$$**

RENTALS   Contact the Fripp Island Property Management Co.

CONTACT   Fripp Island Property Management Co.,
One Tarpon Blvd., Fripp Island, SC 29920
(800/845–4100).

HILTON HEAD ISLAND

Area Code 803
LOCATION   Between the Intracoastal Waterway and the
Atlantic Ocean, north of Savannah, Geor-
gia.

SIZE   12 miles by 5 miles.

ACCESS   *Car:* Bridge; US 278. *Air:* There is a paved
                              3,700-foot airstrip; the island is served by
                              commercial airlines. *Private boat.*

HISTORY AND   Hilton Head Island, 12 miles long and in
DESCRIPTION   places 5 miles wide, is the largest island
                              between New Jersey and Florida. It was
named for an Englishman, Capt. William Hilton, who discovered it in
1663 when he sailed into Port Royal Sound. As early as 1526, Spanish, French, and English colonists had tried to settle on the island, but
were prevented from doing so by raiding Indian and by pirates. Before
the Civil War, prosperous English rice and indigo plantations were established, but were left in ruins after the war (some may still be seen).
The freed slave ("Gullah") population then subsisted on the island by
hunting, fishing, and farming.

Hilton Head is bordered by one of the few surviving unspoiled marine estuaries on the East Coast. The James Byrne Bridge to the island
from the mainland was completed in 1956, and the island was then
developed as an year-round affluent resort. (In 1975, when an errant
barge knocked out the Skull Creek Bridge, helicopters from Savannah
ferried over champagne, filet mignons, and caviar to sustain islanders.) The principal developer was Charles Fraser, whose father, General Joe Fraser of Hinesville, Georgia, had, with his partners, bought
much of the island. Fraser had a true conservationist's vision of developing the island so as not to obliterate the beauty of the natural
surroundings; he abhorred such strip development as had occurred at
Myrtle Beach. For over 3 decades, the island has been visited by a
mixture of Graces and Furies. Fraser's master plan for Sea Pines Plantation, with its quality architecture; the setting aside of green spaces;
and the protection of trees, was carried out with immense success.
Over 3,000 homes and apartments were built on an island that, in
1950, had had only 150 homes. Then the island was visited by the
Furies of several developers who went bankrupt and constructed un-
sightly buildings. Today, Hilton Head is an incorporated municipality,

Aerial View of Harbour Town, Hilton Head

and has regained some control over commercial restrictions. The permanent population is over 17,000, and about two-thirds of the island is owned and controlled by seven "plantations," or planned resort communities, each with a security gate. The island has over 1600 hotel rooms, 22 golf courses, 200 tennis courts, 90 restaurants, 34 shopping centers, 3 equestrian centers, and 7 marinas. The *New Yorker* profiled the typical resident in its famous "Seven Ages of Man" cartoon; it showed 7 panels, depicting a boy at the Dalton School, advancing to Greenwich Country Day, Deerfield, Princeton, Harvard Business School, PaineWebber, and finally as a retiree in a golf cart at Hilton Head. The community is a lively one, however, with an active local theater, 2 excellent newspapers (the *Island Packet* and the *Hilton Head News)*, and many organizations and activities. Such tennis stars as Evonne Goolagong Cawley and Rod Laver maintain residences here.

POINTS OF INTEREST   The wildlife preserves (see Parks) are of interest, as are Calibogue Sound and nearby Daufuskie (see Sightseeing). There are also several historic sites on the island, including an Indian shell ring dating back to 1450 B.C. in Sea Pines Forest Preserve, 2 Civil War forts and Baynard Plantation Ruins, dating from about 1800, on Baynard Park Road in Sea Pines Plantation.

The candy-striped Harbour Town Lighthouse is one of the best-known landmarks along the eastern seaboard among boating people.

SIGHTSEEING TOURS   The *Gypsy* makes narrated sea life and nature cruises from South Beach Marina (842–4155).There are several tours to Daufuskie Island. Two boats leave from Broad Creek Marina, the *Daufuskie Queen* (681–7918) and the *Safari* (785–5654); the *Adventure* leaves from Shelter Cove (785–4558), and the *Vagabond* (842–4155) leaves from the Harbour Town Yacht Basin. The *Vagabond* also makes ocean cruises in the afternoon (842–4155). The *William Hilton* makes deep-sea fishing excursions (671–5909) from the Harbour Town Yacht Basin and the *Drifter* makes fishing trips from South Beach Marina (671–3060).

Two-hour afternoon and sunset schooner cruises leave from Hudson's Restaurant, 1 Hudson Rd. (681–2773).

PARKS, BEACHES AND   **Parks:** There are no public parks on the is-
CAMPING   land, but there are several wildlife and waterfowl habitats, including the Audubon Newhall Preserve, the Sea Pines Forest Preserve, and Hilton Head Plantation's Whooping Crane Conservancy. These attest to the fact that the island has not been completely exploited commercially. **Beaches:** There is 1 public beach, at Coligny Circle. **Camping:** No tent camping is allowed, but there are 2 resorts for self-contained vehicles, the Outdoor Resort RV Resort and Yacht Club, Jenkins Rd.

(681–3256) and the Outdoor Resorts/Motor Coach Resort, Arrow Rd. (785–7699).

MARINAS   The appealing marinas on Hilton Head are too numerous to list in full. Three of the most popular, however, are the Harbour Town Yacht Basin (671–2704); 15 transient slips; maximum length 100 feet; approach depth 6 feet; dockside depth 6 feet; electric power—yes; restaurant within walking distance—yes. Shelter Cove/ Palmetto Dunes (842–7001); 26 transient slips; maximum length 100 feet; approach depth 18 feet; dockside depth 13 feet; electric power—yes; restaurant within walking distance—yes. Palmetto Bay Marina; 25 transient slips; maximum length 100 feet; approach depth 20 feet; dockside depth 20 feet; electric power—yes; restaurant within walking distance—yes.

RESTAURANTS   Hilton Head abounds in interesting restaurants. Among them are Alexander's, Queen's Folly Rd., Palmetto Dunes (785–4999), known for its seafood.**$$**

Ballard's Shrimp House, Marshland Rd. (681–7777), does its own baking and specializes in seafood.**$**

The Café Europa, at the mouth of Harbour Town Harbor (671–3399), has continental cuisine and piano entertainment.**$$**

The Commodore Seafood Restaurant, at Shelter Cove (785-4442), has local seafood specialties.**$$**

Harbourmaster's at Shelter Cove (785–3030) also specializes in good seafood and has a pleasant nautical atmosphere.**$$**

The Landing, One Hudson Rd. (681–3363), has char-broiled seafood (very fresh) and a view of the Intracoastal Waterway.**$$** It is adjacent to Hudson's, a famous restaurant founded in 1968 on the Intracoastal Waterway shrimp boat docks. Both serve very fresh seafood.**$$**

The Overlook, in the Port Royal Clubhouse in Port Royal Plantation

Harbour Town Marina, Hilton Head

(681–4444), has Lowcountry cuisine and specializes in seafood. It offers a *prix fixe* dinner.**$$$**

LODGING   There are accommodations in all price ranges at Hilton Head. A central reservation service handles reservations at most island locations: 800/845–7018 or 785–9050.

The Hyatt Regency Hilton Head Island, Box 6167, Hilton Head 29928 (785–1234), has a private sand beach, balconies, and full resort amenities.**$$$**

Mariner's Inn, Box 6165, Hilton Head 29928 (842–8001; US except SC 800/845–8001) is located in the Palmetto Dunes Resort; it has ocean view rooms with balconies or patios; all the rooms have kitchens.**$$$**

Marriott's Hilton Head Resort, in Shipyard Plantation, 130 Shipyard Dr., Hilton Head 29928 (800/228–9390), has rental boats, saunas, a whirlpool, and 20 tennis courts.**$$$**

The Red Roof Inn, 5 Regency Parkway, Hilton Head 29928 (800/848-7378 or 686–6808), offers more moderate accommodation.**$**

The Sea Crest Motel, 1 Forest Beach, Box 5818, Hilton Head 29928 (785–2121; US except SC 800/845–7014), has competitive family rates and is on the ocean.**$$-$$$**

Sea Pines Plantation, US 278, Hilton Head 29928 (800/845–6131), was the earliest resort. It has 18 pools and 3 golf courses; there are villas with kitchen units, children's programs, and a free shuttle to the beach.**$$$**

A Super 8 Motel with 92 units opened in Spring 1989; 40 Waterside Dr., Hilton Head 29928 (800/843–1991).**$**

RENTALS   Hilton Head Oceanfront Rentals; 800/845–6132, Island Rentals & Real Estate; 800/845–7017 and the Worthy Owner Rental Group, 803/785–5577, all handle rentals. The Chamber of Commerce will send a list of other realtors.

CONTACT   Hilton Head Island Chamber of Commerce, Box 5647, Hilton Head Island, SC 29938 (785–3673).

HUNTING ISLAND
STATE PARK

Area Code 803
LOCATION   16 miles east of Beaufort.

SIZE   3 miles by 1 mile.

ACCESS   *Car:* Highway 21 from Beaufort. *Air:* There
                              is commercial service to Charleston and
                              there is a 3,430-ft. airstrip at Beaufort for
private planes. *Private boat.*

HISTORY AND   The island is one of the barrier islands off
DESCRIPTION   the coast of South Carolina; it has been
                              called a "tropical paradise," with its abun-
dant foliage and 5,000 acres of beach, forest, and marsh. The island
was so named because it was once used for hunting deer, raccoon,
and other small game animals and waterfowl. Much of the redevelop-
ment here has been done to enhance or protect this significant wildlife
habitat. Roads have been moved to avoid fragile areas and to mini-
mize the impact of visitors, while wildlife browse areas have been established. The best developed slash pine-palmetto forest in the state
is here; it is a very good place in which to find the Cabbage Palm or
palmetto in its native habitat. Visitors are asked to respect the vegetation, which has been planted in an attempt to stabilize the sand
dunes.

POINTS OF INTEREST   The Hunting Island Lighthouse, 136 feet
                              high, was built in 1875; three other struc-
                              tures also remain of the original lighthouse
complex. As early as 1859, a brick lighthouse structure was built on
the island to guide vessels along the coast. By the late 1860s, erosion
had destroyed the building. The new lighthouse was made of cast iron
plate; owing to erosion, it also had to be relocated in 1889, one and
a quarter miles southeast of the old site. The lighthouse was active
until June 16, 1933.
    The Paradise Fishing Pier extends 1,120 feet into Fripp Inlet; it is
located on the southern tip of the park. This is a popular gathering
place year-round for anglers. A tackle shop at the pier entrance carries
tackle, bait, and other fishing items.
    In and around Beaufort there are several points of interest, includ-
ing the Beaufort Museum, which has Civil war relics and plantation
handicrafts; the Penn Center on St. Helena Island, the first school for
freed blacks established in the south; the Parris Island, which relates
the history of Parris Island and has a collection of vintage Marine
Corps uniforms and weapons; and the George Elliott House Museum,
built in 1840 and used as a Federal hospital during the Civil War.

SIGHTSEEING TOURS   None, but there is a 2-mile nature trail and
                              a 1,000-foot marsh boardwalk extending
                              into the salt marsh on the north end of the
                              park.

PARKS, BEACHES AND   *Parks:* The entire island is a state park.
CAMPING   *Beaches:* There are more than 3 miles of
                              beach, and numerous boardwalks leading

from the parking lots to the beach are located throughout the north and south beaches. Ocean swimming may be enjoyed in a protected area during the summer. **Camping:** A 200-site camping area with water and electrical hook-ups is located at the north end of the park, along with a park store, recreation/nature center, and 2 play areas for children.

MARINAS   None on the island, but there are several marinas in Beaufort

RESTAURANTS   None on the island, but in Beaufort there is the Anchorage House (524–9392), across from the downtown marina, an historic house with gracious porches.

LODGING   None, but there are motels in Beaufort. Also, you may stay at the Fripp Island resort (see that entry).

RENTALS   The park has 14 vacation cabins within walking distance of the ocean; they are fully furnished, heated, air-conditioned, and supplied with linens. They are rented weekly from Monday to Monday.

CONTACT   Superintendent, Hunting Island State Park, Rt. 1, Box 668, Frogmore, SC 29920 (838–2011).

ISLE OF PALMS

Area Code 803
LOCATION   12 miles north of Charleston.

SIZE   Approximately 7 miles by about ¼ mile.

ACCESS   **Car:** Via Rt. 17 and Rt. 703. **Air:** There is commercial service to Charleston. **Private boat.**

HISTORY AND   The Isle of Palms, once called the Long Is-
DESCRIPTION   land, was developed by J. C. Long. In the early part of the century, it had an amusement park; access was by ferry to Sullivan's Island and by trolley to the Isle of Palms. In 1946, a bridge from the mainland was built to Sullivan's Island; later in the decade, a bridge was built from Sulli-

van's Island to the Isle of Palms. For many years it was accessible only by water and a single railroad bridge, but it was still a favored retreat for the citizens of Charleston. There are many private homes and modest commercial development on the southern end of the island.

Wild Dunes, at the northern end of the island, was developed by Raymon and Henry Finch. The golf course here was designed by Tom Fazio, who lost $1,000 when the club's developer bet him that he'd never laid out a golf course on finer natural terrain—massive oaks, pines, marsh, and sand dunes. Fazio admitted that he had not, and donated the money to charity. The Wild Dunes Beach and Racquet Club stretches along the northern end of the island, with timbered wood houses set back amid the foliage off Palm Boulevard. The development is integrated environmentally and very posh. It is much closer to the attractions of Charleston than Kiawah Island, and is a good choice for families with children, as you can manage Charleston's boat cruises, carriage rides, and historic sites while still leaving time to enjoy the ocean and beach.

POINTS OF INTEREST   Nearby Sullivan's Island is of interest, with its vintage rustic beach houses and wide beach. Fort Moultrie, also on Sullivan's, part of the Fort Sumter National Monument, is well worth touring; here there is a Visitor Center with an audiovisual program depicting the evolution of seacoast defenses. It was here in 1776 that Colonel William Moultrie and his men drove off a squadron of 9 British warships at the Battle of Sullivan's Island. Sullivan's Island is also known as the setting for Edgar Allan Poe's short story "The Gold Bug."

Folly Beach is also of historic interest; George Gershwin lived here for about 6 months while writing *Porgy and Bess*.

Among the many sights in Charleston is the Charleston Museum, the oldest in the nation, dating back to 1773. The old Market features interesting specialty shops and restaurants; it was originally constructed in 1804. The Battery is well worth touring, with its much-

Wild Dunes Resort, Isle of Palms

photographed stately mansions (the newest is Victorian; the rest pre-date the Civil War). Charlestonians are fond of saying the Battery is where the Ashley and Cooper Rivers flow together to form the North Atlantic Ocean (modesty is not a Charleston trait). At Patriots Point there is a large naval and maritime museum, including the aircraft carrier *Yorktown* and other interesting ships, such as the World War II submarine *Clamagore* and the destroyer *Laffey*, as well as the *Savannah*, the world's first nuclear-powered merchant ship.

SIGHTSEEING TOURS   None on the island, but Charleston has many tours, including some by horse-drawn carriage and others by boat (see entry for Fort Sumter).

PARKS, BEACHES AND   **Parks:** There are no formal parks on the is-
CAMPING   land. **Beaches:** The beach is about 6 miles long and extremely wide; there was an erosion problem a number of years ago, but the beach has been successfully nourished and expanded. The surf is gentle. The section of the beach at Wild Dunes is for resort guests only; the beach on the remainder of the island, as well as on Sullivan's Island, is public. **Camping:** No camping is allowed on the island.

MARINAS   Wild Dunes Yacht Harbor (886–5100); 50 transient slips; maximum length 100 feet; approach depth 12 feet; dockside depth 12 feet; electric power—yes; restaurant within walking distance—yes. Cast-A-Way Marina (886–4396); 4 transient slips; maximum length 54 feet; approach depth 12 feet; dockside depth 4 feet; electric power—yes; restaurant within walking distance—yes.

RESTAURANTS   The Atlantic House at Folly Beach (588–9563) is well worth the trip over; it is perched on pilings out over the ocean and is a landmark in the area. The waves gently crash on the beach below, giving rise to decided longings for beach houses, cruises, and, at least, a post-dinner moonlight beach walk.**$$**

Island House Restaurant, within Wild Dunes (see Contact), offers seaside dining and traditional Lowcountry favorites.**$$–$$$**

Long Island Cafe, 1515 Palm Blvd., Isle of Palms (886–8809), offers local seafood and Sunday brunch.**$$**

The Palms Seafood Restaurant, 1010 Ocean Blvd., Isle of Palms (886–8145), has seafood, steak, and chicken.**$$**

The Rusty Anchor, 2213 Middle St., Sullivan's Island (883–9131), specializes in grilled and baked seafoods, cooked in full view.**$$**

The Clubhouse Restaurant at Wild Dunes is open year-round.**$$**

The Wild Dunes Yacht Harbor Marina has a restaurant called Trade-winds (886–5678).**$$**

LODGING   Sea Cabin/Island Realty Oceanfront Villas, 1300 Ocean Blvd., Isle of Palms (800/ 845–2546).**$$**
The Wild Dunes Beach and Racquet Club has beachside and island homes, along with condo units, most of which are oceanside. Altogether, there are over 300 beautifully appointed units, which come with maid service, linens, and complete kitchens. There are swimming pools in the various complexes.**$$$**

RENTALS   At Wild Dunes Beach and Racquet Club, all rentals are handled by the Club (see Contact). There are rental cottages on the part of the island outside the Club (and on Sullivan's Island, adjacent); two realtors handling them are O'Shaughnessy Resort Rentals, Box 465, Isle of Palms, SC 29451 (SC 886–8600; US 800/533–1343); and Resorts, Inc., 1116 Palm Blvd., Isle of Palms, SC 29451 (886–6493). A complete list will be sent by the Charleston Trident Convention & Visitors Bureau (see Contact).

CONTACT   The Wild Dunes Beach and Racquet Club, Box 388, Isle of Palms, SC 29451 (800/ 845–8880 or 886-6000); also the Charleston Trident Chamber of Commerce, 85 Calhoun St., Box 975, Charleston, SC 29402 (577–2510) or the Charleston Convention and Visitors Bureau (east of the Mississippi 800/845–7108; 723–7641).

KIAWAH

Area Code 803
LOCATION   21 miles south/southwest of Charleston.

SIZE   10 miles by 1.5 miles at widest point.

ACCESS   **Car:** Via US 17 and Main Road. **Air:** There is commercial service to Charleston, and Johns Island, 20 minutes away, has an airstrip with 2 5,000-foot runways. **Private boat.**

HISTORY AND   The island is named for one of the Indian
DESCRIPTION   tribes which once inhabited the low country of South Carolina (it is thought that the Kiawahs, Edistos, Stonos, Sewees, and Wandos were offshoots of the Muskogean inland tribe). Robert Sandford, exploring the coast in 1666 for the Lords Proprietors, described the area as "ye land of the Kyawha." The first recorded claimant was George Rayner (or Raynor or

Reiner); the property later passed to John Stanyarne, who built the tall mansion known as the Vanderhorst House. The island was famous as a hunting and fishing retreat during the tenure of the Vanderhorst family, which continued into the 1930s. In the late 19th century, excursion packets from Charleston such as the *Island Boy*, the *Packet Boy*, and the *Islander*, carrying blacks, came to the east end of Kiawah Island, on Stono Inlet, for all-day beach picnics, swimming, and late-night dances on the sand. Kiawah as "Kittiwar Island" is the locale of a scene in Du Bose Heyward's 1925 novel *Porgy and Bess*. The Vanderhorst furnishings were removed from the island by 1942; there was a period of occupancy by the Coast Guard, and in 1952 the island was sold to the C. C. Royal Lumber Company, which bridged the river. In 1974, Royal's heirs sold the land to the Kiawah Island Company. Today the remains of the Vanderhorst plantation still exist; it is said that the ghost of Major Arnoldus Vanderhorst IV inhabits the old mansion. The dunes, savannahs, and marshes have changed little since the island was first visited by Europeans. The indigo and cotton fields which once supported the economy are slowly eroding.

The island was spared the more commercial exploitation which has afflicted many islands, for the company has developed the island in a careful, pro-environmental manner; there is a remarkable harmony between the natural surroundings and the visitors, who seem to cherish the ecology as much as any naturalist. Maintenance is meticulous, and there is nothing garish; even the burgundy stop signs are carved of wood. Speed limits are 23, 33, or 43 m.p.h. and it is has been said that it is an honor to obey them. Some of the original developers had a hand in Sea Pines Plantation on Hilton Head, and knew how to construct a resort which accommodated the natural surroundings yet provide for recreation. Kuwait was the largest investor in Kiawah; a 16-month environmental study preceded any groundbreaking. Only 3,500 of the island's 10,000 acres are slated to be developed; much of the rest has been set aside for the indigenous mammals, reptiles, and birds. Egrets, herons, and osprey are frequently observed; if you collect live shells and leave them on your balcony overnight, don't be surprised to hear little tinkling sounds as the birds pick them clean.

The villas and inn are low and positioned back behind the barrier-dune structure. Long elevated walkways lead to the beach from various access points. The architecture is notably low-key and suitable for the site; it has received praise from many professionals. The first phase, West Beach, was opened in 1976, and East Beach Village, the newest segment of the development, near the center of the island, was opened in 1981. Today there are 2,400 property owners, but only about 200 live on the island year-round. Because the transient resort facilities are discreetly clustered some distance away, they are spared intrusion.

There are conferences at Kiawah of many kinds; they often include delicious buffets on the veranda of the Kiawah Inn and, in lieu of a banquet, an outdoor oyster roast at Mingo Point. The resort has two 18-hole championship courses and a third, designed by Tom Fazio, is under construction. There are 16 tennis courts; Kiawah has received a Five-Star Tennis Resort Award from *World Tennis* magazine. Other activities for guests include swimming, bicycling (there are 12 miles of bike paths), hiking, fishing, crabbing, and shrimping.

Car access to Kiawah is controlled; there is careful security upon entrance and there are other checkpoints.

POINTS OF INTEREST The main point of interest is the old Vanderhorst mansion, which rises like a ghost in a small clearing in the thick live-oak and palmetto forest. Not far from the house, on a tidal creek, is an area where Kiawah Indian pottery lies broken in the mud.

SIGHTSEEING TOURS Kiawah Island Safaris (768–111) offers year-round (7:00 A.M. to 6:00 P.M.) 2-hour jeep tours over plantation trails to discover the unique beauty of the island's creeks, marshlands, and beaches as well as much of its forests that have remained unchanged since the Civil War. Favorite stops include shelling on the undeveloped beach and a visit to the antebellum Vanderhorst mansion.

PARKS, BEACHES AND CAMPING *Parks:* Night Heron Park, 21 acres near the ocean, has playfields, a bicycle rental shop, a 25-meter swimming pool, and an ocean access point with sunning and observation decks. Here, in season, there are beach cookouts, family movies, swimming, a playground, pony rides, and games. *Beaches:* There are 10 miles of very wide beaches fronting on the Atlantic; erosion has not been a problem since jetties were built at the mouth of Charleston Harbor. There is a public beach, Beachwalker Park, located before the first security gate, on the southern end of the island. *Camping:* No camping is allowed.

MARINAS There are no marinas on the island, but some visitors dock their boats at Bohicket Marina Village, on Johns Island (768–1280), a half mile from Seabrook Island. There are 10 transient slips; maximum length 100 feet; approach depth 20 feet; dockside depth 20 feet; electric power—yes; restaurant within walking distance—yes.

RESTAURANTS The inn's restaurants are the Charleston Gallery, an intimate gourmet room with a prix fixe menu (**$$$**) and the Jasmine Porch, an airy and engaging room, serving breakfast, lunch, and dinner (**$$**). The restaurants are accessible to the public, but reservations are recommended. Jonah's, in the Straw Market, just across from the Inn, is also pleasant.**$$** On East Beach, there is the Indigo House in Town Center (**$$**) and the Park Cafe in Night Heron Park (seasonal).**$$**

The Privateer at Bohicket Marina Village, between Kiawah and Sea-brook Island Resorts, serves fresh seafood from the docks and over-looks the river.**$$**

LODGING   Accommodations include villas and cot-tages on West Beach, bordering the Atlan-tic Ocean; and 150 luxurious rooms adja-cent to the Kiawah Inn (call the main resort number; see Contact). The inn has a gracious shaded verandah. There is an adult pool and also one for families with children. At East Beach Village, there is a lake, a pool complex, and an ocean access point; here there are village and cottage accommodations. All rooms and villas vary in price according to location; off-season there are excellent packages.**$$$**

RENTALS   There are condominium units and cottages available for rent through the Kiawah Re-sort office (call 800/6-KIAWAH).

CONTACT   Kiawah Island Resort, Box 12910, Charles-ton, SC 29412 (US except SC 800/845–2471; SC 768–2121).

PAWLEYS ISLAND

Area Code 803

LOCATION   Off the coast of South Carolina, about 25 miles south of Myrtle Beach and 12 miles north of Georgetown.

SIZE   4 miles by ¼ mile.

ACCESS   **Car:** Via Hwy. 17. **Air:** There is commercial service to Myrtle Beach. **Private boat.**

HISTORY AND   The island was named for George, Anthony,
DESCRIPTION   and Percival Pawley, sons of Percival Paw-ley I, who obtained a grant to land here in 1711. At the beginning of the 18th century, many old rice plantations sprang up nearby on the mainland; planters brought their families to the island, during the rice-planting era, to escape the heat and benefit from the therapeutic effects of salt water and sea air. Some of the fine old homes are still on the island, such as the Pawley House, built before 1749, the Ward House, and the Nesbit House (1780). Among the prominent South Carolina families who summered at Pawleys were the Wards, Allstons, Woods, Frasers, LaBruces, and Tuckers. Planters' families were rowed to the island by singing slave oarsmen; many of

their harmonies are thought to have had an African origin. Among the spirituals they sang were "Roll, Jordan, Roll" and "O Zion." Later, there were carriages, railway cars, and automobiles. Planters imported cooks, seamstresses, and nurses for their children, who were required to read classics during their vacation mornings. An orchestra came from Georgetown to play for dancing in the early 1900s. Later there were carriages, railway cars, and, finally, automobiles. Many Georgetown families, descendants of the early planters, still retreat to Pawleys Island each spring and remain until fall.

Pawleys is a different world from the resort islands, such as Kiawah and Hilton Head, developed further south. Here there are picturesque old homes with gabled roofs, handwoven rope hammocks, and a resident ghost, the Gray Man. It has been called "arrogantly shabby" and in many ways has changed little since the 1700s, when plantation owners built summer places to escape the heat. Today the pace is still slow and leisurely; vacationers enjoy swimming, sunning, fishing, and visiting neighbors. There is an active social life among the families staying on the island, many of whom are the third, fourth, or even higher generation to occupy a house.

POINTS OF INTEREST   Brookgreen Gardens, 3 miles south of Murrells Inlet on U.S. 17 (237–4218), is a unique blend of beautiful gardens and impressive 18th- and 19th-century American sculpture; there are more than 400 works of art. The gardens were developed by sculptor Anna Hyatt Huntington and her husband, philanthropist Archer Huntington.

The Hammock Shops at Pawleys Island is a complex of 17 unique gift shops, created in Old South style with brick brought from England. Visitors may see the authentic Pawleys Island rope hammocks made here; the original methods, dating from 1880, are used.

All Saints Waccamaw Episcopal Church, S.C. 255, about 3 miles west of the island, is not the original church attended by the planters, which burned in 1915, but has many similar features.

SIGHTSEEING TOURS   The *Island Queen* makes historic plantation river cruises from the Georgetown Landing Marina (527–3160); there are several cruises each day from March 1 through December 15.

PARKS, BEACHES AND CAMPING   **Parks:** There are no public parks on the island. **Beaches:** There are several beach access points along the island. **Camping:** No camping is allowed.

MARINAS   There are a number of marinas at Georgetown, but the Intracoastal Waterway cuts inland and bypasses this section of the coast.

RESTAURANTS   The Litchfield Inn (see Lodging) offers in-
                         teresting seafood dishes.**$$** Pawleys Is-
                         land Inn Restaurant and Bar, Hwy. 17
(237–8491) has been widely praised and has been written up in *Food
& Wine*, among other magazines. It is a replica of a 17th-century
South Carolina rice plantation home, and was purchased by chef/
owner Louis Osteen and his wife Maureen in 1980. Among the many
specialties are angel hair pasta with local caviar, soft-shell crabs with
fried green tomatoes, hot biscuits, shrimp with orange and pernod
sauce, and a mixed grill of grouper, shrimp, and scallops; the menu
changes daily to reflect the season and products available. One food
writer has called it "imaginative, well-executed cooking based on regional traditions and the local bounty." Reserve well ahead.**$$-$$$**

LODGING   The Litchfield Inn, Drawer 98, Pawleys Is-
                         land 29585 (237–4211), has rooms,
                         suites, and efficiencies, with many ocean-
front accommodations.**$$-$$$**
   Quality Inn Seagull, Hwy. 17 (237–4261), is large and has a pool,
but is not on the ocean.**$–$$**
   There are many motels at Myrtle Beach, north of Pawleys, but for
the full flavor of the island, many people choose to rent a cottage.

RENTALS   Pawleys Island Realty, North Causeway,
                         Box 306, Pawleys Island 29585 (237–
                         4257), handles about 200 cottage listings
each year. E. R. A. Mueller Realty, Island Shops, Hwy. 17, Pawleys
Island 29585 (237-4243), also handles cottage rentals.

CONTACT   South Carolina Grand Strand Chamber of
                         Commerce, Box 650, US 17, Murrells Inlet,
                         SC 29576 (651- 1010).

SEABROOK ISLAND

Area Code 803
LOCATION   23 miles south of Charleston.

SIZE   2,200 acres, bordered by Lowcountry
                         marshes.

ACCESS   *Car:* Via Rt. 17 and Main Rd. *Air:* There is
                         commercial service to Charleston and a
                         private airport on Johns Island with 2
5,000-foot runways (call 559–2401 for information). ***Private boat.***

HISTORY AND   Seabrook was once inhabited by Indians. In
DESCRIPTION   1666, Lt. Col. Robert Sanford explored and
                           claimed the area for Charles II; it was first
part of "Carolina," then named "Colleton" in honor of Sir John Colleton.
Sir Joseph Blake received the first land deed in 1696; he sold it to
John Jones and Samuel Jones in 1732. They renamed it "James Island"; it was then named "Simmons Island" when purchased by Fran-
cis Simmons. Finally it was renamed for William Seabrook, a wealthy
cotton planter who used it as his personal hunting preserve. In 1880,
the Gregg family sold the island to William Andell; the Andell family
owned it until 1938, when part of it was sold to Victor Morawetz, who
deeded it to the Episcopal Diocese of South Carolina for use as a
camp and conference center. In 1970, the Seabrook Development
Corporation, headed by William C. Whitner, acquired part of the
church property and purchased another parcel from the Andell family.
Today, the island's developer carries out the objective of protecting
the environment while creating a community conducive to gracious
living. This is a private resort island; it has been called the "reclusive
little sister" of Kiawah. The Seabrook Island Resort opened in 1971.
There is golf, tennis, and swimming, along with extensive children's
programs from Memorial Day through Labor Day. One golf course was
designed by Robert Trent Jones and another by Willard Byrd.

POINTS OF INTEREST   There are no museums or historic struc-
                           tures, but the endangered brown pelican
                           has one of its largest rookeries in a shallow
sandbank just offshore of the Beach Club.

SIGHTSEEING TOURS   There are no sightseeing tours on the is-
                           land.

PARKS, BEACHES AND   **Parks:** There are no formal parks, but the
CAMPING   island has much wildlife, including a va-
                           riety of birds, and mossy trees and rain for-
est vegetation. **Beaches:** There are 3½ miles of ocean-front beach.
Camping: No camping is allowed.

MARINAS   Bohicket Marina Village, on Johns Island
                           (768-1280), a half-mile from Seabrook Is-
                           land; 10 transient slips; maximum length
100 feet; approach depth 20 feet; dockside depth 20 feet; electric
power—yes; restaurant within walking distance—yes.

RESTAURANTS   The Island House has 2 restaurants, the
                           Deveaux Room, which has gourmet a la
                           carte dining with continental cuisine and a
large wine library (**$$–$$$**), and the Island House Restaurant, serving

breakfast, lunch, and dinner with views of the waterfront.**$$–$$$**
Cap'n Sams has fast food.**$** The public may not eat in these restaurants unless they are guests at Seabrook or accompanying people who are staying there.

The Privateer at Bohicket Marina Village, between the Kiawah and Seabrook Island resorts, serves fresh seafood from the docks and overlooks the river.**$$**

LODGING   There is accommodation in 375 villas; it is all handled through the main Seabrook Island Resort office (see Contact); they rent daily and weekly.**$$$**

RENTALS   All rentals are handled through the main office (see Contact).

CONTACT   Seabrook Island Resort, Box 32099, Charleston, SC 29417 (US except SC 800/ 845–2475; SC 800/922-2401).

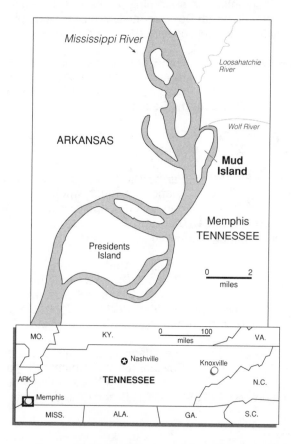

TENNESSEE

The roots of Tennessee go back to the Chickasaw Indians and to Hernando de Soto, who is thought to have visited the site of Memphis in 1541, planting the Spanish flag. Following him were Louis Joliette, Père Marquette, and Sieur de la Salle, who claimed the territory for France in 1673. Fort Assumption, the first permanent structure, was built on the bluffs in 1739. It was not until 1779 that the first permanent settlement, at Jonesboro, was established. Tennessee has been called the "Volunteer State," as so many of its citizens volunteered to fight in the War of 1812.

Memphis has been called an "elixir of the Old South and a modern metropolis." The city is almost synonymous with music; it was here that the blues were born and that Elvis Presley lived and died. W. C. Handy, "Father of the Blues," who said of Memphis, "I'd rather be here than any place I know," first performed in PeeWee's Salon on Beale Street. It was in a Memphis recording studio that Elvis Presley began his career; he has become known as the "King of Rock 'n' Roll." The city has several noted museums, including Brooks Memorial Art Gallery, the Museum of Natural History and Industrial Arts, and the Magevney House, the oldest pioneer house in Memphis.

Mud Island, once a stretch of sand and brush in the Mississippi River in front of downtown Memphis, was converted into a recreational and cultural park in 1982. It is a museum of the Mississippi River, the only "riverama" in the country. It has been completely transformed since 1939, when the WPA Guide to Tennessee described it as the abode of squatters and stated, "a few straggling shanty-boats remain around Mud Island, their occupants the gypsies of the water. Clannish and friendly to river people, but contemptuous and suspicious of land people, they are vagabonds who live meagerly by selling fish in season." Today Mud Island attracts hundreds of tourists each year, who are particularly drawn to River Walk, an outside replica of the entire Lower Mississippi River.

TENNESSEE

MUD ISLAND

Area Code 901

LOCATION   Just off the bank of the Mississippi River from downtown Memphis.

SIZE   52 acres of parkland.

ACCESS   Pedestrian bridge or monorail from downtown Memphis.

HISTORY AND   Memphis was, legend goes, named by An-
DESCRIPTION   drew Jackson for the Egyptian City of the same name, "Place of Good Abode," which is surely true of Memphis. Mud Island, in the river just off the downtown area, belies its own name; it is a revitalized island museum presenting, in microcosm, the history and people of the entire Mississippi River. It is an educational and cultural complex focusing on the river towns and bringing to life the era of the grand old paddlewheel steamers which once plied its length.

POINTS OF INTEREST   River Walk, a popular feature of the island, is a special 2,000-foot-long scale model of the entire Lower Mississippi River between Cairo, Illinois and the Gulf of Mexico, taking in 20 river towns and graced with blooming foliage which duplicates the foliage of the river's regions. One step equals one mile, an equation which will fascinate children. Near the beginning is a 1-acre river-theme playground, Huck's Backyard. Paddlewheel cruises aboard the sprightly green and white *Island Queen*, with smokestacks and a huge red paddlewheel, leave from the Island Queen Docks. There is also an amphitheater where popular entertainers perform.

The 5-story River Center, the terminus of the monorail, is the most prominent landmark on the island and contains the Mississippi River Museum, with 18 galleries setting out various historical aspects of life along the river. Among these are the theater of river disasters, an 1870s packetboat, Indian artifacts, a Civil War battle scene re-enacted, the Hall of River Music with exhibits on music from the Memphis blues to Elvis Presley, displays on river art, and the River Folk Gallery with authentic life-sized figures, such as Mark Twain. The Memphis Belle Pavilion houses one of World War II's most famous aircraft. There are a number of special events on Mud Island, such as a Halloween party and a Catfish Festival in July.

In Memphis itself, sights include the grand old Peabody Hotel with its peacocks in the lobby, the Orpheum Theatre, Beale St. (where W. C. Handy gave birth to the Blues), the Memphis Brooks Museum of Art, the Memphis Zoo, the Memphis Botanic Garden, and Graceland, home of Elvis Presley. The *Delta Queen* and the *Mississippi Queen* begin their week-long river cruises from here.

Note that the principal island attractions are seasonal, from Memorial Day through Labor Day week; some are offered with a varying schedule during the rest of the year.

SIGHTSEEING TOURS   Getting to Mud Island is a sightseeing tour in itself, with a panoramic view of the island and the Memphis skyline from the futuristic cabins of the Swiss-built Monorail. Once there, you can take cruises on the *Island Queen* from mid-April through mid-October. (The *Memphis Queen* also has sightseeing excursions, just across from Mud Island on the Memphis side from the docks at Riverside and Monroe. Their cruises run March through December, but check times).

PARKS, BEACHES AND   The entire island is a park, but there are no
CAMPING   beaches and camping is not permitted.

MARINAS   Boat-docking facilities are available at a nominal charge.

RESTAURANTS   There are several restaurants on the island, ranging from those with table service to those serving fast food.**$**

LODGING   None.

RENTALS   None.

CONTACT   Mud Island Marketing, 125 North Front St., Memphis, TN 38103 (576–7241).

Mud Island's World-famous River Walk

VIRGINIA

The inland sea now known as the Chesapeake Bay was familiar to white explorers in the 16th century, but it was not until 1608, when Captain John Smith and his band of men sailed up the Bay, that its dimensions and flavor were recorded. The natives, according to Captain Smith, "made such descriptions of the Bay, Isles, and rivers, that often did us exceeding pleasure." In the course of their voyage, they came to 2 "Isles in the midst of the Bay," which he named Russels Isles (they are known now as Tangier.) Visitors arriving by boat, gliding over what James Michener, in *Chesapeake*, calls "that glorious body of water," can almost envision the islands as they were in the 17th century when they were discovered by Smith and inhabited by John Crockett and his family.

Chincoteague and Assateague are on the ocean side of the Eastern Shore. Giovanni da Verrazano is thought to have landed on Assateague as early as 1524; the next European to leave a description of his landing on Assateague was Colonel Henry Norwood, who had a brief sojourn on the island in 1650. Later in the century, Colonel Daniel Jenifer established a small stock-raising settlement on the island. Assateague Village, the largest of the communities on the island, had a population of about 200 before the turn of the century, but the islanders all moved to the mainland when they were denied access to Tom's Cove and the seafood ground by an island owner.

The Eastern Shore is an anomaly within the state, remote and rural, with a leisurely tempo; residents greatly fear that, one day, the Chesapeake Bay Bridge-Tunnel toll will be removed and the lower part of the Eastern Shore will become a commuting suburb of Norfolk. Inhabitants of Tangier, Assateague, and Chincoteague, however, have no such fears; they are, to some extent, a further anomaly within the separate culture of the Eastern Shore and the Chesapeake. Douglas Southall Freeman once wrote than all Virginians are "Shintoists under the skin," as "genealogy makes history personal to them in terms of family." Nowhere is this truer than on the tiny island of Tangier, where one-third of the population is descended from the original settler John Crockett and his eight sons. Chincoteague, a small fishing community, and Assateague Island, preserved as part of the Assateague Island National Seashore, are very unlike Tangier. Chincoteague has several museums, inns, motels, and good restaurants; it is an intriguing foil to the haunting environment of Assateague, which has wildlife trails through delicate and rare vegetation and a very long, unspoiled, protected beach. The islands all appeal, in varied ways: Tangier has the charm of a small community with an absorbing spirit and history; Chincoteague invigorates with its energy and serious seafood industry; Assateague invites introspection and solitary exploration.

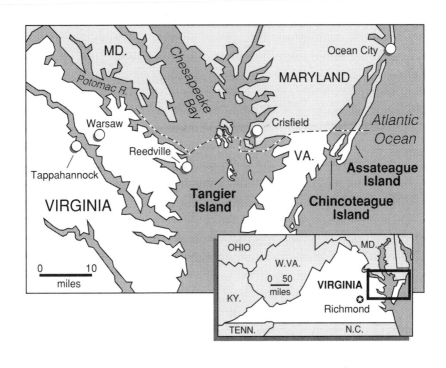

VIRGINIA

ASSATEAGUE ISLAND

Area Code 301 (MD)
Area Code 804 (VA)

LOCATION Off the Virginia and Maryland mainland.

SIZE The barrier island is 37 miles by 3 miles at its widest point.

ACCESS **Car:** The Maryland portion is reached via Rt. 611, from Rt. 50. The Virginia section is reached by Rt. 175, from Rt. 13. **Air:** There is commercial service to Ocean City, MD, and Norfolk, VA. **Private boat.**

HISTORY AND DESCRIPTION Had it not been for the storm of March 1962, Assateague Island might have been another crowded resort like Ocean City, Maryland. Development on that scale was planned; the storm, however, destroyed many vacation homes, few of which were rebuilt, and the government acted in 1965 to make the island a National Seashore. (The Chincoteague National Wildlife Refuge had been created by Virginia on the lower third of the island in 1943.) The Maryland portion begins below Ocean City, with the Assateague State Park. The Assateague Island National Seashore stretches south for over 30 miles. It is a slender finger of land battered by the surf and continually reshaped by the endless struggle of sand and sea. It is for beachcombers, meditators, artists, and naturalists.

Three jurisdictions, the National Park Service, the Maryland Park Service, and the U.S. Fish and Wildlife Service, oversee Assateague. In addition, the Assateague Lighthouse is managed by the Coast Guard. The Virginia portion is reached by Rt. 175, from Rt. 13. No roads run along the oceanfront; most of Assateague can only be penetrated by bicycle, canoe, or foot. The island has no lodging facilities, but there are bath houses for changing, and visitor centers. More than 300 species of birds use the refuge each year, and in November the sky is filled with snow geese, their dark wingtips flapping like frenetic boomerangs. There are also swans, ducks, rare species such as the piping plover and peregrine falcon, and waders like herons, egrets, and sandpipers. In addition, the fox squirrel, an endangered species, is found here. Offshore there are dolphins and pilot whales. Fishermen come to surfcast, troll, or take party boats from Chincoteague or

Ocean City, in pursuit of white marlin, channel bass, and bluefish. Consider coming in spring or fall rather than summer; that way, you will miss the crowds and have a chance to enjoy the wildlife and the chill lapping of the waves on the barren, deserted beach.

Both portions of the island have herds of feral ponies. The Virginia ponies are owned by the Chincoteague Volunteer Fire Company, which, since 1924, has rounded up and auctioned off the excess ponies on the last Wednesday and Thursday of each July. It is said that Pony Penning attracts enough visitors to sink the island. "Gum-boot cowboys" from Chincoteague, riding, as one observer has remarked, "like Cossacks," round up the semi-wild ponies and, the next day, swim the herd across the channel to Chincoteague and drive them to a pen; the foals are then auctioned, with the proceeds going to the fire department. The aura of Marguerite Henry's classic book *Misty of Chincoteague*, written in 1947, rounds up far more devotees each year than there are ponies; they come to relive the book and their childhood. Children plead fervently to take ponies home, but most must be content with a visit to the Chincoteague Miniature Pony Farm or to the 1961 film *Misty*, shown each year at the island theater during pony penning. The Maryland ponies are left to breed on their own, and their growing numbers have caused some concern of late. There is speculation about the origin of the ponies; some legends have it that Blackbeard left a herd in a secret lair on the island; others say that they came ashore when the Spanish ship *Greyhound* was wrecked off the coast. Another story is that they are descended from horses that were put out to graze on the island in order to protect mainland crops.

To enter Assateague from Chincoteague, escaping its low-key but definite commercialism, is to find a new and tranquil domain of ocean, dunes, sand, and wildlife.

POINTS OF INTEREST   The red and white striped Assateague Lighthouse, built in 1857, still stands guard over the Chincoteague shoals and is a colorful landmark.

At the Chincoteague Refuge, there is a 4-mile loop Wildlife Drive; it

Annual Wild Pony Roundup, Chincoteague Island

is closed to cars until 3:00 P.M., but you can hike or bike along it and see the Sitka deer, wood ducks, and ospreys.

There are visitor centers at either end of the island with exhibits on its flora and fauna.

(For attractions in nearby Chincoteague, see that entry).

SIGHTSEEING TOURS — Wildlife Tours (Island Tours, Inc., Box 83, Chincoteague, VA 23336, 336–5593 or 336–5511) offers boat and motorized wagon tours of the wilderness refuge. There are also natural history programs arranged by the Visitor Center, some of which include wilderness hikes and canoe trips.

PARKS, BEACHES AND CAMPING — **Parks:** The island contains the Assateague Island National Seashore (39,500 acres), the Assateague State Park (755 acres), and the Chincoteague Wildlife Refuge (9,460 acres). **Beaches:** The beaches are wide, white, and sandy; they are also wild and lonely, punctuated by skeletons of old wrecks; walkers are reminded not to lose track of the distance back. During the summer season, there may be lines to enter the restricted car lots at the beaches; a "one off, one on" rule applies when the parking lot is too crowded. **Camping:** Camping is not allowed in the Chincoteague National Wildlife Refuge, though Chincoteague has several commercial campgrounds. On the north end of the island, the state park has 311 campsites and the National Park Service offers 150 (60 tent only) sites that are more spacious. For details, contact the National Park Service. In summer, all the campsites fill up; it is best to come early in the week and put your name on the waiting list. Most have a 7-day limit from Memorial Day weekend to Labor Day.

MARINAS — There are no marinas on the island, but the State Park maintains a boat launching ramp on the mainland.

RESTAURANTS — There are no restaurants; the closest ones are in Chincoteague and Ocean City. There is a snack bar in the State Park.

LODGING — The nearest accommodations are in Chincoteague and Ocean City.

RENTALS — There are no rental accommodations.

CONTACT — Assateague National Seashore Headquarters, Rt. 2, Box 294, Berlin, MD 21811 (301/641–1441). For accommodations at the Maryland end, contact the Public Relations Division, Convention

Center, 4001 Coastal Hwy., Ocean City, MD 21842 (301/289–2800). For accommodations in Chincoteague, contact the Chincoteague Chamber of Commerce, Box 258, Chincoteague, VA 23336 (804/ 336–6161).

CHINCOTEAGUE

Area Code 804

LOCATION   On Virginia's Eastern Shore, between the mainland and Assateague Island.

SIZE   7 miles long by 1½ miles wide.

ACCESS   *Car:* Via Rt. 175, then by causeway and bridge to the island. *Air:* There is commercial service to Norfolk. *Private boat.*

HISTORY AND   Chincoteague, the gateway to the Virginia
DESCRIPTION   part of Assateague, is a small seafaring village of about 4,500, with fishing boats chugging about the harbor, and a quiet, welcoming air. It was settled in 1662 but was not incorporated until 1908. It has been known since 1830 for its delicious salt oysters (particularly those from Tom's Cove). Commercial boats continue to dock here between their trips up and down the coast, and shucking houses and seafood companies still process clams and other products of the sea. From the bridge over Chincoteague Channel, the simple white 2-story houses almost have a New England flavor.

Autumn brings hunters; in fall the tidal marshes between Chincoteague and Assateague are a vivid red and purple hue; the red and white striped Assateague Lighthouse is another colorful landmark. The wildlife refuge on nearby Assateague draws immense crowds, who eat, sleep, and camp in Chincoteague (everyone must be off the refuge each night). Spring and fall are an especially good time for birdwatching; over 300 species of birds have been identified on Assateague.

POINTS OF INTEREST   The Chincoteague Miniature Pony Farm, 201 Maddox Blvd. (336–3066), has unusual Falabella miniature horses, miniature donkeys and ponies, and a museum where "Misty" is mounted.

The Oyster Museum of Chincoteague (336–6117) is the world's only oyster museum, showing shellfish farming and island history.

The Refuge Waterfowl Museum (336–5800) has exhibitions on the waterman's life, along with duck decoys, weapons, and boats.

The Chincoteague National Wildlife Refuge, on Assateague Island, has a beautiful beach and an interesting wildlife drive and nature trail (*see* entry for Assateague Island).

SIGHTSEEING TOURS   Wildlife Tours (Island Cruises, Inc., Box 83, Chincoteague, VA 23336, 336–5593 or 336–5511) offers boat and motorized wagon tours of the wilderness refuge. There are also natural-history programs arranged by the Visitor Center, some of which include wilderness hikes and canoe trips.

PARKS, BEACHES AND   **Parks:** Memorial Park is the destination of
CAMPING   ponies during the pony swim. **Beaches:** There are no recreational beaches on the island. **Camping:** There are 4 campgrounds: Tom's Cove, Beebe Rd. (336-6498); Pine Grove, Deep Hole Rd. (336–5200); Maddox, Maddox Blvd. (336-3111); and Inlet View, S. Main (336–5126).

MARINAS   Deep-draft boats can come into Chincoteague Channel and tie up temporarily at some of the fish docks; they have fuel, and there are nearby restaurants. The Curtis Merritt Harbor on the southern tip of the island has deep water and a harbormaster. Small boats may be rented at Snug Harbor Marina (336–6176), Sea Tag Lodge (336–5555), and Captain Bob's Fishing Camp, S. Main St. (336–6654).

RESTAURANTS   The Beachway Restaurant, Maddox Blvd. (336-5590), has its own pastries, an Old English tavern decor, and outdoor dining; there are steak and seafood specialties.**$$**
    The Channel Bass Inn (*see* Lodging) is widely known for its haute cuisine and dishes with a Spanish Basque accent, served with a flair.**$$$**
    Chincoteague Inn, S. Main (336–3314), overlooks Chincoteague Channel. The decor is simple, but the views, clams and oysters are excellent.**$$**
    Don's Seafood Market and Restaurant, N. Main St. (336–5715), has formica tables and very good seafood platters; it is an excellent choice for breakfast; this is where the locals go.**$**
    Oyster Catcher, 116 S. Main St. (336–5316), a tiny place with red geraniums and dishes such as oysters *bienville*. The butter tarts are superb.**$$**
    Pony Pines, Church St., east of town near Assateague Bay (336-8964). Good food in a pleasant country dining room.**$$**
    Spinnakers, Maddox Blvd. (336–5400), has a sailing motif and offers casual dining.**$–$$**

LODGING   The Channel Bass Inn, Chincoteague 23336 (336-6148), is a 100-year-old 3-story frame house with 10 guest rooms without television or telephones. Families with children may not enjoy this quiet inn, but the food is acclaimed.**$$$**

The Refuge Motor Inn, Box 378, Beach Rd., Chincoteague 23336 (336–5511), overlooks the Chincoteague National Wildlife Refuge and has rooms with a pleasant decor, porches, and a whirlpool, sauna, sun deck, and bike rentals. Donald J. Leonard, the owner, belongs to the Volunteer Fire Department, which handles pony penning, and there is a small herd of the shaggy Chincoteague ponies here in a corral. Leonard's wife Martha provides board games for families in bad weather. This is an excellent place for families to stay.**$$**

The Driftwood Motor Lodge, Beach Road (336–6557), is at the entrance to Assateague National Seashore.**$$**

The Island Motor Inn, N. Main St. (336–3141), overlooks Chincoteague Bay.**$$**

There are a number of other motels; the Chamber of Commerce will send a list.

RENTALS   There are many agencies handling cottage rentals, including Island Properties Rentals, Bridge St. (336–3456) and Willow Tree Cottages, Box 353, Church St. (336–3280). Snug Harbor Marina and Cottages, East Side (336–6176) and Sea Tag Lodge, East Side (336–5555) offer cottages with boat rentals. The Chamber of Commerce will send a full list of realtors.

CONTACT   Chincoteague Chamber of Commerce, Box 258, Chincoteague, VA 23336 (336–6161).

TANGIER ISLAND

Area Code 804
LOCATION   In the Chesapeake Bay, about 12 miles south of Crisfield, MD and 16 miles east of Reedville, VA.

SIZE   3½ miles by 1½ miles.

ACCESS   **Ferry:** From Reedville, VA: The *Chesapeake Breeze*, Tangier and Chesapeake Cruises, Inc., Warsaw, VA 22572, 804/333–4656 (May–October 15). From Onancock, VA: The *Captain Eulice*, Hopkins & Bros. Store, # 2 Market St., Onancock, VA 23417 804/787–8220 (June-September). From Crisfield, MD: The *Steven Thomas*, Crisfield, MD 21817, 301/968–2338 Memorial Day-Oct). **Air:** There is a 3,600-foot airport; on some summer days 80 or more planes land, bringing people for dinner. **Private boat.**

HISTORY AND   Virginia's Tangier Island welcomes visitors.
DESCRIPTION   With its tidy little homes, narrow streets,
                         lingering Elizabethan accents, and crab
farms, it seems an island where time has almost been arrested. It was
called by the *National Geographic* "2½ square miles of brine-soaked
tradition." One former islander, Marion Carson, transplanted to Crisfield, says the island is "as close as you can get to God." Tangier
Island was discovered in 1608 by that intrepid explorer, Captain John
Smith. He described the Chesapeake Bay, ". . . a faire Bay compassed
but for the mouth with fruitful and delightsome land. Within is a country that may have the prerogative over the most pleasant places of
Europe, Asia, Africa or America, for large and pleasant navigable rivers. Heaven and earth never agreed better to frame a place for man's
habitation." Tradition holds that he named it Tangier, but the name
does not occur in records until 1713. The Cornish John Crockett family
were well established on Tangier by 1686 (father and 8 prolific sons),
and they make up at about one-third of the population today, so if the
people seem to have a visible similarity, it is not surprising. You will
undoubtedly be enjoying their hospitality if you stay long on the island,
perhaps by staying in or dining at the homey Chesapeake House
(ideally, both). The Pruitts, Parkses, Evanses, Dises, and Dizes are
other prominent families. In 1804, Joshua Thomas arrived in his boat
The Methodist, and proceeded to reform the licentious living which, it
is thought, characterized the early days on the island. According to
Tangier historian and artist Vernon Bradshaw, Thomas held religious
camp meetings that were sometimes attended by thousands of people
(some coming from the mainland). Today, Tangier is a devoutly religious community; Sunday work is frowned upon and businesses close.
   In 1814, British soldiers camped on the island; it was headquarters
for a British fleet ravaging the Chesapeake. Much of the beach from
which the British fleet set sail to bombard Baltimore has been washed
away.
   Since the 1800s, excellent crabs and oysters have been exported
from Tangier Island. The crab "peelers," about to shed their hard
shells, are placed in wooden floats; they back out of their old shells
and are then, as soft shell crabs, packed in ice and seaweed and
exported.
   Residents cherish the Tangier lifestyle, and most have no desire to
live on the mainland; the way of living has been passed down through
many generations as something worth preserving, and they share a
strong sense of community and purposefulness. It would be a mistake
to think the islanders are childlike, on their diminutive island, or
trapped in another century, however; most have television and cars
waiting on the mainland which can whisk them to Washington or Norfolk within a few hours. "Whisking" is in fact a favorite mode of transportation on the island itself; when the mail has been sorted at the
Post Office, young mothers speed up in golf carts with their golden-
haired children, greeting some of the other 850 islanders. There is a

high school on the island; often, graduates go on to college and return to the island to teach.

Most cruises do not allow much time on the island; if you can, stay overnight. If not, make do with a traditional seafood family-style mid-day meal at the Chesapeake House, take a quick golf-cart tour, and browse in the gift shops. If possible, buy, for $1, a delightful guide to the island, *Visitors Guide to Tangier Island, Va.*, by Vernon Bradshaw, an artist who also has a shop with some of his work across from the Chesapeake House. He is friendly, witty, and approachable, and can explain what happened to the picket fences (you hear numerous tales, such as souvenir-seeking, but he says the darting golf carts kept running into them. In any case, they are making a comeback.) In summer, the excursion boat arrivals are staggered so that the tourists do not sink the island. You can also eat a picnic lunch aboard ship or at tables overlooking the harbor. After dinner, if you are staying over-night, you can stroll again about the island, admiring the crape myrtle and oleander and nodding "Evening" to the inhabitants.

POINTS OF INTEREST   The Tangier Museum has items of historic interest collected by Evelyn Day.

SIGHTSEEING TOURS   There are golf cart tours of the island; the golf carts meet the cruise ships and also wait beside the Chesapeake House and at other places on the main street. Try, if possible, to take the forward-facing seats, as the carts fly along the streets and it is hard to take in the sights facing backwards.

PARKS, BEACHES AND   **Parks:** There are no parks on the island.
CAMPING   **Beaches:** There are no recreational beaches on Tangier. **Camping:** There are no campgrounds.

MARINAS   Milton Parks' Marina and Parks' Pier are the main stopping places for pleasure craft.

RESTAURANTS   Fisherman's Corner (891–2571) is a sea-food restaurant specializing in locally caught crabs, fish, oysters, and clams (when in season).**$**

Hilda Crockett's Chesapeake House (*see* Lodging) is the vintage, and justly famous, eating place on the island. Mrs. Crockett has been succeeded by her daughters, but the menu is still superb—crab cakes, fritters, fresh vegetables, corn pudding, and other homemade dishes, served family style at long tables.**$**

Dennis' Pilot House and Ray Crockett's Double Six (named for the domino games played inside) are technically sandwich shops but far more than that. According to Vernon Bradshaw, they are favorite gathering spots in the evening for islanders "engaged in the quaint pastime of talking and joking with one's fellow man."**$**

LODGING   Hilda Crockett's Chesapeake House, Main St. (891–2240), has 8 rooms.**$**

RENTALS   The island does not have realtors as such.

CONTACT   Eastern Shore of Virginia Tourism Commission, Box 147, Accomac, VA 23301 (787–2460).

The Tiny Fishing Village of Tangier Island

ACKNOWLEDGMENTS

This venture has been reinforced and strengthened by the contributions of many people. My aunt, Dorothy Williams, a lifelong island enthusiast, has cheerfully tolerated rain, missed boats, and misplaced camera bags in the interest of seeking out a variety of southern islands. I am indebted to my brothers, Oscar and Martin Grant, who shared a happy childhood at Wrightsville Beach, North Carolina, and my sister-in-law, Jane Grant, for their ample knowledge of North and South Carolina islands. In their company, I have visited a treasure trove of special islands, many of them aboard Oscar and Jane's ketch, *Sea Fever.* Martin's diligent historical research was very welcome.

Jean Davis has given support and encouragement from the earliest stages of the endeavor. Bob DuCharme and the staff of the Academic Computing Center, at the University of Richmond, especially Gilpin Brown, Lois Morley, Louise Bickerstaff, Carolyn Racliffe, Edith Tiller, Bob Littlepage, and Salonge Moses, have helped me unstintingly and at all hours, giving invaluable assistance with laptops, lasers, and file transfers. Kate DuVal and Lucretia McCulley of the Boatwright Library at the University of Richmond provided expert bibliographic assistance and saved me from many errors. Jo Anne Triplett of the Smithsonian sent much appreciated documentation on various artists.

I am very grateful to Greg Yon of the State of Florida for his expertise on the islands of Florida and for facilitating travel and providing information. Rosemary Heffernan of the St. Augustine and St. Johns County Chamber of Commerce delved into the history of Anastasia Island with considerable aplomb under great pressure. Beth Cooke, of Kentucky, was, as always, a fountain of information, as were Jerry Eubanks of Ship Island, Mississippi, and Craig Ogilvie and Kerry Kraus of the Arkansas Department of Parks and tourism. Janette Hunt and Ellen Kennedy of Lee County, Florida, provided extensive assistance.

As always, I am infinitely indebted to Mary Ann Caws, who has shared innumerable pilgrimages to islands of fact and fancy. Peg Rorison instilled a very early appreciation of islands, a cicerone *sans pareil* on midnight swims and dawn beach walks. Margaret Devereaux Lippitt Rorison was unfailingly inventive in providing varied island excursions, supplemented by extraordinary food for mind and body, throughout my childhood. I shall always be grateful to Edith Register, who led my brothers and me, when we were children, on forays by boat to uninhabited islands, giving us a unique appreciation of wildlife and natural vegetation. I also owe many thanks to my aunt Virginia White, who imparted her knowledge of the Florida Keys and helped shape my trip there, and to Lois Reamy, whose advice as to ways I might round out and substantiate my original idea was extremely welcome. My heartfelt thanks are also due Leslie Glassberg, a connoisseur of elite and elusive islands, and to David and Darlene Trent, who provided vignettes of St. Simons and Sapelo. Prudence Heller, a specialist in islands, deserves special thanks for sharing her knowledge so generously. Susan Urstadt, my agent, and her colleague Helen Pratt have supported the project from its earliest days, making valuable suggestions for improvements and additions. Special thanks are due to

Peachtree editors: Margaret Quinlin, for shaping the overall concept of the book and envisioning its ultimate focus, and Susan Thurman, for her sensitive and meticulous editing; she has been, at all times, accessible and sympathetic about editorial problems, both trivial and major. Estelle Crump has smoothed out many rough edges and saved me countless time with her aid and succour. As in all my undertakings, I have an inestimable debt to my husband, Lewis, for his wise counsel, unfailing interest, patience, and understanding, and to my son Alex, who helped with research and correspondence, and who always sees things clearly; they make it all worthwhile.

SOURCES
FOR FURTHER READING

Non-Fiction

Burgess, Robert H. *This Was Cheaspeake Bay*. Cambridge, MD: Cornell Maritime Press, 1963.

Brewington, M.V. *Chesapeake Bay: A Pictorial Maritime History*. New York: Bonanza Books, 1953.

Cronkite, Walter. *South by Southeast*. Birmingham, AL: Oxmoor House, 1983.

DeBlieu, Jan. *Hatteras Journal*. Golden, CO: Fulcrum, 1988.

East, Marguerite. *Island of the Mind: Gasparilla*. Boca Grande, FL: Ink and Images, 1976.

Firestone, Linda and Whit Morse. *Florida's Enchanting Islands: Sanibel and Captiva*. Richmond, VA: Good Life, 1980.

Firestone, Linda and Whit Morse. *Virginia's Favorite Islands: Chincoteague and Assateague*. Richmond, VA: Good Life, 1982.

Georch, Carl. *Ocracoke*. Winston-Salem, NC: J. F. Blair, 1956.

Gibson, Charles Dana. *Boca Grande: A Series of Historical Essays*. Boca Grande, FL: privately published, 1982.

Gleasner, Diane C. and Bill. *Sea Islands of the South*. Charlotte, NC: East Woods, 1980.

Hall, Lewis Philip. *Land of the Golden River: Historical Events and Stories of Southeastern North Carolina and the Lower Cape Fear*, Vol. I, *Old Times on the Seacoast*. Wilmington, NC: Wilmington Printing Co., 1975.

Kidder, Chris and Dave Poyer. *The Insiders' Guide to the Outer Banks of North Carolina*. Manteo, NC: Storie/McOwen, 1988.

Lockwood, C.C. *The Gulf Coast: Where Land Meets Sea*. Baton Rouge, LA: Louisiana State University Press, 1984.

MacNeill, Ben Dixon. *The Hatterasman*. Winson-Salem, NC: J. F. Blair, 1958.

Puterbaugh, Parke and Alan Bisbort. *Life is a Beach*. New York: McGraw Hill, 1986.

Russell, Anne. *Wilmington: A Pictorial History*. Norfolk, VA: Donning Publishing Co., 1981.

Salter, Ben. *Portsmouth Island*. Atlantic, NC: privately published, 1972.

Sherrill, Chris and Roger Aiello. *Key West: The Last Resort*. Atlanta, GA: Villa Press, 1981.

Stick, David. *Bald Head: A History of Smith Island and Cape Fear*. Wendell, NC: Broadfoot Publishing Co., 1985.

Stick, David. *The Cape Hatteras Seashore*. Charlotte, NC: McNally and Loftin, 1964.

Stick, David. *The Outer Banks of North Carolina*. Chapel Hill, NC: University of North Carolina Press, 1958.

Sullivan, Buddy. *Sapelo: A History*. Darien, GA: McIntosh County Chamber of Commerce, 1988.

Vanstory, Burnette. *Georgia's Land of the Golden Isles*. Athens, GA: The University of Georgia Press, 1956.

Williams, Joy. *The Florida Keys: A History and Guide*. New York: Random House, 1987.

Works Projects Administration guides to the states included.

Wrenn, Tony P. *Wilmington, North Carolina: An Architectural and Historical Portrait*. Charlottesville, VA: University Press of Virginia, 1984.

Wroen, William H., Jr. *Assateague*. Cambridge, MD: Tidewater Publishers, 1972.

Yeadon, David. *Secluded Islands of the Atlantic Coast*. New York: Crown Publishers, 1984.

Fiction

Barth, John. *Sabbatical: A Romance*. (Chesapeake Bay islands). New York: Putnam, 1982.

Conroy, Pat. *The Prince of Tides*. (Hilton Head; Daufuskie, SC). Boston: Houghton Mifflin, 1986.

Conroy, Pat. *The Water is Wide*. (Daufuskie, SC). Boston, MA: Houghton Mifflin, 1972.

Grau, Shirley Ann. *The Hard Blue Sky*. (Grand Isle, LA). New York: Knopf, 1958.

Hemingway, Ernest. *To Have and Have Not*. (Key West, FL). New York: Scribner's, 1937.

Henry, Marguerite. *Misty of Chincoteague*. (Chincoteague and Assateague, VA). New York: Random House, 1947.

Heyward, Du Bose. *Porgy*. (Kiawah, SC). New York: George H. Doran, 1925.

Michener, James. *Chesapeake*. (Chesapeake Bay islands). New York: Random House, 1972.

Powell, Padgett. *Edisto*. (Edisto Island, SC). New York: Farrar Straus and Giroux, 1984.

Price, Eugenia. *The Beloved Invader*. (St. Simons Island, GA). Philadelphia: Lippincott, 1965.

Photo Credits

Fort Gaines, Courtesy Alabama Bureau of Travel and Tourism, Page 6

DeGray State Lodge and Convention Center, Courtesy Arkansas Dept. of Parks and Tourism, Page 9

Anna Maria Island, Courtesy Manatee County Convention and Visitors Bureau, Page 23

The Inn at Cabbage Key, Courtesy Florida's Lee Island Coast, Page 28

Caladesi Island, Courtesy Florida Dept. of Commerce, Page 31

Fisher Island, Courtesy Fisher Island Club, Page 43

The Hemingway House, Courtesy Florida Keys and Key West Visitors Bureau, Page 58

The Conch Tour Train and Sloppy Joe's Bar, Courtesy Florida Keys and Key West Visitors Bureau, Page 60

The Seven Mile Bridge, Marathon, Courtesy Florida Keys and Key West Visitors Bureau, Page 62

Pine Island, Photo by Sarah Bird Wright, Page 81

Redington Long Pier, Indian Rocks Beach, Photo by Sarah Bird Wright, Page 89

"The Sanibel Stoop," Sanibel Island, Photo by Sarah Bird Wright, Page 93

Sanibel's J.N. "Ding" Darling National Wildlife Refuge, Photo by Sarah Bird Wright, Page 95

Useppa Island, Courtesy Lee Island Coast, Page 102

Ruins of Dungeness Mansion, Cumberland Island, Courtesy Georgia National Park Service, Page 107

The Clubhouse, Jekyll Island, Courtesy Jekyll Island Authority, Page 110

Crane Cottage, Courtesy Jekyll Island Authority, Page 111

Hunting Lodge on Little St. Simons Island, Courtesy Little St. Simons, Page 114

Fort Frederica, Courtesy Brunswick's Golden Isle of Georgia Tourist and Convention Bureau, Page 116

St. Simons Lighthouse, Courtesy Brunswick's Golden Isle of Georgia Tourist and Convention Bureau, Page 117

The Cloister Motor Entrance, Sea Island, Courtesy The Cloister, Page 121

Horseback Riding on the Beach at Sea Island, Courtesy The Cloister, Page 123

General Burnside Island, Courtesy Dept. of Travel Development, Commonwealth of Kentucky, Page 126

Louisiana Heron, Grand Isle, Courtesy Louisiana Office of Tourism, Page 130

Rhodes Point, Smith Island, Photo by Sarah Bird Wright, Page 135

West Ship Island, Courtesy Gulf Islands National Seashore, Page 145

"Old Baldy," Bald Head Island, Photo by Sarah Bird Wright, Page 150

Cape Hatteras Lighthouse, Photo by Sarah Bird Wright, Page 156

Ocracoke Lighthouse, Photo by Sarah Bird Wright, Page 160

Portsmouth Island, Photo by Sarah Bird Wright, Page 164

Wrightsville Beach, Photo by Sarah Bird Wright, Page 169

Aerial View of Harbour Town, Hilton Head, Courtesy Hilton Head Chamber of Commerce, Page 179

Harbour Town Marina, Hilton Head, Courtesy of Hilton Head Chamber of Commerce, Page 181

Wild Dunes Resort, Isle of Palms, Courtesy Wild Dunes, Page 185

Mud Island's World-famous River Walk, Courtesy Mud Island, Memphis Park Commission, Page 197

Annual Wild Pony Roundup, Chincoteague Island, Courtesy Virginia Division of Tourism, Page 201

The Tiny Fishing Village of Tangier Island, Courtesy Virginia Division of Tourism, Page 208

INDEX

Sarah Bird Wright is a noted travel writer whose work has appeared in *Travel-Holiday*, *The New York Times*, *The Christian Science Monitor*, *Woman's World*, *The Toronto Globe and Mail*, and many other publications. Her **FERRIES OF AMERICA** (Peachtree) was named by *Library Journal* as "one of the best reference works for 1987." She teaches part-time at the University of Richmond and makes her home in Midlothian, Virginia.